BROADWAY AND ECONOMICS

Economics has often been described as "the dismal science," with TV and movies reinforcing this description. However, economics is a powerful tool that can be used to understand how the world works, helping to answer confusing puzzles and solve the world's problems. Surprisingly, Broadway musicals are an excellent way to show this.

Musicals tell engaging stories through song and many are rich with economic concepts. This book analyzes 161 songs from 90 musicals to explore what they can teach us about supply and demand, monetary policy and numerous other core economic concepts. While some songs have an obvious connection to economics, other connections may seem less apparent. When you hear "Let it Go" from *Frozen*, does your mind think about a firm's production decisions? After reading this book, it will. Whether showing how *Hamilton* can illustrate concepts of central banking, or how "Stars" from *Les Miserables* provides a perfect example of inelastic demand, the author presents complicated topics in an understandable and entertaining way.

Featuring classic songs from some of the most popular shows ever produced, along with some hidden gems, *Broadway and Economics* will be of interest to anybody studying an introductory economics course as well as theatre aficionados.

Matthew C. Rousu is Professor of Economics at Susquehanna University, USA. He is a prolific researcher and frequently contributes to or is quoted by news outlets, including *USA Today*, *The Washington Post*, *Bloomberg*, and *Forbes*.

Routledge Economics and Popular Culture

Series Editor: J. Brian O'Roark, *Robert Morris University, USA*

Broadway and Economics
Economic Lessons from Show Tunes
Matthew C. Rousu

Dystopia and Economics
A Guide to Surviving Everything from the Apocalypse to Zombies
Edited by Charity-Joy Revere Acchiardo and Michelle Albert Vachris

For a full list of titles in this series, please visit www.routledge.com/Routledge-Economics-and-Popular-Culture-Series/book-series/REPC

BROADWAY AND ECONOMICS

Economic Lessons from Show Tunes

Matthew C. Rousu

LONDON AND NEW YORK

First published 2018
by Routledge
2 Park Square, Milton Park, Abingdon, Oxon OX14 4RN

and by Routledge
711 Third Avenue, New York, NY 10017

Routledge is an imprint of the Taylor & Francis Group, an informa business

British Library Cataloguing-in-Publication Data
A catalogue record for this book is available from the British Library

Library of Congress Cataloging-in-Publication Data
Names: Rousu, Matthew, author.
Title: Broadway and economics : economic lessons from show tunes / Matthew C. Rousu.
Description: Abingdon, Oxon ; New York, NY : Routledge, 2018. | Series: Routledge economics and popular culture | Includes bibliographical references and index.
Identifiers: LCCN 2017052879 (print) | LCCN 2018010981 (ebook) | ISBN 9781315168364 (Ebook) | ISBN 9781138051218 (hbk. : alk. paper) | ISBN 9781138051232 (pbk. : alk. paper)
Subjects: LCSH: Economics—Case studies. | Musicals—Economic aspects—Case studies.
Classification: LCC HB171.5 (ebook) | LCC HB171.5 .R7738 2018 (print) | DDC 330—dc23
LC record available at https://lccn.loc.gov/2017052879

ISBN: 978-1-138-05121-8 (hbk)
ISBN: 978-1-138-05123-2 (pbk)
ISBN: 978-1-315-16836-4 (ebk)

Typeset in Bembo and Stone Sans
by Florence Production Ltd, Stoodleigh, Devon, UK
Printed by CPI Group (UK) Ltd, Croydon CR0 4YY

CONTENTS

ACKNOWLEDGMENTS

As with any book project, I am grateful to many. Thanks to Brian O'Roark who reached out to me with this opportunity. Thanks to Elanor Best, Anna Cuthbert, and Andy Humphries at Routledge for making this idea a reality and helping me throughout the process. Thanks to my #teachecon friends who helped inspire me to create the Broadway Economics website, including Dirk Mateer, Lee Coppock, Abdullah Al-Bahrani, Kim Holder, James Tierney, Jadrian Wooten, and the others I should be mentioning but have forgotten. Thank you to the Broadway World community for recommending songs that discuss economic themes. Several students helped me as well. Mikalah Potvin helped with editing and the references. Torin McFarland was incredibly helpful in finding appropriate references and background materials. And thanks to Courtney Conrad for assisting in producing the videos that helped make the Broadway Economics website a reality. And she also helped on the book with editing, references, formatting – basically everything.

I was blessed to have the best and most supportive parents anybody could hope for. My mom was never afraid to jump into new ventures – starting a new business in her mid-thirties, earning her CPA in her late forties, and becoming a great poker player in her fifties, all while being the nicest person on the planet. My dad showed me the value of a strong work ethic and helped instill in me a confidence that I could always accomplish my goals with hard work.

Last but most important are my wife and kids. My children, Jacob, Allison, and Ezekiel are my favorite actors and are incredible human beings. They inspire me to be a better person. My beautiful wife Amanda is the best partner anybody could want and my best friend. She's also the smartest theatre person I know and puts up with my crazy schedule. On top of love and support, everybody in my family contributed to finding songs for the book, debating the topics in the songs, and reviewing the manuscript.

INTRODUCTION

Economics is often considered dull. In TV and movies it is characterized by teachers like Ben Stein from *Ferris Buehler's Day Off* droning "Buehler? Buehler? Buehler?" The image is that economics is boring, complicated, and dismal. This is unfortunate as economics helps explain how the world works and can come up with explanations to many problems and puzzles. That so many think it is dull should not be acceptable.

While some teachers might teach economics in a dull way, I know many professors who find amazing and creative ways to teach. This is also my goal when teaching: to find engaging ways to help students learn about the subject I love. I think this is crucial, as economics is the single most important subject in terms of explaining how the world works.

This is where musicals can help. Musicals tell engaging stories through songs and many of these stories are rich with economic concepts. Let's think about some of the most famous shows. *Fiddler on the Roof* shows how a family's traditions and livelihood are changed because of oppressive government restrictions (bad) and innovative change (good). *Hamilton* has songs that help illustrate the concepts of central banking, trade-offs, labor economics issues, opportunity costs, and many other topics. Other shows have songs that illustrate economic concepts well but are less obvious. When you hear "Let it Go" from *Frozen*, do you think about a firm's production decisions? After reading this book, I hope you do.

Broadway and Economics contains 161 songs from 90 musicals that help to teach dozens of different economic concepts.

Sometimes the songs discussed will have an obvious connection to economics. Other times the connection might not seem as apparent. But my goal with this book, like with my classes, is to help make otherwise complicated topics more understandable. And more fun!

I have two audiences in mind for this book. I hope those in introductory economics will find that by hearing about complicated topics explained through musical theatre songs, they will better understand the topics. Economics can be complicated but by seeing examples of economic ideas presented in Broadway songs, I'm hoping the ideas will come easier. This book should make for an excellent supplementary text for anybody in an introductory economics course.

I also think theatre aficionados will enjoy this book. With 161 songs from musicals included, it contains many standards from some of the most popular shows ever produced, along with some hidden gems. I think the theatre fan should find it fascinating to see how a song illustrates economic concepts.

For those who want to explore this a bit more, I encourage you to visit my website, BroadwayEconomics.com. There you'll find more than fifty different videos of show tunes that contain lyrics and often callouts, discussion questions for instructors to use, and more. I also plan on updating the website with songs from musicals that didn't make it into the book.

I want to note a couple of points on the book's organization. I have sorted the songs alphabetically by show – starting with *1776* and ending with *You're a Good Man Charlie Brown*. When there are multiple songs in a show, they are presented in the order they appeared in the show. When a musical covers several economic topics or has economic themes consistently presented throughout the show I will sometimes present a separate section discussing the musical itself.

I have also included several songs that are from off-Broadway shows, the West End (London's theatre district), or movie musicals. While not technically "Broadway" shows, the songs from these musicals, like the other songs, help illustrate economic principles.

At the end of each song description is a listing of topics. If you're studying economics and want to see examples of songs by topic, page 187 has a directory. So, for example, if you're interested in songs that illustrate international trade, you will be able to easily find the five songs that will help you learn this topic.

1776

"Molasses to Rum"

Edward Rutledge, a representative from South Carolina, sings about the slave trade. He and his other southern colleagues do not want a clause about it included in the Declaration of Independence, and tell the northern representatives that their prosperity is a result of the slave trade as well. As Robert Morris University economist Brian O'Roark noted: "It is fairly safe to say that ["Molasses to Rum"] is the only song ever written about the triangle trade."[1] The Triangle Trade could refer to a trade between any three regions; however, in practice it usually refers to the slave trade.

In the slave trade, sugar plantations in the United States colonies made the molasses that was used to produce rum. The rum was traded to African nations for slaves. The slaves then were used as low-cost labor in the Caribbean to produce more molasses – which provided the ability to manufacture more rum to trade for more slaves.

Topics: International Trade, Gains from Trade, Opportunity Costs, Slavery

A FUNNY THING HAPPENED ON THE WAY TO THE FORUM

"Everybody Ought to Have a Maid"

As the title indicates, Senex sings that everybody should have a maid to "putter around the house." But getting a maid actually brings up an interesting point with how Gross Domestic Product (GDP) is calculated. GDP is the market value of all final goods and services produced within a country in a given period of time. It is used around the world to help compare the economic well-being across countries and across time. As you might expect, the United States, the United Kingdom, and Canada all have large GDPs per capita (ranging from $43,000 to $56,000 in U.S. dollars). This is higher than many other countries, like South Korea (GDP per capita of $34,500 per capita), China ($8,000 per capita, although it has been growing at a quick pace), India ($1,600) and Mexico ($9,000).[2]

By hiring a maid who provides services described in the song, like "tidying up the dishes" and "fetching" slippers, the money spent on a maid will count towards a country's GDP. The reason is that hiring a maid is a purchase done through a market: a legal one at that. However, if these same tasks are done by a family member – like a stay-at-home parent or child – for no payment, it does not add to a country's GDP. Housework is not counted in GDP even if the work is exactly the same as work done by a maid. The definition for GDP means that anything that doesn't go through a legal market, like housework and illegal drug sales, will not count towards GDP.

The other interesting connection to economics is that a maid is what economists would call a luxury good. Economists define a luxury good as a product where people spend a greater percentage of their income on it when they make more money. Items like vacations, maids, and jewelry are all items that poorer households will spend next-to-nothing obtaining, meaning that a small percentage of their income is spent on them. But richer households not only spend more money on luxury goods – they spend a higher percentage of their income.

Hiring a person to do your work like that isn't cheap and few households could afford a full-time maid. According to the U.S. Bureau of Labor Statistics, the median income for maids or housekeepers in the U.S. in 2015 was $20,740.[3] To hire a maid full-time would actually cost quite a bit more, as the person hiring would have to pay employment taxes, insurance, and more. Because of this, we would expect that very few households earning under $200,000 a year could afford a full-time maid.

Topics: Gross Domestic Product (GDP), Luxury Goods

A GENTLEMAN'S GUIDE TO LOVE AND MURDER

"I Don't Understand the Poor"

Lord D'Ysquith does not understand the poor and feels it is necessary to inform us of his views. He sings that the poor seem to be poor because of "nothing but stubbornness." The musical is set in England in the year 1909, and the song seems to show the audience his view as a member of the idle rich who arrogantly sings that the only poor people who are "rising above" with "work they love" are "beggars, pickpockets, and whores."

His comments do allow us to raise a good question – are the rich working hard while the poor are not? Data from the U.S. shows that those with the highest incomes in the U.S. work the most hours while those with the lowest work least.[4]

This is quite different than what historically was true. Estimates vary, but economic historians seem to agree that the poor worked more than the rich. Hans-Joachim Voth, an economic historian at the University of Zurich, found that in 1800 the average English worker labored for 64 hours a week.[5] This prompted Mr. Voth to say "In the 19th century you could tell how poor somebody was by how long they worked."[6] Other sources indicate that U.S. factory workweeks averaged about 60.1 hours per week.[7]

As obnoxious as Lord D'Ysquith seems to be, we must concede that he might have a point when he sings that "Why accept charity? . . . I contend we extend them too much latitude." While the idea of "how much" funding the poor should receive is an opinion-based question where reasonable people disagree, one thing about the current welfare state, at least in the United States, is that it does provide bad incentives for the working poor. For example, in Pennsylvania in 2016, a single mother of two children who works and is earning $29,000 could receive about $28,000 in assistance from the government.[8] This assistance comes from childcare, negative income tax subsidies, free health care, SNAP (formerly known as food stamps), and housing assistance. A big problem happens if she gets a raise, however. If she were to get a $1,000 raise – that is to earn $30,000 instead of $29,000 – she actually loses more in benefits than her $1,000 increase in salary. In fact, she'd lose about $8,000 in benefits, making her $7,000 worse off by getting that raise. It keeps getting worse, as the drop in benefits when going from $29,000 to $30,000 is mainly from losing housing assistance and food stamps. By continuing to get raises, this single mother would continue to lose other benefits, like the negative income tax subsidy and child health care, which includes a dramatic drop off at $43,000 of earnings of all childcare assistance. In fact, in order to be as well off as she was when earning $29,000, this single mother's income would need an increase to $69,000![9] This provides a negative incentive to working and could damage the prospects of obtaining a higher-paying job in the future.

Why does our government have incentives that discourage work? It does because there are so many different and independently run programs. The U.S. federal government has over 100 programs designed to aid the poor, including housing assistance, SNAP, energy assistance, and much more. Each program has rules about how much money a person could receive based on what that person is earning – and as incomes increase, the benefits these programs provide drop. This makes some sense, as each program is designed to help those who are struggling, not those who are earning high incomes.

Most of these programs, in isolation, cut benefits in a way that would still provide reasonable incentives to continue working hard and getting promotions. However, when taking all programs together, the cuts to benefits often exceed the increase in pay.

While intended to help those with lower incomes, the design of these programs helps keep the poor from becoming wealthier. It is in the short-term best interest of many who are working with low incomes and receiving government benefits to not seek promotions, raises, and to work fewer hours. These perverse incentives help prevent the working poor from ever attaining higher-income jobs.

Topics: Poverty, Inequality

"Better with a Man"

Henry D'Ysquith and Monty Navarro are singing about how things in life are always "better with a man." The reasons vary, from women being "too complex" and that men are more fun to be spend time with at a sporting event. Henry and Monty's message is clear and the song provides a good example of utility. If things indeed are always "better with a man," then Henry and Monty would always gain higher satisfaction, or what economists call utility, every time an activity involves another man.

But are things *always* better with a man? For most people, the first unit of a product is the most valuable, and each subsequent unit becomes slightly less valuable. For example, at an all-you-can-eat pizza restaurant, the first slice of pizza is the tastiest. The second is often good, but not quite as good as the first slice. As one keeps eating, eventually he or she won't want to eat another slice – even though it comes at no additional monetary cost. This is the idea of diminishing marginal utility – each subsequent unit is less valuable than the one before.

In "Better with a Man," Monty and Henry sing as if the law of diminishing marginal utility does not apply to them as things are always "better with a man." Or perhaps they just have almost no time with a man now. If they don't get much time with a man, then those first moments would be incredibly valuable!

Topics: Utility, Diminishing Marginal Utility

"Lady Hyacinth Abroad"

Lady Hyacinth wants to give her time and money to a charity, but she has a problem. Her rivals, Lady Sitwell, Lady Beach, Margaret Guest, and especially Daisy Greville have snatched up all of the "good" charities. Lady Hyacinth wants a charity of her own, and one that is prominent enough to get the recognition she feels she deserves. In the song, she goes through several options of how she could give. For each option she considers how her charity will further her own social status.

This song provides a great opportunity to think about why people give to charity, an area receiving recent attention from economists. Many who give to the poor are engaged in what economist James Andreoni coined "impure altruism."[10] By giving to the poor, they are being altruistic, but they also have ulterior motives. In the case of Lady Hyacinth, she wanted recognition for her generosity. Donors to universities or hospitals often want their names on buildings or want to be acknowledged in some other way. And as almost all theatregoers know, many people donate to their favorite theatres or theatre companies. Those theatres, in return, print the names of their donors in the playbills.

There are other ways one could be impurely altruistic. The "warm-glow" theory of giving suggests that people who give don't allocate their donations to maximize the impact of their giving, but instead will give to maximize the good feeling (warm glow) they receive from making donations.[11]

Topics: Charitable Giving, Utility

ANNIE

"We'd Like to Thank You Herbert Hoover"

The crowd is sarcastically singing a thank you to Herbert Hoover – saying that "prosperity was 'round the corner" but then they "paid through the nose." They blame him for the conditions of the Great Depression – which allows us to ask a question: how much blame does Herbert Hoover deserve?

First let's examine the stock market crash of 1929 – which many credit as the main cause of the Great Depression. Herbert Hoover took over in March 1929 – just seven months before the October 1929 stock market crash. The stock market bubble predated his presidency. Another factor that helped make this depression a "great" one was the collapse in the banking system. But the crash and banking system regulations that are credited with causing the crash could hardly be blamed on Hoover.

It is also interesting to look at Hoover's actions while in office. While Hoover was labeled as a "do nothing" president by his opponents, that label was inaccurate. During his administration, spending by the federal government increased from about $3 billion annually to almost $5 billion annually in just four years! From 1931 to 1932, the increase was almost $1 billion – almost a 20% increase in the federal budget in just one year![12] This included a budget deficit that was almost 4% of GDP in 1931–1932.

So why did the downturn that started in 1929 turn into the "Great Depression"? Economists still debate this. Some think the government didn't respond enough to the depression. John Maynard Keynes thought that the depression was caused by the total demand dropping so quickly and severely. He argued that it would only recover with significant government spending.[13] He and others argue that the government didn't do enough to get the economy out of the depression. Those who agree with this view would point to the fact that the economy seemed to recover when World War II started, given the increases in military spending.[14]

Milton Friedman thought that the depression was mainly from bad monetary policy – that the Federal government reduced the money supply. Friedman notes that from August 1929 to March 1933, "the stock of money fell by over a third."[15] This caused deflation in the United States – where prices are decreasing, instead of inflation, where prices are increasing. In theory, if all prices are completely flexible, inflation or deflation won't cause any problems. But deflation can cause problems. One problem deflation causes is that because the value of money is now higher, firms are suddenly paying workers more. (And it is tough for firms to cut the pay of workers.) With deflation, firms are essentially giving workers large raises. Couple this with an economic downturn and you have firms paying workers more when in reality they need to pay workers less to survive. Deflation helped spur mass layoffs.

Herbert Hoover might not have been the best president and his actions might not have helped end the Great Depression, but to be sarcastically thanked for causing the depression seems unreasonable.

Topics: Unemployment, Recessions, Great Depression

"A New Deal for Christmas"

The term, "New Deal" was coined in President Franklin Roosevelt's (FDR's) reforms – specifically in his 1932 inauguration speech.[16] It describes programs FDR implemented during his presidency. There were many new laws created and an unprecedented increase in government spending. But did this help? Once again, economists still debate this.

Those who argue that the New Deal programs helped end the Great Depression often refer to Keynesian economic analysis. This analysis indicates that if you increase government spending or cut taxes during a downturn you will get a boost to GDP. Those who argue that the New Deal programs helped the economy often cite the increases in government spending and look at the change in the U.S. unemployment rates, which are shown in Figure 1.[17]

The unemployment rates dropped from their massive highs of 25% once the New Deal policies were implemented. They didn't drop below 10%, however, for the remainder of the decade. But those who advocate for government spending to get out of a recession will also cite that government spending again increased dramatically when World War II started, and that's when unemployment rates finally went back to "normal."[18]

Those who argue that The New Deal programs did not help the economy will point out that there were several "ordinary" depressions in U.S. history but never a "great" one before The Great Depression. They will argue that a big factor in making this depression so bad was the government's involvement.[19] The argument is that both Hoover and Roosevelt expanded government so quickly and changed laws so rapidly that firms had no confidence in the laws to increase output.[20] This caused lower production than normal and a much slower recovery than what

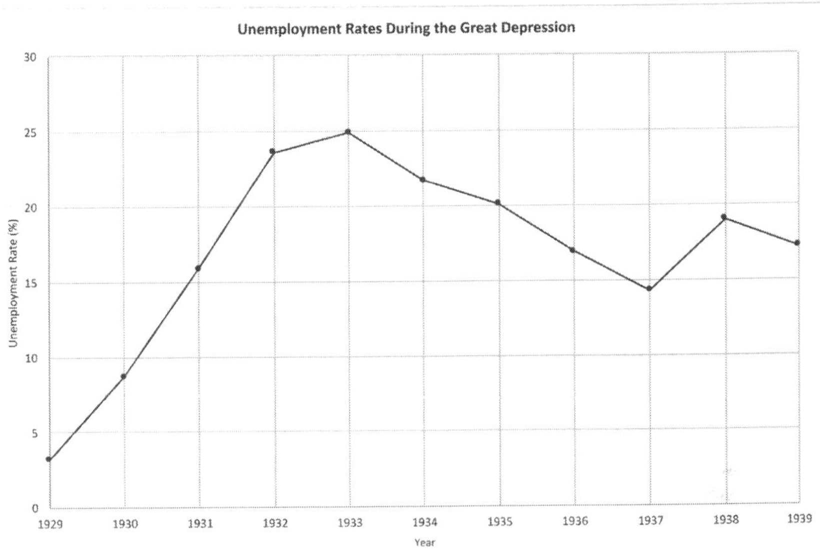

FIGURE 1

would have otherwise happened. Those arguing this position would say that once World War II started, firms knew the government would be more supportive and less likely to change laws and that's why the economy rebounded.[21]

Topics: Great Depression, Fiscal Policy

ANNIE GET YOUR GUN

"Anything You Can Do"

In "Anything You Can Do," Annie Oakley and Frank Butler playfully claim they can outdo each other with increasingly complex tasks. From singing softly to buying cheaply, Annie and Frank assure the other that they can complete the given task(s) best (with the exception of baking a pie).

If you can do anything and everything better than somebody else, you have what economists call an absolute advantage. For example, suppose a father might be better at both vacuuming and doing dishes than his child. When somebody can do all tasks better than somebody else, he is said to have an absolute advantage. But thankfully there can still be specialization and gains from trade even when somebody has an absolute advantage.

The principle of comparative advantage is the idea that a person should specialize in the area where he or she has the lower opportunity cost of production. The opportunity cost is the cost of an activity in terms of foregone options. The cost can be monetary, non-monetary, or both. For example, for a college student, attending an 8 a.m. class doesn't usually cost extra money (the class is paid for), but it does require giving up sleep! If a person goes to the theatre instead of working, she will pay for the ticket at the theatre AND give up wages – so the opportunity cost is monetary but involves more than just the ticket.

To illustrate comparative advantage, let's look at an example. Consider an adult who can wash 20 dishes or vacuum two rooms in ten minutes. He has a child who could wash six dishes in ten minutes or vacuum one room. The parent has an absolute advantage as the parent could either wash more dishes or vacuum more rooms in ten minutes. But the child has a comparative advantage in vacuuming – as the child is only giving up six dishes per room when he/she vacuums, whereas the adult is giving up ten dishes per room. This lower opportunity cost for vacuuming means there can be gains from trade. The parent has the comparative advantage in doing dishes. There can be gains from mutual exchange here, as the child should vacuum and the parent should do dishes.

This is one interesting insight into trade. Even if one economy is more efficient at virtually every task – with trade and the principle of comparative advantage trades that benefit both economies can still occur. In the song, both Annie and Frank claim to be better than the other in every task. Even if one of them is correct, they could still gain from trading with each other and specializing because of the principle of comparative advantage.

Topics: Comparative Advantage, Absolute Advantage, Trade

ANYONE CAN WHISTLE

"Me and My Town"

The Mayoress, Cora, is overseeing a struggling town and she sees people who are "poor, starving, cold, miserable, dirty, dreary, (and) depressing." Yet that doesn't seem to concern her, as she admits she just wants "to be loved." Cora's main concern appears to be gaining popularity, not improving the lives of the citizens in her town. While popularity and good decisions sometimes go hand-in-hand for elected officials, they don't always.

Public Choice Theory is the study of government decision making using economic analysis.[22] It assumes politicians do not take actions that are best for society but instead act like rational economic agents who seek to maximize their chances of re-election. One way that public officials might take an action that could help their re-election chances but be bad for society is by taking advantage of the short-sightedness effect. This assumes that people will focus more on shorter-term benefits and costs, which gives politicians a chance to enact laws that are bad in the long term but might give short-term benefits.

A great examples of the short-sightedness effect occurred in 2010 when a bipartisan committee headed by Former Democratic Senator Erskine Bowles and Former Republican Senator Alan Simpson recommended a plan to reduce the national debt. Their bipartisan plan presented many things that are unpopular in the short term, like tax increases and spending decreases, along with curbs to entitlement spending. Republican Paul Ryan was opposed, claiming it wouldn't curb future health care costs enough.[23] Democrat Jan Schakowsky opposed because it made too many cuts to "expenditures that benefit the middle class."[24] While the deficit is seen as a long-term problem by almost all Americans, the short-sightedness effect would make it logical for these politicians to vote against deficit reduction.

Topics: Public Choice Theory

AVENUE Q

"What Do You Do with a BA in English?"

Princeton, a new college graduate singing about life, is wondering what he'll do with his "useless degree" in English. He sings "four years in college and plenty of knowledge have earned me this worthless degree." The singer is being a bit dramatic, as there still is a great value in attaining a college degree – any college degree. Recent studies have found that the average college graduate in the United States earns 70% more annually and 84% more over a lifetime than somebody with just a high school degree.[25]

But there is some truth behind the singer's worries, as different college majors have different average starting salaries. According to a recent study published in Forbes, English majors ranked 21st out of 22 majors that were examined with starting salaries averaging just under $40,000 per year. This contrasts with Finance, Economics, Engineering, and Computer Science, all of which have starting salaries that average over $58,000 per year.[26]

Part of the reason for the higher salaries for some majors could be the skills that are acquired while another part might be the result of the supply and demand of graduates of each major. For example, while fewer students major in English in the United States than in accounting, for example – about 52,000 degrees in English vs. 82,000 in accounting in 2012[27] – accountants earn higher starting salaries based on higher demand.

Topic: Labor Economics, Education

"It Sucks to be Me"

Brian begins the song by discussing his dismay at losing his job from the catering company. He has skills to work as a caterer, but is now unemployed. Economists will classify a person into one of three types of unemployment: (i) cyclical unemployment – which occurs when somebody becomes unemployed due to a downturn (recession/depression) in the economy; (ii) structural unemployment – which occurs when someone's skills don't match up with the available jobs; and (iii) frictional unemployment – which occurs when somebody becomes unemployed due to normal frictions in the labor market (like searching for a job).

We don't know which one applies to Brian without more information. If he became unemployed because of a downturn in the overall economy, economists would consider that cyclical unemployment. If Brian is unemployed because his skills as a caterer no longer match the skills that employers are looking to hire, economists could consider that as structural unemployment. Finally, if Brian is unemployed because of general frictions in the labor market (perhaps this firm is losing business to another catering firm) but Brian's skills as a caterer are still in demand, then economists would consider this as frictional unemployment.

Toward the end of the song we find out that another character Princeton is looking for an apartment. He discusses that he cannot find any apartments in his price range from Avenue A through Avenue P, but when he gets to Avenue Q things finally look affordable. *Avenue Q* is set in New York City and the problem Princeton encounters finding reasonably priced housing emulates a problem many New Yorkers have encountered: expensive rent prices.

So why are rent prices in New York City so expensive? While the large population will likely ensure that housing prices will always be reasonably high, many economists place much of the blame on New York City's rent control policies.[28] At first, it might sound ironic that a program that is titled "rent control" doesn't control rent prices but inflates them. Let's look at why it was both tough for Princeton to find a place and why rent seemed so expensive.

First, standard economic theory shows that when a government puts in a maximum price for a product – like what is done with rent control – the result will be a cheaper price but the quantity of housing demanded will exceed the quantity of housing supplied, as we see in the graph on the next page.

This explains why there is a shortage of housing – but not why the price is higher, as standard economic theory predicts a lower price. To see why there is both a shortage and a high price, we need to look specifically at the laws of New York City. New York City's system of rent control places no restrictions on the initial price a landlord could charge a tenant for rent, but does restrict how much the price could increase each year. This poses a major problem for landlords, because if the value of the house or apartment decreases or becomes less valuable, the tenants could simply leave – and the landlord would have to find a new tenant at a lower price. But if the value goes up, the landlord cannot raise prices to reflect the change in value. So the landlord faces all of the downside risk and none of the potential benefits if the value increases because they cannot increase the prices to market value. Because of this, two things would happen. First, we'd expect fewer people to wish to become landlords. This by itself will increase rent prices. Second, those that do become landlords will also want to

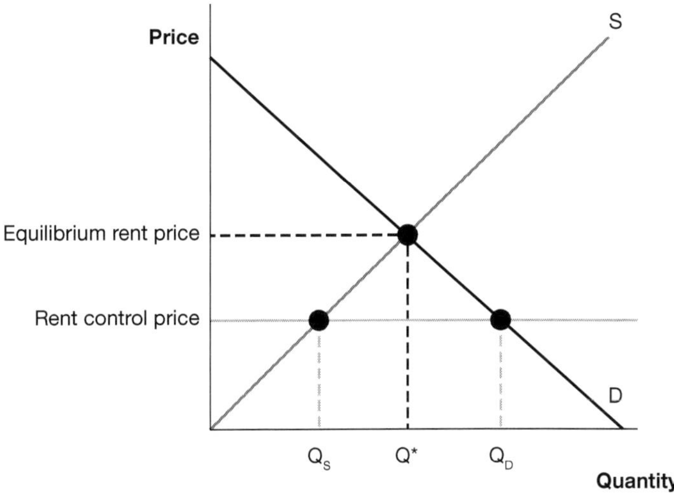

FIGURE 2

charge much higher initial prices to compensate themselves for taking the downside risk without receiving the upside benefit. These two factors will help increase rent prices and helps to explain the high prices in New York City and in the musical *Avenue Q*.

Topics: Unemployment, Price Ceiling, Rent Control

"Money Song"

Princeton decides to give to a charity, Kate Monster's Montessori School. Later, we see that Princeton is able to obtain a $10 million gift for the school. Major charitable gifts are not rare in the United States and many other countries. For example, in 2015 alone, U.S. citizens gave over $370 billion to charities.[29] To put this in perspective, in 2015 the charitable giving of U.S. citizens exceeded the total GDP of 166 countries.[30] Additionally, the charitable giving of U.S. citizens exceeded 2% of U.S. GDP.[31] Furthermore, from the years 2010 to 2015 the growth in charitable donations in the United States have exceeded GDP growth – in fact, during that time frame, total giving grew at a rate of 3.6% while GDP only grew at a rate of 2%.[32]

While Princeton's donation was a private charitable gift, there are parallels to his decision and to what governments decide with their fiscal policies. Fiscal policy is the way governments choose taxing and spending policies to influence the economy. When the government chooses spending programs to help the economy – like it did with the stimulus plan that was passed in response to the Great Recession in 2009 – there are two things it must determine. It must determine how much money to spend overall along with how to spend that money. These are the same issues that Princeton had to deal with when deciding to give money to Kate Monster's school.

Topics: Charitable Giving, Fiscal Policy

BEAUTY AND THE BEAST

"Gaston"

No one does anything like Gaston. He's the best! (If you doubt it, just ask him!) In "Gaston," we learn about how Gaston is better than anybody else at just about any task. Economists would say that Gaston has an absolute advantage in production. An absolute advantage occurs when a person (or country) can do any task better than another person (or country).

However, just because Gaston has an absolute advantage, that does not mean that Gaston cannot benefit from trading. Trading occurs based on the theory of comparative advantage, which occurs when a person/country can produce a product or service at a lower cost relative to the other items they can produce. So just because no one "fights like Gaston" or "matches wits like Gaston" does not mean that Gaston cannot enjoy the benefits of trading with others.

Topics: International Trade, Gains from Trade, Absolute Advantage, Comparative Advantage

BIG FISH

"Closer to Her"

Leo Bloom wants to find a girl he recently met but he knows nothing about her. He wants to find her so badly that he has agreed to work for free. This is in exchange for a new piece of information about how to find her every month. "Closer to Her" illustrates a couple of interesting concepts. First, there is no minimum wage where Leo is working (or perhaps the law is being violated), because if there was any minimum wage, he could not work for free. If there was a minimum wage, the firm could not legally hire Leo and he wouldn't be able to obtain the information about the girl – which he views as more valuable than money. The minimum wage could actually hurt both the employer and employee. This happens when somebody is unemployed who would work for less than the minimum wage and the firm cannot afford to hire a worker for the higher wage.

The U.S. currently has a minimum wage of $7.25, and many U.S. States have implemented a higher minimum wage. However, there is a way employers get around this law and have employees work for free – unpaid internships. An internship is an opportunity for a prospective worker (often a student) to work for a firm for a defined but limited period of time. While many firms do pay their interns, many do not. But employers often value hiring workers who have had an internship. Many workers think the non-monetary benefits of an unpaid internship, mainly the experience in a particular job or industry, make them worth pursuing. There is not an official estimate for how many people take unpaid internships but estimates vary between 450,000 to 1 million people annually in the United States.[33]

Topics: Minimum Wage, Labor Economics, Internships

"I Don't Need a Roof"

Sandra is singing to her sick husband, Leo. She sings that she doesn't need adventure or a roof over head. All "she needs is [Leo] forever." She is expressing that she has an inelastic demand for Leo – she wants him and nothing else. Preferences are considered to be inelastic when a change in the price (whether monetary or in terms of foregone opportunities) does not affect the quantity demanded. Sandra seems willing to forego almost any other comfort to have Leo – so we could even say that her demand for Leo is perfectly inelastic.

Topics: Elasticity, Preferences

BILLY ELLIOT

"Solidarity"

The coal miners are on strike and are singing about staying unified. This is important, because if a union can maintain their cohesion they can exert significant bargaining power. They do this because they have the ability to strike and prevent all workers from working a particular job. The strike prevents workers from earning wages, but it also prevents the firm from earning money. This should make both sides more frantic to negotiate.

A key elements of bargaining theory is illustrated here – and that is the impact of an entity's "best alternative to a negotiated agreement." Nobel Prize-winning economist John Nash[34] showed that the best alternative to a negotiated agreement for a person or organization when entering a negotiation is crucial, and there are three key ways a person could improve his or her outcome when bargaining. The first is the person could raise their best alternative to a negotiated agreement – that is they could ensure that their alternative to an agreement is stronger. For example, suppose a recent graduate from college has applied for a job and received a job offer. If there is bargaining over the salary, the recent graduate will be in a much stronger position if he or she has another job offer on the table. With a second offer, the best alternative to a negotiated agreement for the recent graduate is higher. That will likely allow him or her to command a higher salary after bargaining. With no other offer, he or she will likely feel more pressure to simply accept a lower salary offer.

A second strategy one could employ to gain more from a bargaining situation is to make the other entity's alternative to the negotiated agreement worse. If a person can somehow take away their counterpart's options, that person will be worse off if they don't reach a solution through bargaining. This will make them more likely to reach a deal. Thinking back to job offers, if an employer could figure out a way to have other job offers revoked (which would likely be illegal

– but let's just assume they figure out a way), the applicant will have fewer options if he or she refuses the job offer. That will make him or her more desperate and the applicant would probably accept a lower salary.

But the strikers in the song "Solidarity" take a third approach that can sometimes work – by striking, they harm both themselves and the company simultaneously! If the strikers and the employer don't come to an agreement, the strikers are going without income, but so is the firm. The strikers are just hoping that the firm is hurt more and feels more pressure to negotiate. By doing that, they hope that they will have more bargaining power and receive higher wages.

Topics: Unions, Bargaining, John Nash, Game Theory

"Merry Christmas Maggie Thatcher"

Billy Elliot

These striking coal miners are not singing kind words. They sing "Merry Christmas Maggie Thatcher, we all celebrate today 'cause it's one day closer to your death." The song brings a good opportunity to discuss a bit of economic history between the U.K. government – and in particular the Thatcher administration – and unions.

Margaret Thatcher, who served as the first female Prime Minister of the U.K. from 1979 to 1990, was suspicious of union behavior in the U.K. She viewed union actions as borderline illegal and felt that non-union citizens were subsidizing one political party by paying higher wages to union members – who in turn were forced to pay union dues to political parties.[35] Unions in the 1970s, prior to her taking office, had gone on strike often, with significant production losses a result of the strikes. Thatcher said in July 1984 about the trade unions: "We had to fight the enemy without in the Falklands. We always have to be aware of the enemy within, which is much more difficult to fight and more dangerous to liberty."[36] Thatcher's actions made her a divisive figure – even after her death in 2013.[37]

Topics: Unions, Economic History

BONNIE AND CLYDE

"What Was Good Enough for You"

Bonnie and Clyde sing to their parents about how they want a better life. Throughout history, parents have wanted better lives for their children. Worldwide, this has generally happened due to economic growth and innovation. Between increased agricultural productivity, the benefits of the assembly line, and computers, incomes have increased dramatically. Figure 3 shows the average incomes in the United States (all incomes are adjusted for inflation and presented in 2017 U.S. dollars).[38]

While the U.S. and many other countries have experienced significant growth in wages, unfortunately this isn't true for all countries – especially countries that shunned free markets in favor of communism. The former Soviet Union experienced declines in average incomes annually for many years. A look at North Korea vs. South Korea also shows this fact. Both countries were in about the same economic position at the end of the Korean War in 1953 and North Korea became communist while South Korea embraced the mixed economy with a heavy dose of economic freedom in the mix. The GDP per capita today in South Korea (in U.S. dollars) is about $34,500, while in North Korea it is $1,800.[39] North Koreans are starving and without electricity at night. South Koreans are thriving.

Topics: Economic Growth, Capitalism, Communism

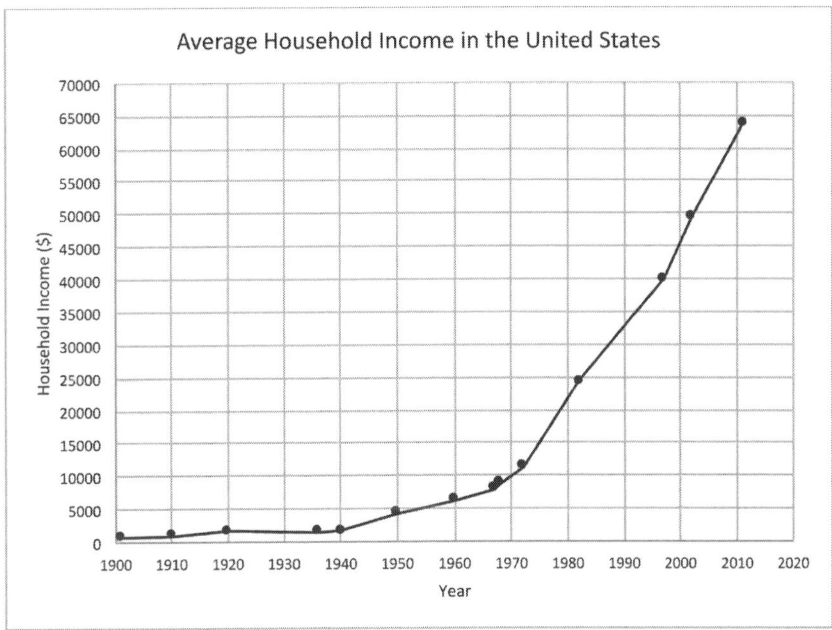
Average Household Income in the United States
Household Income ($)
70000
65000
60000
55000
50000
45000
40000
35000
30000
25000
20000
15000
10000
5000
0
1900
1910
1920
1930
1940
1950
1960
1970
1980
1990
2000
2010
2020
Year

FIGURE 3

CABARET

Set in the early 1930s, the patrons of the Kit Kat Club and others who lived in Berlin were very much influenced by the economic conditions of the time. After World War I, the allied countries had asked Germany to make large reparation payments to compensate the allied countries for lost lives and property from the war. The Weimar government chose to pay back Great Britain and France in part by printing massive amounts of their currency.[40] That caused a bout of hyperinflation, unfortunately. We can see the consequences when we compare the value of the German mark to the U.S. dollar.[41]

The consequences of this and other cases of hyperinflation in our world's history have been devastating. Families with savings see them wiped out. Further, because the currency is no longer trusted, fewer people are willing to use it and many people begin to resort to bartering or using foreign currencies instead of

TABLE 1

Date	*Number of German Marks Needed to Buy One U.S. Dollar*
1919	4.2
1921	75
1922	400
Jan. 1923	7,000
Jul. 1923	160,000
Aug. 1923	1,000,000
Nov. 1, 1923	1,300,000,000
Nov. 15, 1923	1,300,000,000,000
Nov. 16, 1923	4,200,000,000,000

domestic currencies – both of which will greatly decrease economic output. Economist John Maynard Keynes said about hyperinflation:

> Lenin is said to have declared that the best way to destroy the capitalist system was to debauch the currency . . . [he] was certainly right. There is no subtler, no surer means of overturning the existing basis of society than to debauch the currency. The process engages all the hidden forces of economic law on the side of destruction, and does it in a manner which not one man in a million is able to diagnose.[42]

On top of the hyperinflation, Germany also faced a severe depression between 1929 and 1933. These economic conditions would have been in the minds of every German, including those at the Kit Kat Club. The impact went far beyond a fictional musical, however as many historians think these economic conditions were big factors in creating the groundswell of support that helped Adolf Hitler rise to power.[43]

"So What"

Fraulein Schneider begins "So What" by illustrating the idea of producer surplus and the supply curve. She says "You say fifty marks. I say one hundred marks, a difference of fifty marks. Why should that stand in our way?" She accepts Cliff's offer of 50 marks by singing "as long as the room gets let [rented], the 50 that I will get is 50 more than I had yesterday."

Producer surplus is defined as the amount of money a seller receives above and beyond the minimum she needed to sell the product. If she would have let him stay for free – or if it is costless for him to stay – then the 50 marks that Fraulein Schneider receives is entirely producer surplus. Most people have received producer surplus, often when working at a job. For example, suppose a person applies for a job and was willing to work at that job for $8 per hour. But if the firm offers $10 per hour, the worker would receive $2 per hour in producer surplus. The worker is receiving $2 per hour more than he or she requires.

Topics: Producer Surplus, Supply

"Money"

While money might not "make the world go round," as the Emcee in *Cabaret* sings, it certainly has value. One of the main reasons money does help the world operate is that people can avoid using bartering. Bartering is incredibly inefficient, as the only way that a trade can happen is if the two people both happen to have something the other person wants – which economists call a double coincidence of wants. Prior to using money, exchanges had to occur where people bartered, or traded with each other. Without the use of money, we'd be back to bartering – so the Emcee isn't far off when he's singing of the value of money in helping the world operate.

If a society had to rely on bartering, their economic output would drop dramatically. This has happened in the 20th and 21st centuries in several countries that have had severe bouts of hyperinflation, including Greece in 1944, Hungary in 1946, Yugoslavia in 1994, and Zimbabwe in 2008.[44] But having a stable currency allows money to function as a medium of exchange – one of the three key functions for money.

Another role for money is as a store of value. People often choose to hold onto money instead of spending it immediately and know that it will have value at a later point in time. Finally, money also is used to quote prices – or as economists like to say, money serves as the unit of account. (When you've gone to purchase a cup of coffee in the morning – they give you a price in dollars and cents, right? They don't tell you how many paperclips you must pay.)

In addition to extolling the value of money, the discussion of different types of currency in the song is valuable. Four types of currency are discussed: The German mark, Japanese yen, buck (slang for American dollar), and British pound. Of these, the German mark doesn't exist any more, as it has been replaced by the euro. It is one of an estimated 600+ currencies worldwide to once be used but is now retired.[45] Approximately 25% of the currencies no longer in circulation went defunct because of hyperinflation, which is what the Emcee would have been dealing with in 1930s Germany.

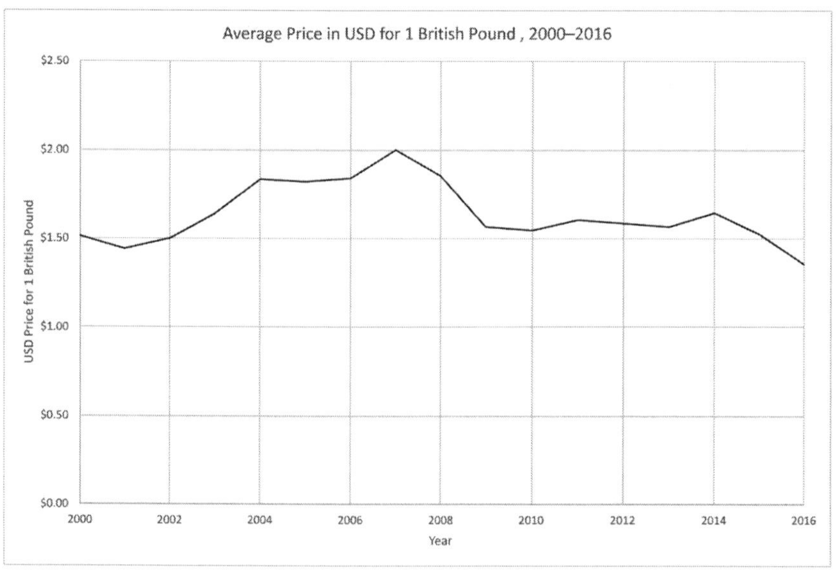

FIGURE 4

This song also highlights the value of exchange rates between currencies. An exchange rate is the price of a foreign currency – indicating how much of one currency must be exchanged for one unit of another. These prices often fluctuate. Right now, Germany uses the euro, Great Britain uses the British pound, while the United States uses the dollar. A currency is said to appreciate when it goes up in value relative to a foreign currency. For example, if the U.S. dollar can suddenly buy more British pounds, then we say that the dollar has appreciated. Conversely, the value of the British pound has decreased, so we say the pound has depreciated.

Currency prices fluctuate based on several factors, including demand for a country's goods and services, inflation rates affecting prices in one country, and speculation. The prices can vary significantly. Figure 4 shows the number of U.S. dollars it takes to purchase a pound from 2000 to 2016.

Topics: Money, Bartering, Exchange Rates

CANDIDE

"Make Our Garden Grow"

Candide and Cunegonde decide to get married. They aren't singing about their romance or love for each other, but instead on the tasks they'll be able to accomplish like chopping wood and working in the garden. Marriage historically has been viewed, at least in part, as an economic arrangement. This includes Kings and Queens marrying off their children to maintain power.[46]

For many today, economic factors still help to determine marriage. Harvard sociologist Alexandra Killewald's research indicates that economic wealth serves to help to ensure a comfortable marriage, and also that the level of wealth before marriage helps people to find a suitable partner.[47]

Assortative mating, the practice of people tending to sort when finding marriage partners, has economic implications. University of Pennsylvania economist Jeremy Greenwood and his colleagues found that in the U.S. there has been a rise in assortative mating. And with college-educated women now more likely to marry college-educated men (and similarly, high-earning women more likely to marry high-earning men), income inequality has also increased.[48]

Topics: Income Inequality, Assortative Mating

CAROUSEL

"When Children are Asleep"

Enoch is dreaming big. He is a fisherman with a boat and wants to reinvest his profits until he has a "big fleet of great big boats" selling fish. Economists define capital as a product that is used to make other valuable goods and services.[49] A boat is a fisherman's capital and Enoch understands that by investing in more boats that he will be more productive and be able to increase his family's standard of living. This is a key economic fact – increases in capital makes people and societies richer and leads to more economic growth.[50]

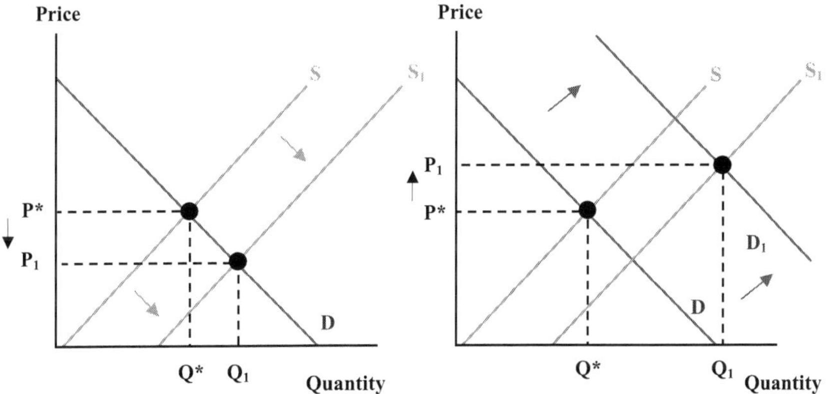

FIGURE 5

But Enoch's fiancée, Carrie, has a keen sense of economics and asks "Who will buy all those fish?" This is an important question as it seems that the increased supply of fish will cause the price to drop dramatically. But Enoch is also pretty smart – he wants to can the fish he catches to make sardines! By canning and distributing the fish across the country, Enoch could increase the demand and raise the price again as we see in Figure 5.

"When Children are Asleep" also highlights a key fact that time preferences for consumption can make a big difference in the lifetime standard of living for people. People who are willing to invest their time and money when younger can live much richer when older. This is true for people who are willing to put significant time and effort into attaining their education, as those with higher education levels earn higher wages.

This is also true for people who choose to invest the money they earn from working when young. In fact, a person who starts investing as little as $2,000 per year when in their late teens or early twenties and earns a reasonable interest rate could retire as a millionaire – and this could occur even if the person stopped saving in their early thirties.[51] The important point is that investing when young, whether in one's own education, saving money, or in capital to produce other products yields significant returns for most people later in life.

Topics: Capital, Demand, Supply, Investment, Savings, Time Preferences

"Real Nice Clambake"

The community sings "Our bellies are full . . . and we had a real good time." They are excited that they had a clambake and that everybody got enough to eat. Few modern musicals have songs where people sing for joy because they are full after a good meal. But in 1945, when Carousel was written, food wasn't as abundant in the U.S., or anywhere else, for that matter. For some perspective – in the 1928 election, Herbert Hoover campaigned for "a chicken in every pot."[52] The campaign for a chicken in every pot implies that not every family could afford a chicken. What makes that campaign pledge so striking is that this was during the economic boom of the 1920s and before the Great Depression started.

Despite the advances in economic growth, there is still some food insecurity in the U.S. according to the federal government, although the causes are debated.[53] The U.S. Department of Agriculture estimates that about 13% of households had food insecurity in 2015.[54] But in the U.S., obesity is actually a bigger problem. The Centers for Disease Control and Prevention (CDC) estimates that 36.5% of U.S. adults are obese.[55] This problem has enormous economic consequences. Economist Eric Finkelstein from Duke University estimated that the costs were estimated to exceed $78 billion annually in 1998 and rose to about $147 billion per year by 2008.[56]

Topics: Economic History, Economic Growth

CHICAGO

"When You're Good to Mama"

Mama Morton sings "they say that life is tit for tat and that's the way I live." She is in prison and her introduction to the new prisoners involves telling them she plays a tit-for-tat strategy. A tit-for-tat strategy occurs when a person will initially choose to cooperate with another person. However, if the other person chooses to no longer cooperate – he or she will then be uncooperative in the next round. So Mama Morton is approaching each new prisoner with a game theoretic mind-set and an offer to them – she will cooperate and attempt to help them out in return for the new prisoners cooperating with her. But if a new prisoner ever becomes uncooperative, Mama Morton will also choose not to cooperate. This is summed up by her lyrics at the end: "when you're good to mama, mama's good to you."

When games are repeated, a tit-for-tat strategy can often lead to cooperation between players with competing interests. But when a game is played only one time (often called a one-off or one-shot game), cooperation is tougher to sustain.

Topics: Repeated Games, Tit-for-Tat Strategy

CINDERELLA

"Impossible" and "It's Possible"

Cinderella and her Fairy Godmother are singing. Initially, the song focuses on Cinderella's opinion of what is impossible. Cinderella notes that it is impossible for a mouse to become a horse, a pumpkin to become a carriage, and she also notes that she cannot obtain a beautiful gown or great slippers given all the other tasks she has to do. Relating this to economics, Cinderella desires a combination of products that are beyond the boundaries of what is producible. In economics, we would say that she is seeking to consume beyond her production possibilities frontier, which shows the efficient combinations of products that are attainable.

As the song progresses, we see that "it's possible," at least if you have a fairy godmother who can work magic. When a person initially has a consumption bundle that isn't possible, one key way to obtain that bundle is by obtaining or creating a new technology. Thankfully for Cinderella, this is exactly what happens when her Fairy Godmother works her magic.

For those of us without magic, there are plenty of examples, however. Those who went to high school in the mid-1990s or earlier would have thought it was impossible to have a full-powered computer available on a telephone that fits in your pocket – and that you could look up virtually any fact at any time. New technology made that possible as well.

Topics: Production Possibilities Frontier

CLOSER THAN EVER

"Life Story"

In "Life Story" a middle-aged lady reflects on some of the big things that have helped define her life. Many moments are sad while some are uplifting. Fortunately for us, many provide economic lessons. The song starts with a discussion of her "sensible divorce." While it might have been sensible, divorces are costly and also have an economic impact. There is the financial cost of lawyers, which can be expensive. When a couple gets a divorce, assets are often split. But that sometimes means that large assets must be sold quickly and therefore below market prices, so the divorced couple is not only losing out on the lawyer fees but is also getting less money for their assets.[57]

The largest costs may be to children of divorced parents. Researchers Catherine Ross and John Mirowsky at the University of Texas at Austin found that

> Compared with individuals who grew up with both parents, adult children of divorce have lower levels of education, occupational status, and income, higher levels of economic hardships (both current and past), more often marry young, divorce and re-marry several times, find themselves in unhappy relationships, and mistrust people in general.[58]

These and other factors led Auburn University family studies researcher David Schramm to estimate that the economic consequences of divorce cost the United States more than $33 billion annually.[59]

Towards the end of the song, the lady sings about her adult son in college, and how she "pays tuition like a fine." Tuition is a major expense. In 2016–2017 tuition with room, board, and fees cost an average of about $20,000 per year at a public university (with in-state tuition). At a private university, it was much higher on average, about $45,000.[60] When this musical was set, in the early 1990s, she was likely paying a lot less. In today's dollars (i.e., after adjusting for inflation), in 1990–1991, tuition with room, board, and fees cost an average of about $6,000 at a public university and $15,000 at a private university. The costs for a college education have gone up much more than the overall inflation rate.

While the price of college has gone up, more people are attending college now than ever before. The total number of students enrolled at institutions of higher education increased from 14.5 million to 20.4 million from 1992 to 2013.[61] The singer hints at the reason for this when she sings that she is being interviewed by "MBAs making fifty thou." This is much less a person with an MBA earns now. The average starting salary for somebody with an MBA is $91,940 and the average mid-career salary is $121,417.[62]

Other topics are also brought up. She sings that she "turned down jobs with salaries" to "stay freelance." This might have actually limited her ability to gain human capital – the skills to earn higher incomes – if staying freelance cost her opportunities to further develop her career. She also discusses how she fought for equal pay for women and "faced down chauvinistic slobs."

Topics: Discrimination, Labor Economics, Trade-offs, Human Capital, Education

CURTAINS THE MUSICAL

"What Kind of Man"

The actors performing *Robbin' Hood of the Old West* here describe a job that is so terrible that nobody would possibly want to take it. At least that's what they think about critics after a few bad reviews come through. (OK, so they may be overreacting just a bit.)

This offers a good and humorous insight into compensating wage differentials. A compensating wage differential is a premium that somebody is paid to work a

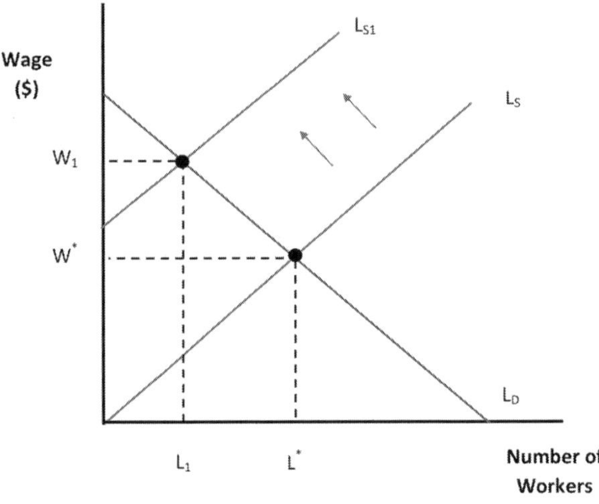

FIGURE 6

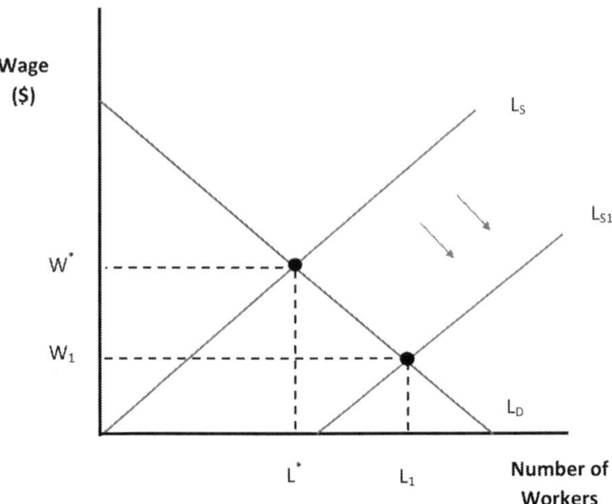

FIGURE 7

dangerous or less-desirable job. If being a critic is such a terrible job, we'd expect fewer people to want to be critics. That means a lower supply of workers, and with a lower supply, a higher wage! (See Figure 6.)

The idea of compensating wage differentials can work the other way as well – where jobs that offer tremendous non-pecuniary (non-monetary) benefits see a large supply of workers, which would increase the supply and drive down the wage. (See Figure 7.)

Understanding compensating wage differentials will help us understand why people in some professions earn higher or lower incomes.

Topics: Labor Economics, Compensating Wage Differential(s)

DAMES AT SEA

"Wall Street"

Mona is singing that she wants to go where the "green stuff grows" on Wall Street. About one kilometer long, Wall Street contains many of the leading financial institutions of the world. This includes the New York Stock Exchange and Nasdaq. Large amounts of money work through Wall Street. In 2015 the New York Stock Exchange along had trading volume worth $18 trillion – about 20% of the value of the world's output for that year.[63]

For somebody who is looking for a job to earn significant amounts of money – going to a financial firm on Wall Street (or elsewhere) is a good bet. According to the Wall Street Oasis's 2013 Compensation Report, third-year analysts on Wall Street earned an average of $111,000 with an average bonus of over $50,000.[64] The average *bonus* for a third-year analyst is approximately the same as the median *family* income in the United States. Naturally, vice presidents and managing directors earned much more (an average of well over $300,000 annually after bonuses).

Topics: Financial Markets

DEAR WORLD

"The Spring of Next Year"

If you don't listen to the lyrics, you might think "The Spring of Next Year" is a joyous song. Then you hear the lyrics, talking of "industrial waste in the air" along with a "black slick" and sludge on the Rhine river.

When firms produce a product that causes pollution, the firm usually only has to worry about the costs to produce the product. However, pollution imposes another cost to every member of society that is affected by it. When there are side-effects like pollution – where people incur a cost but aren't buying or selling the product – this is called an externality. In "the spring of next year," each person will have eyelids that sting from the smog and know about the "black slick" on the Rhine.

Pollution is an externality, and when firms pollute they are normally producing more than the efficient amount of a product. The reason is they don't bear the full cost of production. Let's consider firms that produce go-carts. The firms have a cost of producing go-carts – and each firm has its minimum price they will accept to product the go-cart. There is also a demand for go-carts, and when supply and demand interact, that will determine the price.

But suppose each go-cart emits a small amount of pollution – let's say the cost of pollution to the each person in the United States, due to slightly more particles in the air is 1/10,000 of a penny. One-ten thousandth of a penny certainly isn't a large effect per person, but given each person in a country is affected, the cost per go-cart isn't trivial. Given about 300 million people in the United States, that would mean each go-cart has a pollution cost of $300. If we examined the supply curve and added in the costs the firms face and the external cost of $300 per go-cart, we see that the equilibrium – and in this case, the efficient quantity of go-carts sold – would be lower than what was actually sold. Similarly, we see that the price should be higher!

Supply and Demand of Go-Carts

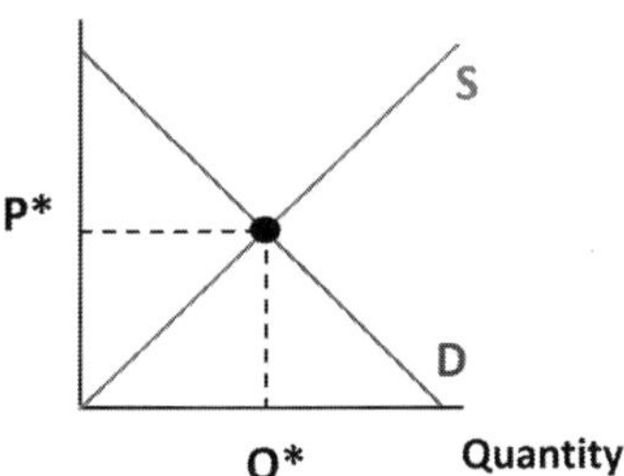

FIGURE 8

Supply and Demand of Go-Carts – Accounting for Pollution Costs

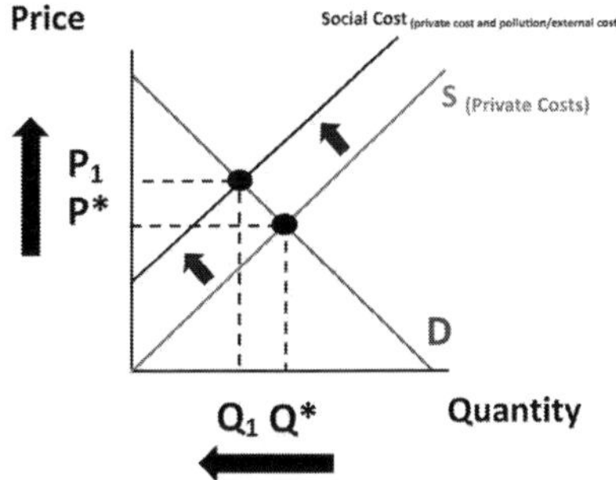

FIGURE 9

But the firms producing the go-carts do not have to pay that $300 cost, and therefore will ignore it – and an inefficient quantity will be produced. This leads to one of the central lessons when there is a negative externality. Too much will be produced if a negative externality is not corrected. How do economists recommend fixing a negative externality? Usually with a per-unit tax that is exactly equal to the cost of the pollution. In this case, a tax of $300 per go-cart! That would prompt firms to consider the full cost of producing a go-cart and would reduce the quantity produced to the efficient level.

There are two important lessons to remember regarding externalities that we see illustrated with this example. First, when there is a negative externality, like pollution, an unrestricted market will usually produce too much. Second, the optimal amount to produce is not zero – as that would also be inefficient.

Topics: Externalities, Pollution

DIRTY ROTTEN SCOUNDRELS

"Giving Them What They Want"

Lawrence and his bodyguard sing about how they will con money out of their wealthy victims. Lawrence is preying on desperate ladies and trying to give them the impression that he will help them live out their fantasies.

While Lawrence is attempting to con these ladies out of money, the advice he sings to "give them what they want" is great for legitimate businesses. In capitalist markets, the most successful firms supply consumers with the products they are demanding. Sometimes firms create products that customers don't even know they yet want, like iPhones, Beanie Babies, and FitBits. The firms that are most successful at giving customers what they want end up making the most money!

Topics: Markets, Competition

"Great Big Stuff"

Freddie is asked what he wants – and he doesn't hesitate to answer. He wants all sorts of things, including a mansion, "unnecessary surgeries," and his "own personal Zamboni." Given how much he wants, one wonders if the normal law of diminishing marginal utility applies to him. The law of diminishing marginal utility says that as you have more of an item each subsequent unit you obtain will be less important.[65] Most economists will contend there is also a diminishing marginal utility of wealth.

Clearly, an extra $10,000 means an enormous amount to somebody who earns $20,000 per year. It still likely means quite a bit to most people who make $100,000 per year, but it should be less important for these people. This is an example of diminishing marginal utility – and in particular, diminishing marginal utility of wealth. Each extra dollar is appreciated but less important than the previous dollar received.

Taking this to the extreme – if you make $10 million a year – how much would an additional $10,000 change your life? Probably not much, although maybe you could afford your own personal Zamboni!

Topics: Utility, Marginal Utility

DO I HEAR A WALTZ?

"Bargaining"

Renato teaches Leona how to bargain with Italian shopkeepers and is told "you wonder, you frown, you dwell on what is poor." She is told after she hears the price that she should not immediately accept it. We learn the shopkeepers are attempting to charge each customer as much as they possibly can, and those who won't go through the hassle of bargaining will pay more. Economists would say that the shopkeepers are price discriminators. They are attempting to charge each person a different price based on their maximum willingness-to-pay, instead of charging each person the same price. In fact, since the shopkeepers might literally charge a different price to every customer, we could call these shopkeepers first-degree, or perfect, price discriminators. There are also other ways firms could price discriminate.

Second-degree price discrimination occurs when firms offer different menus of products with different prices to all customers. Discounts for bulk purchases are the most common way second-degree price discrimination is practiced. Third-degree price discrimination is price discrimination where people in different groups are given different prices. When firms charge working-age adults more than children or senior citizens, this is an example of third-degree price discrimination. (They won't normally say they are charging more, but instead will say they're offering a "senior discount" or "student discount," but it has the same result.) Another example of third-degree price discrimination would be lower matinee prices at movie theatres.

Topics: Price Discrimination

EVITA

"And the Money Kept Rolling In"

Eva Peron is loved – in part because of the money she's giving away. "And the money kept rolling out in all directions. To the poor, to the weak, to the destitute of all complexions." The items she is spending money on bring up a good opportunity to discuss fiscal policy. Fiscal policy refers to the way a government taxes and spends in order to influence the economy. Peron (Eva's husband) and Eva were receiving money in and spending it on what we might think of as welfare programs – helping the poor. That is one way to stimulate the economy. Another is to lower tax rates so those who are working keep more of their money – and then either spend or save (which turns into investments).

Those who obtain the money love Eva Peron – even though it isn't actually her money that they are given. The money was obtained from taxing others. The themes of this song are relevant today. Is somebody compassionate when they tax some individuals in order to give that money to others?

Topics: Fiscal Policy, Size of Government

"A New Argentina"

In "A New Argentina," Juan and Eva Peron are nervous about being arrested by the military. They decide to make a political arrangement with the unions to help Juan in his re-election efforts. These types of arrangements between unions and political parties are common. For example, in the United States between 2005 and 2011, unions spent $4.4 billion on political causes. Unions and union members also spend significant amounts of time – with an estimate of over 6 million hours spent during the 2010 mid-term elections.[66] The unions donate their time and money hoping to help elect politicians who will enact policies that strengthen unions and the politicians support the aims of the unions and hope for their support to stay in power.

This is a good song to introduce public choice theory, as the unions represent a special-interest group receiving privileges in exchange for votes. Public choice theory is a branch of economics that examines political decisions as if the decision makers face trade-offs (much like trade-offs faced by private citizens). Through public choice theory, we realize that politicians might not always make the best decisions for society, because when they make decisions they also consider their re-election changes. With union donations, this means that sometimes politicians enact laws that benefit unions – thus ensuring continuing political donations – even if they don't think the laws are best for society as a whole.

Topics: Public Choice Theory, Unions, Labor Economics

FIDDLER ON THE ROOF

In what might be the most beloved musical of all time, Fiddler on the Roof's original production set a Broadway record by running for 3,242 shows.[67] After it closed in 1972, it was revived five times on Broadway. It has played in dozens of countries and thousands of U.S. high schools have performed it.

As an added bonus – the show gives us many economic lessons. The songs themselves – "Tradition," "If I Were a Rich Man," and others give us the opportunity to explore economic concepts, some of which are rarely seen in songs. But beyond the songs, the show itself also reveals many economic issues. We see Tevye and his family living a meager existence in 1905 Russia. The fact is, as a dairy farmer who owned property, their family is still wealthier than many of the poorest in the world at that time. But by today's comparison, they seem very poor. *Fiddler on the Roof* provides lessons about dispute resolution, matching markets, poverty, inequality, economic growth, and so much more.

"Tradition"

"Tradition," the opening number of *Fiddler on the Roof,* goes through the importance of traditions in the town of Anatevka. The economy of Anatevka is based on traditions, they do not necessarily organize to be economically efficient. There are several alternative ways that an economy could be set up – but all societies either explicitly or implicitly decide answers to the following three questions: 1) What products and services get produced?, 2) How do these products and services get produced?; 3) For whom are the products and services produced?

A market economy is one way these questions are answered. In a market economy, there isn't a government answering the questions – the questions of what, how, and for whom are answered by the hundreds, thousands, or millions of individuals and firms. Each person and firm in the economy makes their own decisions, based on price information which is also determined through market forces, and that helps determine what gets produced, how it gets produced, and who receives the products and services that are produced. Market economies have several benefits including that there rarely are shortages or surpluses, products are allocated efficiently based on consumer willingness-to-pay, and that the profit motive helps to spur economic growth. The downsides of markets include market failures and inequality of incomes.

A command economy is another way that the "what, how, and for whom" questions could be answered. In a command economy, a central government will play a heavy role in determining what is produced, how it is produced, and for whom the products are produced. While at first glance it might appear that this would allow for more efficiency, in practice it does not. It is very difficult to determine, for example, how many pairs of pants might be needed for a country in a given year – not to mention sizes, styles, colors, etc. Throughout history, command economies have been notorious for having too many of some products and too few of others, which often led to very long lines.[68] With markets, for-profit firms can adjust quickly to price changes, which helps prevent shortages and surpluses.

In contrast to market and command economies, traditional economies choose their way of operating based on the way things have always been done. Anatevka is an example of a society that placed a great value on traditions. Another example of a traditional economy would include (some of the activities of the) Amish communities in the United States. The Amish often make choices that are going to reduce production efficiency but are consistent with traditions. This includes decisions not to use outside electricity or motor vehicles.

A traditional economy will be less efficient at creating goods and services than a market economy. That doesn't mean that those in traditional economies are making poor choices. If members of the society value traditions more than the additional material goods and services it could gain by changing their systems, this type of system could be rational.

Topics: Economic Systems, Market Economy, Command Economy, Communism, Capitalism, Traditional Economy

"Matchmaker"

Two of Tevye's daughters, Chava and Hodel, are discussing how they hope the town matchmaker will find them a great husband and they are excited. Tzeitel, their oldest sister, chimes in to discuss some problems with their thinking. Tzeitel helps convince her sisters that their dreams of being paired with their ideal match are unlikely by telling them "you're a poor girl from a poor family so whatever Yenta brings, you'll take, right?" In 1905 Russia, where the musical is set, young men and women didn't pick their own marriage partners. Instead, marriages were arranged.[69] Historically, this was the norm and arranged marriages still occur in parts of the world today. For example, over 85% of marriages in India are arranged marriages.[70] While a much, much smaller percentage, there are also still some arranged marriages in developed countries as well. For example, there are approximately 14,000 forced marriages in the U.S. and 1,400 in the U.K. annually. The differences between an arranged marriage market and one that is free mirrors many differences between free markets and restricted markets in other areas.

One of the areas where economists have made an impact is in the creation of matching markets. A matching market is one in which economic models help pair up those that wish to be matched. Economist Alvin Roth won the 2012 Nobel Prize in Economics for his work on market design. In one of his papers, entitled "Repugnance as a Constraint on Markets," Roth discusses many markets where society won't allow a free market to emerge. One example of a market that is illegal because of repugnance is the market for human organs. This is despite the fact that much research shows that markets are much more efficient than alternative mechanisms and thousands of people die annually because of a shortage of available kidneys.

Economists have worked to help create matching systems for some products where open market exchanges are not allowed by law, including organ donation. If people could legally buy and sell organs, when a person needed a transplant he or she could simply choose to buy (or not) an organ on the open market for the going price. With organ sales being illegal, the person instead needs to find an organ donor. When the person finds a donor that is a match, e.g., the kidney can be taken without complications, things are easy. Matching markets can come into play when a person is willing to donate an organ to a friend, but he or she is not a "match."

The idea behind the matching market is simple – you might want to donate a kidney to your friend but you aren't a match. But somewhere else, somebody needs a kidney of your type and they have a friend who matches your friend's type. The match occurs where you donate the kidney to the anonymous recipient who matches your type in exchange for the anonymous recipient's friend who donates to your friend. In fact, you could have more than two people. With three people you would donate a kidney to an anonymous recipient, whose donor gives to a second anonymous recipient, whose donor gives a kidney to your friend. In 2015, a chain like this of 70-transplants was conducted in the United States.[71]

The market for kidneys is not the only place where matching markets have helped society. Economists have also been instrumental in creating matching markets for college admissions, public school choice matching, and markets that help match medical residents with hospitals.

Topics: Game Theory, Market Design

"If I Were a Rich Man"

Tevye dreams of what it would be like to be rich. He sings that he wants three staircases – one going up, one for walking down, and one that is "just for show."

A poor person dreaming of becoming rich is a common theme and this song is relevant when considering income inequality. Tevye is poor, and others are wealthier. In the United States and many other developed countries, income inequality has grown in the past 30–40 years, prompting popular movements such as "Occupy Wall Street" and other protests against income inequality. While "If I Were a Rich Man" is a good song to play when thinking about income inequality, the real value of this song lies in its ability to show the importance of economic growth.

Fiddler on the Roof is set in the year 1905. It is instructive to think about what it meant to be rich in 1905, and many people today would find Tevye's view on being rich staggering. In this song, Tevye sings about wanting chickens and other small farm animals in his yard, a well-fed wife, some free time, and three staircases in his house. This would not sound rich to the average American today.

However, the song presents a realistic view of what dreams of being rich would have seemed like in 1905 Russia. In 1905, the average income in the United States (adjusting for inflation) was under $1,000/year.[72] It was lower in Russia.[73]

The average poor person in America and most first-world countries today has an income that is considerably higher than Tevye's, and may even be wealthier than the lifestyle Tevye imagines. In this way, "If I Were a Rich Man" is incredibly valuable for showing us the importance of economic growth. In 1905, most of the world was impoverished by today's standard of poverty. Economic growth has caused the standards of living to improve by a factor of 20 or more in many countries.

Why has this happened? Why are average incomes in the United States, Japan, Great Britain, Germany, so much higher than they were in the early 20th century while other countries have seen little to no economic growth? We don't know all the reasons yet, and many people devote their lives to studying economic growth, but it is clear that rules and the government's structure matter.

The ability of economic growth to move millions from poverty to prosperity helped lead Nobel Prize-winning economist Robert Lucas to state "Once you start thinking about growth, it is hard to think about anything else."[74] "If I Were a Rich Man" gives us a great illustration of the power of economic growth.

Topics: Economic Growth, Income Inequality, Poverty

"Dear Sweet Sewing Machine"

Motel and Tzietel are singing a love song. Not to each other, but to their sewing machine. That may seem a bit odd to us now, but getting a sewing machine in 1905 Russia was indeed a reason to celebrate. The sewing machine allows Motel to be a more efficient tailor and increases his production ability.

A sewing machine is considered capital – one of the factors of production – as it is a product that can be used to create other products. (The other factors of production are land and labor.) By getting a sewing machine Motel will be more

Motel's Original Production Possibilities Frontier (PPF)

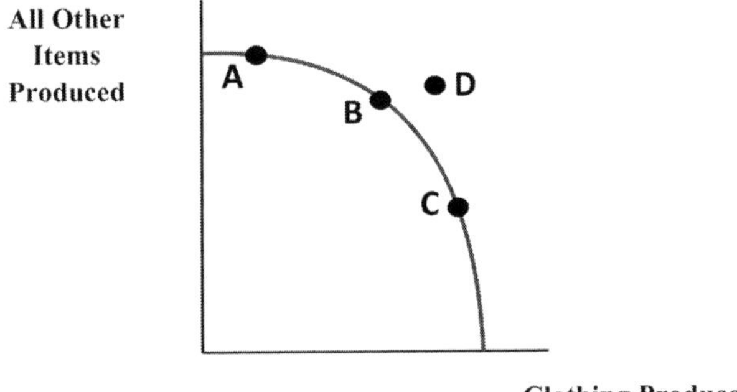

Clothing Produced

Motel's Production Possibilities Frontier (PPF) – Rotation on the X-Axis for Clothing Produced

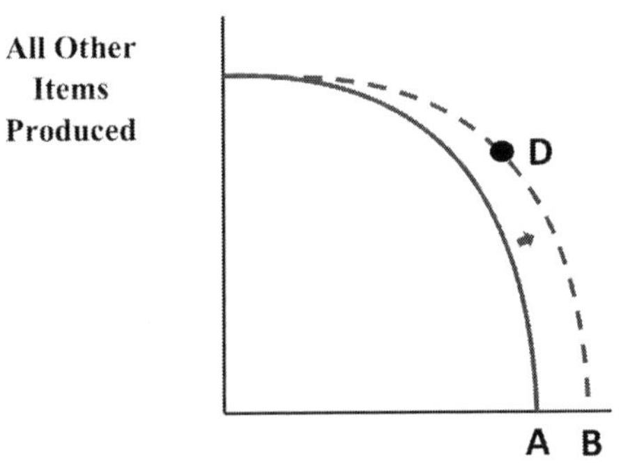

Clothing Produced

FIGURE 10

productive and, as he and Tzietel sing, his family will be able to acquire more food. For those looking at the production possibilities frontier, which graphically shows how much of two items could be produced, we see that a sewing machine would cause an increase in production possibilities. In the first graph, production point D, which contains more of clothing produced and all other items, is not attainable. The current level of technology just won't allow Motel and his family to have that. But with the new sewing machine, Motel is much more productive at sewing and could actually have more of both clothing and other items.

New capital inventions over the past 200 years, like sewing machines, have helped our world produce more and become much, much wealthier.

Topics: Capital, Factors of Production, Production Possibilities Frontier, Economic Growth

FROZEN

"Let it Go"

Elsa has had an affliction – being able to turn things into ice. (I think many people would claim they've had exes for whom that applies . . . but for Elsa this is literal!) But the fact that Elsa has had a past shouldn't influence what decisions she makes going forward and she realizes this when she sings "the past is in the past." Elsa uses good economic logic when singing that she will "let it go."

Elsa's past is what economists call a sunk cost, which is a cost that has already been incurred and cannot be recovered, and stays the same regardless of the next course of action.[75] Because her past is a sunk cost, she should simply "let it go" and ignore her sunk costs. Much like Elsa, individuals and firms that want to make good decisions should not factor sunk costs into their analyses. Because the cost is not retrievable, the only thing that should influence a person's/firm's decision to move forward is the expected benefit/loss from each possible action that is still possible.

There are several real-world examples where people make better decisions when ignoring sunk costs. First, consider a person in a relationship with somebody who is considering breaking up the relationship. If he or she wanted to stay in the relationship "because we have a history," that is bad logic. What the person should be thinking about is whether the benefit of staying in the relationship is worth the costs (the benefits and costs here are non-monetary). The sunk costs of the days, months, or years in a relationship should not influence the choice.

Let's consider a second example. Suppose that you want to try a new restaurant. You arrive and are told it will be a one-hour wait – which is about the longest you would wait, but you decide you will stay and wait for a table. After 30 minutes of waiting, the host has bad news, telling you that because of something unexpected that happened, it will take one additional hour before you get a table

(30 minutes longer than anticipated). In this case, the 30 minutes you've already waited should be thought of as a sunk cost. It isn't recoverable and it shouldn't change your decision process going forward. Maybe you think you should wait for an additional hour. Maybe you think you should find another restaurant. Or maybe you think it is better to eat at home. All options could be reasonable, but regardless of what you choose, you waited for 30 minutes and that cost is not retrievable. It is a sunk cost and should not factor into your decision.

Topics: Costs, Sunk Costs

FOLLIES

"Broadway Baby"

Hattie Walker, who is now elderly, sings about what it takes to be successful on Broadway. It involves "learning how to sing and dance" – obvious, but not easy given Broadway is the pinnacle for stage acting. She also discusses that it requires "slaving at the five and ten" which is slang for working at a discount retail outlet, indicating that many who are successful on Broadway have to hold down other jobs. Hattie is trying to convey that there are trade-offs to pursuing a dream career on the Broadway stage.

This song presents a realistic view at the prospects of those seeking acting work in New York. Mitch Weiss, author of the book *The Business of Broadway*, wrote that "at any one moment, approximately 88% . . . of Actors' Equity Association union actors are not employed in the theatre." That doesn't include the fact that there are many "nonunion actors living in New York without an income from theatre."[76] Many aspiring actors take up side jobs while pursuing their dream of an acting career.[77]

Topics: Trade-offs, Business of Broadway

FUN HOME

"Come to the Fun Home"

The children of the Bechdel Funeral Home decide to make a commercial. In "Come to the Fun Home" they attempt to differentiate their family's funeral home from the competition. The children mention several reasons people should use the Bechdel Funeral Home, including their smelling salts, folding chairs, and car magnets.

This song provides a good example of a firm in a monopolistically competitive industry. A monopolistically competitive industry is one where there are many small sellers, there are few or no barriers to entering the market, and firms sell similar but slightly differentiated products. The funeral home business is one with relatively low barriers to entry and can have many smaller firms. While funeral homes all provide the same general service, their services are slightly different, so they are in a monopolistically competitive market. The kids in the commercial are doing everything they can to help differentiate the Bechdel Funeral Home from their competitors.

In addition, the Bechdel Funeral Home is a small business, started by the father of the family, which is a good example of the value of entrepreneurship. The family earns extra money by running the funeral home, but the community benefits from another option for funeral home needs. And while the kids in the song are singing about some odd innovations, like "smelling salts for if you're queasy," entrepreneurial innovations have added a tremendous amount of value to society.

Topics: Market Structure, Monopolistic Competition, Entrepreneurship, Innovation

GREASE

"Beauty School Dropout"

In "Beauty School Dropout," Frenchie is dreaming. In her dream, she hears about the consequences of flunking out of beauty school. Frenchie initially dropped out of high school to attend beauty school but then also flunked out of beauty school. The teen angel who is singing to Frenchie explains the consequences, singing that her future is "so unclear now" and that nobody except a prostitute would patronize her business. The teen angel then recommends that Frenchie goes back to high school. The teen angel is giving good advice, as those without a high school degree on average earn $25,000 annually. Those who earn a high school degree earn $30,000 annually – 20% more!

Topic: Human Capital, Labor Economics, Education

GYPSY

"You Gotta Get a Gimmick"

The ladies are singing about how someone could become a better stripper. While entertaining and funny, this song illustrates a couple of economics concepts. First, this song illustrates the returns to human capital, as the ladies all invested time and energy to "get a gimmick" in order to receive higher wages. Whether it was Miss Mazeppa, who figured out how to "bump it with a trumpet" or Tessie Tura who does "it with finesse," they all invested. Education and training usually do result in higher wages, and according to this song – these strippers are no exception.

Second, this song illustrates the benefits of product differentiation in a monopolistically competitive market. While it may seem odd to think of stripping in this manner, the market for strippers is monopolistically competitive. (Very low barriers to entry, many small "firms," and product differentiation as no two strippers are identical.) In a monopolistically competitive market, you can earn more money by successfully differentiating yourself in a positive way.

Topics: Human Capital, Monopolistic Competition, Product Differentiation

HAMILTON

Hamilton is perhaps the best single album – musical or otherwise – ever produced to teach economics. The musical, based on Ron Chernow's book, contains a variety of genres, including pop, hip-hop, rhythm and blues, jazz, and more to showcase the life of U.S. founding father, Alexander Hamilton. The musical's use of current music styles has attracted many younger fans – including many college students. Yet it is not solely younger fans who like the show. The wide variety of music styles presented and the focus on American history have made this one of the most popular musicals of all time. In fact, Barack Obama once said: "*Hamilton* is the only thing Dick Cheney and I agree on."[78]

Hamilton has become what *The Wall Street Journal* describes as "the best and most important Broadway musical of the past decade."[79] *Hamilton* earned #1 Billboard 200 ranks for Cast Albums, Rap Albums, Digital Albums, and a #3 rank for Top Album Sales,[80] only the sixth cast album to reach the Top 20 in the last 50 years,[81] and it set the record for most Tony Award nominations.[82] It won the Tony Award and Grammy Award for best musical, along with a Pulitzer Prize in Drama – one of only nine musicals in history to win this accolade.[83] *Hamilton*'s popularity is so great that tickets on the resale market routinely were selling for over $1,000. In fact, best-selling economics textbook author, Greg Mankiw, reported paying $2,500 per ticket (and said it was worth it)![84]

In addition to being a well-decorated show, the songs in *Hamilton* can be used to illustrate trade-offs, opportunity costs, acquisition of human capital, monetary policy, labor economics, discounting the future, and more.

"Alexander Hamilton"

The words in the opening sentence of the musical Hamilton asks an important question. The song asks "how does a bastard, orphan . . . impoverished in squalor,

HAMILTON
RODGERS
HAMILTON
RICHARD
RODGERS

BACKGROUND ON ALEXANDER HAMILTON'S SIGNIFICANCE IN U.S. HISTORY AND ECONOMIC POLICIES

It is worthwhile to briefly discuss Hamilton's role in U.S. economic policies. Scholars of American history acknowledge Alexander Hamilton to be a progressive founding father whose contributions shaped the United States as a republic. Therefore, when considering utilizing songs from *Hamilton* to introduce economics concepts, it is crucial to note Alexander Hamilton's significance and influence not only in U.S. history but also in economic policies of the past and present United States.

With numerous contributions to U.S. monetary policy, it is rather ironic that Alexander Hamilton has been so overlooked in U.S. history. Award-winning historian and Alexander Hamilton biographer Ron Chernow noted of him: "Except for [George] Washington, nobody stood closer to the center of American politics from 1776 to 1800 or cropped up at more turning points."[85] Alexander Hamilton's importance is in part because of his official government appointment. He was the Nation's First Secretary of the Treasury and is credited as being the "architect of the department." Hamilton advocated for a strong centrally controlled treasury – often pitting himself against the likes of Thomas Jefferson (Secretary of State at the time) over how much control the treasury should wield.[86]

One area where Hamilton and Jefferson clashed was over whether the U.S. should establish a national bank. Coinciding with the establishment of the First Bank of the United States in 1791, Hamilton also fought for the assumption of state debts by the federal government and to create a mechanism for collecting taxes.[87] The implementation of these three elements of Hamilton's financial plan ultimately provided the foundation for the Nation's future economic and monetary policies. Through his financial plan and service as U.S. Treasury Secretary, Chernow argues that Alexander Hamilton blazed a trail for trade, industry, the stock market, and banks and "was the messenger from a [economic] future we now inhabit."[88]

grow up to be a hero and a scholar?" The full answer to this question is complicated and is answered in the musical, but the short answer is income mobility, which is the degree to which a society has people from lower income groups moving to higher income groups. America has traditionally been a country with high income mobility.

While we don't know the perfect recipe to ensure that a country has a high degree of income mobility, economists have argued that strong access to education, being raised in a nurturing environment, and a stable rule of law are key to allow those in lower income groups to rise to greater incomes.[89] In "Alexander Hamilton" we hear that Hamilton's work ethic and willingness to devour books helped put him in a situation where people in his home country (the island of Nevis) contributed to send him to America.

Topics: Income Mobility

"My Shot"

"My Shot" contains lyrics that illustrate several economic concepts. One main theme throughout the song is the value of acquiring human capital. Early in the song Hamilton is talking about going to King's College (which is now Columbia University) to gain skills, as he claims "the problem is I've gotta lotta brains but no polish." Education is one of the main ways that individuals can improve their human capital to get better jobs and live better lives. That was true in the late 1700s and is still true today. But a university education certainly is not the only way to advance in one's career.

In "My Shot" we are introduced to Hamilton's best friends and his personal outlook on life. In the song, the character Mulligan sings:

> Yo, I'm a tailor's apprentice.
> And I got y'all knuckleheads in loco parentis.
> I'm joining the rebellion cuz I know it's my chance
> to socially advance, instead of sewin' some pants.

To Mulligan, hard work, along with showing his value in the Army, is a way to increase his future income. His view is still true today – in 2017, 15 Fortune 500 CEOs were military veterans.[90] The Army offers programs in accounting, computer engineers, nursing, and many more fields where there is significant demand for jobs.[91]

Other economic topics are also discussed in "My Shot." The character Laurens sings that "we'll never be truly free until those in bondage have the same rights as you and me." Slavery was common in the colonies in the late 18th century despite the efforts of abolitionist movements. In fact, when discussing the "capital" that was owned in the United States, Thomas Piketty showed that slaves were a large portion of the capital base in the United States in the late 1700s and the first half of the 1800s.[92] Taxation and the size of the government are also briefly discussed when Hamilton sings that Britain taxes the colonies "relentlessly, then King George turns around and runs a spending spree."

Topics: Human Capital, Economic Freedom, Taxes, Slavery

"You'll be Back"

In "You'll be Back," King George sings to the colonists warning them not to leave the union. He sings that "When push comes to shove, I will send a fully armed battalion to remind you of my love." In addition to sending a fully armed battalion, he threatens that he will kill "friends and family to remind you of my love." Clearly, King George doesn't want the United States to separate from Britain. To encourage them not to secede, he very clearly indicates the opportunity cost that the colonists will incur should they ignore his advice. Recall that opportunity cost is defined as what someone must give up to get something – monetary and non-monetary. In this case, the cost of independence will be war with one of the most formidable armies of the time and will result in thousands of colonists losing their lives. Along with the opportunity cost, the trade-offs are quite clear: Remain as a colony and live with British oppression, or attempt to become free at the cost of many lives. King George attempted to make the first option sound better. As we know, the U.S. chose the second.

Topics: Opportunity Cost, Trade-offs

"Right Hand Man"

Alexander Hamilton sings that he wanted a war when he was so young that he would "either die on the battlefield in glory or rise up." Hamilton gives an example of somebody considering compensating wage differentials when making choices. A compensating wage differential is a higher payment someone receives for a job that is more dangerous or unpleasant. Judging from Alexander Hamilton's words, he is willing to face the increased risk of death in order to have a better life.

There are more economic lessons from "Right Hand Man." Later in the song, we also hear that Hamilton is judicious about his choices for jobs. Hamilton turns down job offers from Nathaniel Green and Henry Knox, now legendary figures in American history, because he isn't being offered a job that he wants. If Hamilton is choosing unemployment while looking for a better job, this is an example of what economists call frictional unemployment – Hamilton has skills to be employed, but is unemployed while searching for a job that better fits his skill sets and interests.

Topics: Labor Economics, Compensating Wage Differentials, Unemployment, Frictional Unemployment

"Satisfied"

The song "Satisfied" has Angelica Schuyler (the daughter of prominent U.S. general Philip Schuyler) singing a toast to her sister Eliza and her sister's groom, Alexander Hamilton, at their wedding. While singing the toast, Angelica has a flashback to when she first met Hamilton. Angelica actually met Hamilton first, and she and Hamilton shared a mutual attraction. She considered pursuing him but instead decided to give up her chance of courting Hamilton by introducing him to her sister, Eliza. Angelica is pained by this decision, but provides three justifications as to why she made her decision: 1) As the eldest daughter, she must marry somebody wealthy; 2) Hamilton is only interested in her because of her family's status; and 3) She genuinely cares about her sister's happiness and potential love interest in Hamilton. Even with these rationales in mind, it is clear that Angelica's choice of giving up her chance with Hamilton was tough, especially since she seems to be in love with him. A careful analysis of Angelica's thought process shows that the rational part of her mind still believes that she made the correct choice in the situation – there were just costly emotional trade-offs.

Many trade-offs have nothing to do with money and that's often the case with some of the most important decisions in life. For example, some cancer patients face a terrible decision on whether or not to receive chemotherapy. Chemotherapy can lengthen the lifespan but often significantly reduces the quality of life. This is an unpleasant trade-off, but one that many people face.

Topics: Trade-offs, Opportunity Cost

"Ten Duel Commandments"

In the "Ten Duel Commandments," we learn about the rules that people in the late 1700s followed when agreeing to engage in a duel. At first glance, this song might not appear to have anything to do with economics – but in fact it's a great song to highlight how spontaneous institutions might emerge without government intervention.

Without government rules, market rules and institutions tend to form, and tend to form quickly. These institutions can seem trivial, like in a farmers' market where the buyer and seller agree on a price. But they could also be much more complicated – like the institutions that have been created the governing of payments made for items bought on eBay. Users on eBay make transactions, and payments are made using PayPal. If there is a case where somebody feels they did not get what they should have received in a purchase – the police are not involved, instead there are procedures in place that eBay and PayPal follow. This has worked well and PayPal now processes over $100 billion per year in payments.[93] Other examples where complicated institutions arose without government guidance or intervention include the London Stock Exchange and private police forces.[94]

Topics: Public Choice Theory, Institutions

"Guns and Ships"

Marquis de Lafayette and George Washington are discussing what they must do to ensure that the colonies win the Revolutionary War against Britain. Both agree there is only one man who can help them achieve their mission of winning the war: Alexander Hamilton. In this respect, they have an inelastic demand for Alexander Hamilton's services.

Topics: Elasticity

"Cabinet Battle #1"

How did the U.S. first form a central bank? Why did the U.S. decide to run a national debt, where the federal government assumed the debts of all states? Of course there were congressional debates, and the musical *Hamilton* portrays these debates through rap-battles. In "Cabinet Battle #1," Alexander Hamilton and Thomas Jefferson debate Hamilton's financial plans for the new nation. Hamilton's plan contained three recommendations: for the U.S. to create a central bank, for the U.S. to assume the debts of the individual states, and for the U.S. to pay back the national debt accumulated during the revolutionary war.

The debate we hear in the song covers the first two items of the plan and is fun yet fierce. Jefferson was clearly suspicious of the plans to have a larger national government with financial power and did not like the idea of having a central bank. In the late 1700s many (like Jefferson) viewed federal government power suspiciously, which certainly was one reason why forming a central bank was controversial. We could make the parallel to today – where many still disapprove of the Federal Reserve and find it controversial – with part of the reason being that the Federal Reserve has control over monetary policy without having to go through the usual legislative checks-and-balances. According to a 2015 Pew Research poll, 47% of Americans had a favorable view of the Federal Reserve while 39% had an unfavorable view (Maniam 2015). Poll questions among economists are not asking for whether economists had a favorable vs. unfavorable view, rather, their questions address specific policies. Responses in recent years illustrate a nearly even split of economists thinking the Federal Reserve's policies are "about right" (The Associated Press 2014, 2016).

Jefferson goes on: "This financial plan is an outrageous demand and it's too many damn pages for any man to understand." This line has relevance to politics today, where politicians have passed laws worth hundreds of billions of dollars without reading them – often because the bills are hundreds or thousands of pages long. For example, in 2014, Congressman Earl Blumenauer of Oregon's 3rd District voted for the 1,528-page $1.1 trillion government spending bill and admitted he hadn't read the bill.[95] A year later, to take a stand against politicians voting for bills or laws without reading the fine print, Senator Rand Paul actually voted against the 2015 $1.1 trillion spending bill (that was eventually passed by Congress) on the basis that "nobody had a chance to read the behemoth [2,242 pages] legislation."[96]

Hamilton counters Jefferson by singing: "If we assume the debts, the union gets a new line of credit, a financial diuretic." In true rap-battle style, Hamilton also slips in the fact that Jefferson is a slave owner, so it's hypocritical for him to talk about freedom.

Topics: Federal Reserve, National Debt, Slavery, Public Choice Theory

"Take a Break"

Hamilton has been working long hours trying to figure out a way to get his financial plan through Congress. But Eliza wants more time with him, and she can't understand why he'd want to keep working when he's achieved so much success, doesn't have a war to fight, and is earning a decent salary.

Hamilton has important work to do, and faces a tough trade-off. He is surely earning more money, so he can afford to take time off. But each hour of leisure time he takes also is incredibly costly given his productivity and earnings. Hamilton is facing what economists call a labor/leisure trade-off.

When people start to earn more money there are competing forces that provide different incentives regarding how many hours to work. When a person earns a higher wage, he/she can afford to "buy" more leisure time. This will provide an incentive to work less, and economists call this the income effect. However, while a person might be able to afford more leisure, it is also more expensive to "buy" an hour of leisure time. For example – if someone earns \$10/hour, an hour of leisure means giving up \$10. But someone who earns \$100/hour will have to give up \$100

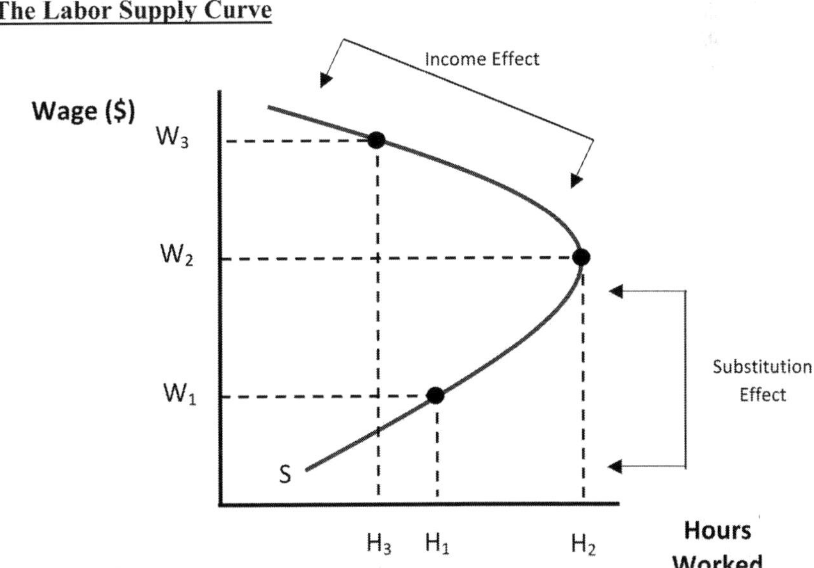

FIGURE 11

for that same hour of leisure. The fact that leisure is more expensive will provide an incentive to work more, not less. Economists call this the substitution effect.

The income and the substitution effects counteract each other, and because of these competing effects there is no guarantee the labor supply curve will look the same as a conventional supply curve. In fact, these competing effects lead to what economists have called the backward bending labor supply curve. The idea is that at low wages, increases in pay do induce more hours worked (the substitution effect dominates). But there is a point where that will change, and higher wages will lead to fewer hours worked and more leisure time (the income effect dominates). The resulting supply curve will then bend backwards.

While in the song we do not necessarily hear that the money is driving the decision, clearly Hamilton is facing trade-offs similar to the labor/leisure trade-off as he gets more successful. Ultimately, he decides to keep working – a lot – so the substitution effect still seems to be dominant for Hamilton.

Topics: Labor Economics, Labor-Leisure Trade-Off

"Say No to This"

In the song "Say No to This," the trade-offs of having an extra-marital affair are highlighted. Hamilton was alone and was propositioned by Mrs. Maria Reynolds. After a month of having an affair with her, Mrs. Reynolds's husband notifies him that Hamilton either has to make payments to keep seeing her or Mr. Reynolds will tell Hamilton's wife about the affair.

Later in the show, we see that Hamilton did choose to keep seeing Mrs. Reynolds, and in the process paid over $1,000 to Mr. Reynolds. For Hamilton, paying Mr. Reynolds meant being able to continue seeing Mrs. Reynolds and ensuring sure his wife did not find out about the affair. For Mr. Reynolds, receiving $1,000 meant consenting to allow his wife to have an affair.

It could also be that Hamilton viewed the short run as more important the long run. Perhaps he assumed the affair would go public and that relationships and his career would be damaged – but that would be in the future. If that was the case, the short-run satisfaction gained through the affair might have outweighed the costs he expected in the future. If that was the case, then economists would say that Hamilton's discount rate for the future was high.

Topics: Trade-offs, Short Run vs. Long Run, Discount Rate

"The Room Where It Happens"

"The Room Where It Happens" highlights an issue that can be analyzed using public choice theory, which studies how governments can fail based on political agents acting in their personal best interest. In the song, Burr enviously speculates about Hamilton's financial plan negotiations with Jefferson and Madison during a dinner meeting. During the dinner meeting, Hamilton ultimately agreed to a compromise (The Compromise of 1790) that allowed his financial plans to pass in exchange for the United States capital moving from New York City to its current location in Washington D.C.[97] The following is the show's breakdown of these negotiations:

Madison: A quid pro quo
Jefferson: I suppose
Madison: Wouldn't you like to work a little closer to home?
Jefferson: Actually, I would
Madison: Well, I propose the Potomac
Jefferson: And you'll provide him his votes?
Madison: Well, we'll see how it goes
Jefferson: Let's go

Madison and Jefferson evaluate if they should allow the creation of the central bank, which they did not think was good for society. They will agree to it as long as they could move the capital closer to Virginia (which shortens Jefferson's commute). The decision making between Madison and Jefferson is a strong example of politicians not necessarily working for the good of the people – but instead working in their own interest.

Later, Aaron Burr and the other non-participants sing "the art of the compromise, hold your nose and close your eyes." Burr expresses disdain and overall disgust in their lack of voice with politician's decision making – lending to outcomes benefiting politicians but not the people in which they serve. According to the song, Jefferson did not think that Hamilton's plan was good for the country, but he thought getting the capital near Virginia was enough of a win for his constituents and for him that he would allow it. The real-life Jefferson later stated that this compromise was one of the worst mistakes he ever made.[98]

These types of compromises still occur today. For example, Nebraska Senator Ben Nelson played an integral part in drafting President Barack Obama's health care law.[99] In what is now referred to as the "Cornhusker Kickback," Senate Majority Leader Harry Reid offered Senator Nelson and the state of Nebraska $100 million in Medicaid funding, with one outcome in mind – Senator Nelson's vote for the Senate's health care reform bill.[100] Quite similar to Madison and Jefferson looking out for their self-interests, Nelson had only voted for the health care bill in order to achieve Medicaid expansion in his home state.[101]

Topics: Public Choice Theory

"Your Obedient Servant"

"Your Obedient Servant" occurs near the end of the musical and Hamilton's life. It begins with Aaron Burr trying to comprehend how Alexander Hamilton could have endorsed Thomas Jefferson for president (instead of him). It then quickly moves to the back-and-forth between Hamilton and Aaron Burr at the end of Alexander Hamilton's life before their fateful duel.[102] The song decides to portray these letters through song, and it fantastically illustrates trade-offs. Hamilton and Burr are writing letters to each other and Burr is angry because he thinks Hamilton is slandering him. He threatens Hamilton with a duel, and Hamilton's decision is whether to apologize or risk his life in a duel. Hamilton decides "Burr, your grievance is legitimate, I stand by what I said, every bit of it, you stand only for yourself, it's what you do, I can't apologize because it's true."

"Your Obedient Servant" could also be used as to start a discussion about the role of a culture, the traditions within a culture, and how culture influences perceived benefits and costs. In 21st-century America, the idea of dueling to defend one's honor seems silly to most people. But it very much mattered to Hamilton and Burr in the early 1800s.

The opportunity cost to Hamilton of avoiding the duel is to apologize when he doesn't think it is warranted, which he views as dishonorable. Hamilton placed a value on his honor, and apologizing would indeed be incredibly costly to him. The opportunity cost to Hamilton to save his honor is to engage in a duel and risk his life. Clearly Hamilton viewed apologizing as so costly that he was willing to risk his live by engaging in a duel.

Topics: Trade-offs, Opportunity Costs

HANDS ON A HARDBODY

In a story that is based on an actual event, ten contestants in rural Texas are in a contest to win a truck. To win the truck, a contestant must keep his/her hands on the truck longer than any other contestant. When a contestant removes his or her hands from the truck, he/she is removed from the competition. The last one standing wins. Sound easy? It will not be. When ten people start with their hands on a truck and the prize is the truck itself, the contestants will do everything they can to win.

Some of the musical focuses on contestants' jobs, including jobs at Walmart and UPS. Some contestants are unemployed and searching for work, while others are attempting to finance a college education. In addition to labor economics, other economic topics are covered, including military work, the rent seeking that occurs when a prize is available, and more. *Hands on a Hardbody* has some fantastic songs and provides an opportunity to examine many economic issues. Other than winning a new truck, what could be better?

"Human Drama Kind of Thing"/"If I Had This Truck"

In "Human Drama Kind of Thing" and "If I Had This Truck," the ten contestants sing about what winning a truck means to them – implying they are willing to spend a significant amount of energy and effort to win the truck. This is an example of rent seeking, which is the process where people or firms expend valuable resources (time, money, energy, etc.) while attempting to win a competition. This is often considered a market failure but rent seeking can be a government failure as well. One common real-world example is when a government offers grants or projects and firms must bid for them. Firms collectively will spend more effort than is optimal to win the project. Other examples are when scholarships are offered and students must apply, or when lawyers fight over signing up clients for class-action lawsuits. In these cases, economic theory predicts – and real-world results verify – that too much effort will be expended to win the prize.

"If I Had This Truck" provides a good example of rent seeking, as the contestants are engaging in a non-productive activity to win a prize. While their hands are on the truck, they aren't working or producing anything useful for society. (And these competitions last for several days!)

Topic: Rent Seeking, Government Failure, Market Failure

"I'm Gone"

Kelli and Greg are singing about their work and life dreams. Kelli sings about her job at the local UPS and appreciates that "there's no better job to get" in her small town. But she isn't inspired by her work and has dreams of living by the ocean. Greg has been out of work for two years and also dreams of moving to the west coast, to become a Hollywood stuntman.

While Greg is wants a job, whether he is considered unemployed isn't certain. To be considered unemployed, a person must be out of work and must have actively looked for a job in the past four weeks. So if Greg has looked for work in the past four weeks he is considered unemployed. If Greg has not, he would be considered out of the labor force. Workers who want a job but aren't looking any more are also called discouraged workers.

Topics: Unemployment, Labor Economics, Labor Force

"Born in Laredo"

Jesus Pena sings about how people view him. He is Mexican-American – born in Laredo, Texas – but thinks people see him as an illegal immigrant. He sings that people think he "steals your jobs living here illegally." While Jesus is not an immigrant – undocumented or otherwise – his song gives us a good opportunity to examine the debate on the economic benefits (or costs) of immigration – in particular immigration from Mexico to the United States, where workers are primarily taking lower-skilled jobs.[103]

General economic theory shows that when the supply increases, we generally expect the price to fall. So if the supply of low-skilled workers decreases, we would expect the wage for lower-skilled workers to increase. This is straightforward supply-and-demand analysis (see Figure 12), and this argument is used by those who wish to cut back on the number of low-skilled immigrants into a country. Their claim is that domestic workers would have higher wages if there were fewer immigrants.

But many argue that simply looking at the supply increase is too simplistic[104] and there are many benefits to immigration, even for domestic workers. For example, with an increased supply of labor, firms might expand their capacity and invest more money increasing the demand for jobs. This could increase the demand for workers and push the wages for workers back up. (See Figure 13.)

A second benefit cited is that immigrants are more likely to relocate from areas that have high unemployment rates to areas with low unemployment rates –

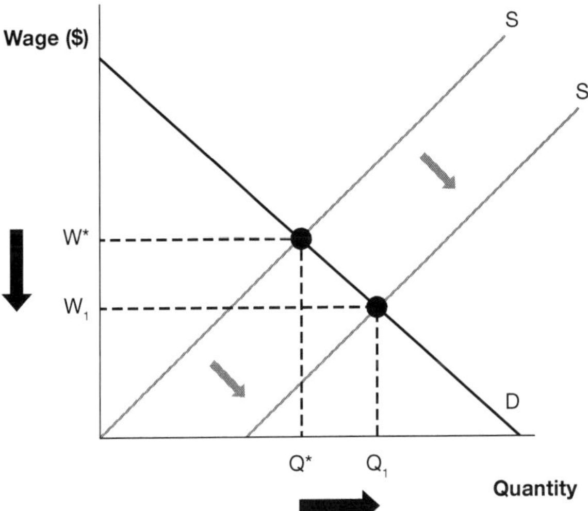

FIGURE 12

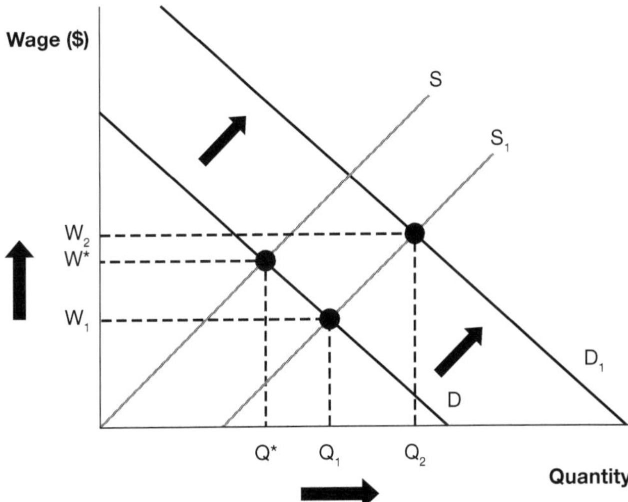

FIGURE 13

which helps both regions. Proponents of immigration also argue that the increased supply of labor that might push down wages could also help to push down costs for products – which could result in lower prices. Lower prices mean more purchasing power and greater well-being for society.

Economist Patricia Cortes examined how immigration affected purchasing power – which is the ability to buy products when factoring both wages and product prices. She found that prices for many products dropped with an increase in low-skilled immigrants. She found that the increase in low-skilled immigration in the 1990s increased the purchasing power of U.S. citizens with high-skilled jobs by 0.65% but decreased the purchasing power of high school dropouts by 2.66%.[105] In the 2016 U.S. Presidential election, Donald Trump pushed for more restrictive immigration policies than Hillary Clinton. He won the vote among non-college graduates but lost the vote among college graduates – which seems to make sense given Dr. Cortes's findings.

Topics: Immigration, Demand and Supply

"Used to Be"

J.D. Drew and Benny Perkins are thinking about the small town they live in and reminiscing. What they notice is all the changes. They sing "That used to be the barbershop next to what used to be the five-and-dime" and notice small mom-and-pop businesses have been replaced by Stuckey's, Best Buy, and Applebees.

They seem to feel that there has been a cost to all the changes in their town. Economists might have a different opinion, however. If a chain store like an Applebees comes into a town and is successful – yes, it might cause an independent diner to go out of business. The independent diner would have closed because customers started viewing the Applebees as a better place to eat, whether it be because the food is better, the price is lower, the atmosphere is fun, or for some other reason. Best Buy's success could also cause some stores to close, but once again, if other businesses close it is because consumers prefer shopping at Best Buy.

This is what economists call creative destruction. When there is economic growth and new products and services are invented, the new product or service usually does lead to an improvement in the lives of consumers. However, consumers will often stop using the old product or service, which can cause the destruction of businesses or even entire industries. In this case, the chain stores – Best Buy, McDonalds, Applebees, and Starbucks – are providing products and services more efficiently and push the other stores out of business.

Topic: Creative Destruction, Economic Growth

HAPPY END

"Bilbao Song"

The singers are singing about Bill's place in Bilbao, an old hangout for the crowd that has gathered. They reminisce about the good times they used to have at a low cost and lament the higher costs that they must pay now that their favorite establishment is respectable. The singers also lament that their hangout was "cleaned up and . . . middle class" and is too "bourgeois." It appears that Bill's place is a victim of gentrification.

Gentrification occurs when a run-down (usually urban) neighborhood is revived after wealthier residents move into the area. That usually brings about an increase in investments and housing values along with lower crime rates. However, one negative consequence is poorer residents of the area often are forced to move away. This is because increased prices, including rent prices, could make the newly gentrified area unaffordable for poorer residents.

Topics: Gentrification

HEATHERS THE MUSICAL

"Candy Store"

> Say goodbye to Shamu, that freak's not your friend.

Heather Duke, Heather Chandler, and Heather McNamara, the most popular girls in the school, have invited Veronica into their gang. But for her to get in, she has to pull a prank on her old best friend, Martha. Veronica faces a trade-off. Like many trade-offs, this one is non-monetary, and it is unpleasant. Veronica wants to be friends with the Heathers, as they are popular and she thinks her life would be better if they were friends with her. But she doesn't want to hurt her best friend.

In the beginning of the song, the Heathers also illustrate that different people get utility from different products. They'd rather buy expensive items and "pound rum and coke" than play with dolls, for example.

Topics: Trade-offs, Utility

HEDWIG AND THE ANGRY INCH

"Sugar Daddy"

Hedwig is singing to potential suitors and she wants a Sugar Daddy so she can obtain "whiskey and French cigarettes, a motorbike with high-speed jets," among other items. A Sugar Daddy is a wealthier older man who wishes for the company of (and sometimes sexual favors from) a younger woman. For this, the Sugar Daddy provides the younger woman with many gifts. In this case, the young woman could be thought of as the supplier – she is supplying the company – and the rich older man as the consumer. They are simply engaging in a transaction for prostitution (or simple companionship) services.

While prostitution is illegal in much of the U.S. and the world, economic analysis can still explain much of the behavior in the prostitution market.

Prostitutes charge based on market conditions and charge different rates based on the sexual act performed,[106] the build and hair color of the prostitute,[107] and the race of the prostitute.[108] Research by Economists Scott Cunningham and Todd Kendall has even found that prostitutes who have graduated from college earn 31% more, on average, than non-graduate prostitutes.[109]

Topics: Markets, Economics of Prostitution

HELLO DOLLY

"Just Leave Everything to Me"

This song showcases Dolly, who provides valuable services for a price. She's willing to arrange almost anything, including a "roof inspected, eyebrows tweezed" or a "daughter dated." She'll do it "for a rather modest fee." Dolly works in the service sector. In the United States and most other economies, the number of manufacturing and agricultural jobs has been declining dramatically over the past 100 years, while the number of service sector jobs has increased.

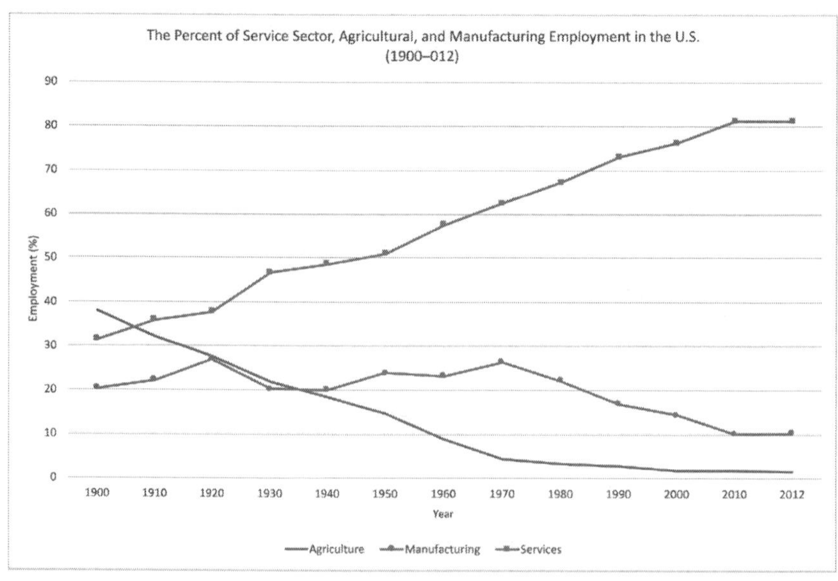

FIGURE 14

While Dolly's job seems to be a "do it all" type of service job, other examples of service sector jobs are restaurant workers, financial industry executives, and teachers. Almost everybody who works on a Broadway show is in the service sector, including the actors, ushers, and directors.

Topics: Labor Economics, Service Sector Jobs

HONEYMOON IN VEGAS

"Airport Song"

Jack has to get from Hawaii to Las Vegas, Nevada as quickly as possible. When the airline employee tells him the next flight that is leaving has a price of $8,000, Jack responds "are you insane?"

The airline employees then find other routes that would get Jack to Las Vegas for a lower price. This song provides a great introduction to price discrimination which is the process where a firm will charge different prices to different people for the same product. In order for price discrimination to occur, a firm must: 1) have some pricing power – i.e., the market can't be too competitive; 2) be able to differentiate between customers willing to pay higher and lower prices; and 3) ensure the consumers cannot resell the product.

Airlines attempt to price discriminate as they will charge customers different prices, even though the cost to the airline is basically the same. Airlines price discriminate in several ways. They are able to charge different prices by charging based on when the ticket is purchased. People who purchase their tickets at the last minute usually have less travel flexibility and therefore airlines can charge them more than those who book in advance. Airlines also price discriminate by charging more to travel at peak times relative to slower times, charging different prices for bulk purchases or for children's tickets, charging to check bags, and in other ways.

Topics: Price Discrimination

HOW TO SUCCEED IN BUSINESS WITHOUT REALLY TRYING

"Happy to Keep His Dinner Warm"

Rosemary sings that she would be happy to be in a marriage where she is the homemaker while her husband "goes onward and upward." The musical is based on a 1952 book – and in the 1940s and 1950s, a much larger percentage of women stayed at home (90% in 1950 compared to 29% in 2012).[110]

Today, far more women are part of the labor force, 57% in 2015 compared to 34% in 1950.[111] The increased number of women joining the workforce since 1950 has been cited as one of the main drivers for strong GDP growth we saw in the United States and several other countries.[112] This is because of the massive influx of highly productive workers into the labor force.

Topics: Labor Economics, Women in the Workforce

"The Company Way"

Mr. Twimble is sharing his advice with Frump on how to build a career within the company. He says to do whatever the boss says and to play it safe. He goes on to sing that he is willing do to anything he can to make sure he avoids unemployment. This includes always losing at gin (card game) with Mr. Bratt (the boss) and not complaining about the company restaurant or letterhead.

Some of the things he mentions indicate that he isn't working for an efficient company, however. Most companies should want their employees to give ideas on how to improve its operations. Mr. Twimble seems sure that if "a man of genius make suggestions, watch that genius get suggested to resign."

Topics: Labor Economics

I CAN GET IT FOR YOU WHOLESALE

"I'm Not a Well Man"

Mr. Pulvermacher is singing about his ailments and the costs of curing those ailments. He sings that his "bills for only pills alone would chill you to the bone." Many could sympathize with Mr. Pulvermacher. Health care in the U.S. and across the world is expensive. In the U.S. in 2015, health care spending was almost $10,000 per person, or 17.8% of the country's GDP.[113] Economists have different views over what this indicates. Harvard health economist David Cutler argues that there are three reasons for high health care costs: that U.S. citizens pay too much on health care administration, pay more for drugs and medical equipment than consumers in other countries, and that U.S. citizens consume more health care than people in other countries.

Cutler's Harvard colleague, Greg Mankiw, focuses on the latter issue. He thinks it is prudent that Americans demand so much health care. He argues that as a country gets richer, that country will want to spend more on the highest-quality health care. He argues that as people get richer and reach a certain income threshold extra material items won't have as much value because of diminishing marginal utility. For example, at some point people simply won't need an additional flat screen TV! But, an extra year of life in good health is something almost everybody would want. Given there is almost no diminishing marginal utility for another year of health, demand for health care should go up and we would expect rich countries with free markets to spend more on health care.

Topics: Health Care

IF/THEN

"A Map of New York"

Beth and Stephen are city planners in New York City. They dream that as government officials they can create plans, rules, zoning restrictions, and regulations to make New York a better place to live. Many cities in the United States and across the world, like New York, Minneapolis, and Chicago, employ economic planners whose goal is to make their cities a more attractive place to live.

But there have been many who are critical of the actions of government economic planners. Pierre Desrochers and Joanna Szurmak (2016) discuss the actions of Jane Jacobs – who is known for her influence on urban studies. Jane Jacobs found that urban renewal plans, i.e., trying to "draw a map" for a city, had several negative impacts on cities. They destroyed social networks, churches, and more.[114] Though the intentions were good, she argued the results were disastrous.

Jacobs noted that cities would set themselves up spontaneously when not arranged by planners, and that spontaneously created cities tended to be better. As noted by Callahan and Ikeda:[115]

> Early in the morning, workers head off to their jobs in other neighborhoods as well as entering the neighborhood to work. Soon thereafter, parents transporting their children to school appear on the street. Shops open, and shopkeepers, anxious that the area of their business not frighten away customers due to dangers present in the area, keep a close eye on the sidewalks. Mothers with preschool children head to the parks, workers come out to eat lunch in them, and shoppers come and go from area stores. In the early evening workers again come and go from the neighborhood. As night falls, restaurants, bars, and nightclubs keep the sidewalks lively – and generally safe.

Topics: Economic Planning

IN THE HEIGHTS

In the Heights, the first musical that Lin-Manuel Miranda brought to Broadway, has economic themes woven throughout the story. It is set in the early 2000s in Washington Heights, a neighborhood in northern Manhattan – just north of Harlem. The musical tracks a few days in the life of Usnavi, Benny, Vanessa, Nina, Abuela, and others as they struggle with choices about their careers, their schooling, where to live, whether to pursue their dreams, and more.

"In the Heights"

Usnavi opens his store, discusses his neighborhood, and introduces us to the people we will see in the musical. Early on we hear how Usnavi's refrigerator is broken which means he won't be able to keep cream, which is essential for his coffee as he is "not making any profits if the coffee isn't light and sweet." Those who sell coffee are in a monopolistically competitive market: it is easy for a new firm to enter, each firm sells only a small portion of the total coffee purchased, and each seller's coffee tastes slightly different. Usnavi is worried his coffee won't be as tasty – which is a legitimate concern as his customers will likely go elsewhere if the quality of his coffee drops.

Later he sings that "neighbors started packing up . . . the rents went up." That could be because of gentrification –when a previously run-down area is renovated because wealthier people move into it and financial investments are made. This often makes the area safer and more appealing for many. But with this increased appeal comes higher demand for housing and higher rents, forcing some poorer people to move.

Kevin and Camila Rosario run the local taxicab company and "their daughter Nina is off to college, tuition is mad steep so they can't sleep, everything they get is mad cheap." Nina is from New York but has gone to California to attend Stanford. We find out later that she got a scholarship to cover some of her costs but Kevin and Camila also helped out with the costs. They are trying to be frugal in their other purchases while paying for their daughter's college, and they view that as a trade-off worth making. Paying for college often does require sacrifices, as college expenses have gone up dramatically over the past 25 years in the United States[116] and are among the biggest expense a family can incur.[117]

In 2008, shortly after the timeframe for when *In the Heights* was set, Stanford actually started paying the entire tuition bill for all students with family incomes that were low enough. For the 2015–2016 academic year, Stanford provided scholarships to cover the full cost of tuition for all families with incomes less than $125,000. For families earning $65,000 or less, Stanford covered not only tuition but also room and board.[118]

Benny sings that he is "the number one earner, the fastest learner" and that his boss "can't keep (him) on the damn back burner." If Benny is correct that he is the best employee, he probably is also correct that he won't be on the "back burner" for long. In labor markets that are competitive – and in New York City there are many employees and employers so it is very competitive – if a good employee is underpaid he or she could likely find a higher-paying job elsewhere.

Topics: Human Capital, Monopolistic Competition, Product Differentiation, Gentrification, Trade-Offs

"Inutil"

Kevin, from a generation of farmers, is recalling his childhood. His father wanted Kevin to be a farmer, but he wanted to pursue a different profession. This isn't unique to Kevin, as recently there are far fewer farmers than there used to be. In America, over 90% of the workforce was in farming in 1790, now it is under 5%.[119] This trend is not unique to America. For example, Mexico and China have seen dramatic decreases in the percentage of farm workers over the past 30 years, with Mexico seeing the percentage of farmers cut in half since 1993 (26.9% to 13.4% in 2013) and China seeing a drop from 60% in 1987 to under 5% today.[120] This occurred because of the technological innovations that improved efficiency, meaning that fewer people were needed to produce the amount of food required to feed everybody. With fewer workers needed for farming, those workers took jobs producing other goods and services, which helps the economy grow.

As Kevin keeps singing, he transitions from focusing on his life and starts thinking about his daughter, Nina. Nina had to drop out of college because she couldn't afford it without working, but working while attending college was too difficult. Kevin swears that he will do whatever it takes to make sure Nina can succeed. He correctly recognizes the tremendous value of a college education for his daughter – as the average college graduate in the United States earns 70% more annually than somebody with just a high school degree.[121]

Topics: Economic Growth, Education

"96,000"

At the beginning of the song, Usnavi is checking whether his store has sold any winning lottery tickets. He finds out that he sold somebody a winning lottery ticket worth $96,000. As Usnavi starts to tell his friends and neighbors, everybody sings about what they would do if they won $96,000 – with each person having a different dream.

Benny leads off by sharing his dream of using the money to go to business school. He recognizes that if he invests the money in himself – to gain what economists call human capital – he could become wealthier. Statistics on earnings confirm Benny's suspicions. The average graduate from an MBA program earns a starting salary of over $90,000– and starting salaries from top MBA programs often average well above six figures.[122]

Daniela, who owns a beauty salon, would use $96,000 to open up a shop in Atlantic City. Like Benny, she would invest the money, but her investment would be in physical capital – a new store location – rather than human capital. Physical capital allows for greater production – and greater earnings.

The others have different ideas. Usnavi thinks everybody is overestimating how much $96,000 really is – especially after taxes. He would just use it to help keep his shop running. Usnavi's cousin Sonny would use the money to help fund protests while Vanessa would move to a nicer area. Everybody thinks that the lottery win will make them happier, but is that assured? The research is mixed; some studies indicate that people could be less happy after winning the lottery. The reasons for this are that people get used to a standard of living and then it doesn't bring them joy any more,[123] that lottery winners are more likely to go bankrupt than non-winners,[124] and that lottery winners become targets for criminals.[125]

Topics: Wealth, Lottery, Capital, Human Capital

"Pacienca y Fe"

Grandma Claudia is singing about her life and the need for *pacienca y fe* (Spanish for patience and faith). She begins with a look at her life in Cuba, where her family could not find work and therefore often went hungry. There were some aspects of Cuba that she loved compared to New York, but they were going hungry in Cuba. The transition wasn't easy, as it required hard work and learning English, but there were jobs available in New York for Grandma Claudia and her mother. Clearly the trade-off of not being able to see the stars in New York City was offset by the ability to work. Hence, Grandma Claudia's family, like millions of others, emigrated to the United States in search of a better life.

Topics: Trade-offs, Immigration

"Piragua (Reprise)"

In this short song, the character Piragua Guy sings "New block of ice, hike up the price." He is singing about the market conditions for piragua, a Puerto-Rican treat similar to a snow cone. It is shaved ice that is flavored and it is typically shaped like a pyramid.[126] There is an electricity failure in New York City on a hot day, so people can't use their air conditioning to cool down. That means the Piragua Guy's shaved ice should be in high demand. Better yet for Piragua Guy, one of his main competitors – Mr. Softee – has shut down. So business is really good!

During the song, you can hear him singing about how he's raising his prices. This will because the demand for piragua is increasing – allowing Piragua Guy to sell a greater quantity for a greater price. This is illustrated by basic supply-and-demand analysis (see Figure 15 below) – having hotter weather and a main competitor being out of business will increase the demand for piragua, which in turn increases the price. It is tough to think of a better reason to sing!

Topics: Demand, Supply and Demand

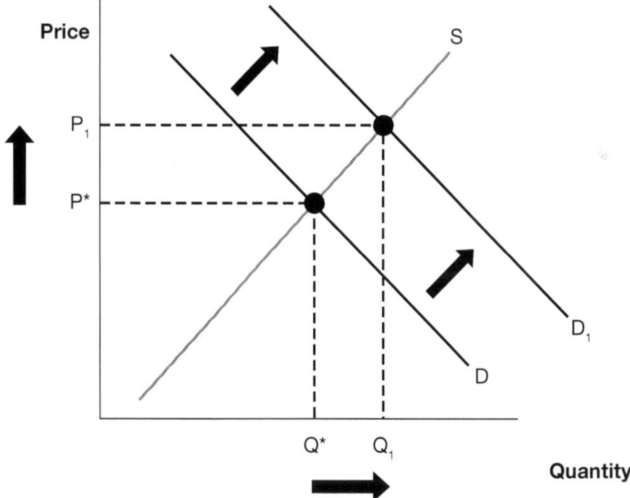

FIGURE 15

INSIDE U.S.A.

"Rhode Island is Famous for You"

"Every state in the U.S.A. has something it can boast of" according to this song. If this is correct and each state has a sought-after product, then there is a big incentive for states to trade with each other. The singer talks about the product that each state is famous for producing but is attempting to be funny, not truthful. For example, he sings that tents are from "Tent-a-see" and coats are from "Da-coat-a." Regardless of intent, the song works well at illustrating gains from specialization and trade. Because each state has a specialty, there are significant gains possible with free trade.

Trade occurs because of the theory of comparative advantage as each region has a lower opportunity cost of producing an item. While this song lists fictitious items each state is good at producing, different states within the U.S. do have different products they produce efficiently and export. For example, Colorado's top exports are electronic circuits and meat. For North Dakota, it is oil and New Hampshire's top export is cellular telephones.[127]

And of course, Rhode Island is famous for more than what the song says, as it exports precious metal scraps![128]

Topics: International Trade, Gains from Trade, Comparative Advantage

JOSEPH AND THE AMAZING TECHNICOLOR DREAMCOAT

"Pharaoh's Dreams Explained"

The Pharaoh explained his dreams to Joseph, who is an expert at dream interpretation. Joseph tells Pharaoh his dreams mean that the next seven years will bring about robust crops. However, after those first seven years, there will be poor crop yields for the following seven years. The Pharaoh then assigns Joseph to handle the economic planning.

While Joseph is singing about cycles in food – the economy also goes through cycles where things are good and bad. There are four phases of a business cycle: recovery (or expansion), peak, recession (or contraction), and trough. The recovery/expansion occurs when real gross domestic product (GDP) is increasing. This is when the economy is expanding. A peak of the business cycle occurs when GDP increases to a high point before starting to drop. A recession or contraction occurs when real GDP is falling, resulting in a trough as the bottom point of the recession, before real GDP begins expanding again.[129]

Joseph sings that Pharaoh needs to "find a man . . . with a flair for economic planning." Ignoring the fact that economists rarely have anything close to "flair," this is an instructive lyric, as governments can try to minimize the pain of recessions, much like Pharaoh wants to minimize the pain of the famine. This can be done by Congress and the President using fiscal policy – where changes in taxes and spending can help an economy get out of a recession.

Actions to help minimize the pain of economic downturns can also be done by the Federal Reserve, which uses monetary policy. In general, during a recession, the Federal Reserve might want to go with policies that lower interest rates – which will give firms a greater incentive to invest in capital which can boost the economy. But the Federal Reserve has dual mandate to try to minimize unemployment and inflation. So it will sometimes take actions not to cut unemployment, but to prevent inflation.

Topics: Economic Cycles, Fiscal Policy, Monetary Policy

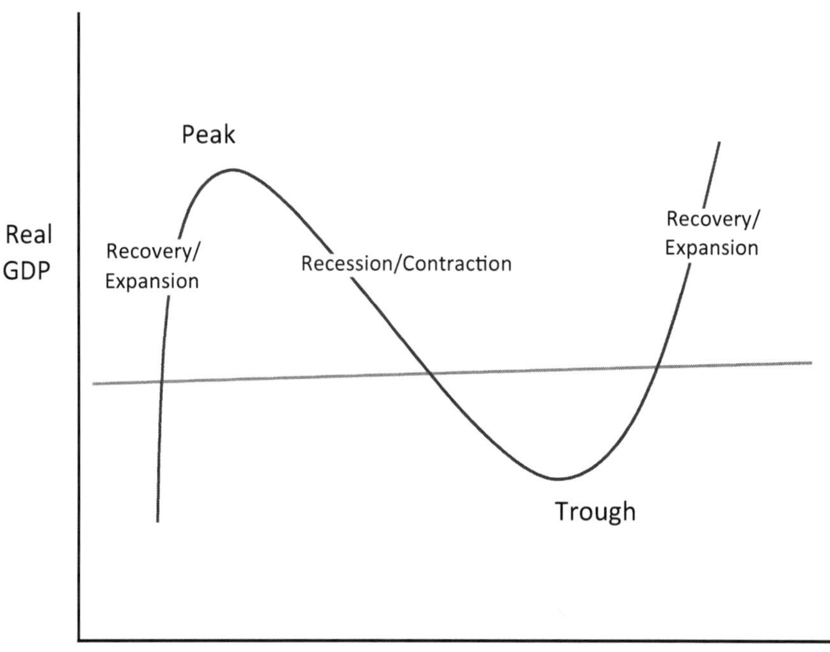
The Business Cycle
Peak
Real GDP
Recovery/ Expansion
Recession/Contraction
Recovery/ Expansion
Trough
Time

FIGURE 16

KINKY BOOTS

"Everybody Say Yeah"

Charlie's dad owned the family shoe business, but now it is Charlie's after his father's death. In order to turn the business around, Charlie and the workers transition to making "kinky boots." By doing so they hope to differentiate their products. They don't have a monopoly, because there is more than one firm producing footwear. They are competing in what economists call an oligopoly. An oligopoly occurs when a market is dominated by a few large firms. Because there are so few firms, the actions of one firm will matter to the other firms.

Shoe manufacturing companies compete against each other in an oligopoly. The oligopoly is most evident with athletic shoes, as Nike and Adidas make up 80% of the share of U.S. athletic shoes sold and 49% of athletic shoes sold globally. Given this, Nike and Adidas will try to do anything they can to differentiate themselves – including hiring celebrities to endorse their products, creating a better shoe, creating customizable shoes, and more.[130]

Topics: Oligopoly, Product Differentiation

KISS ME KATE

"I've Come to Wive it Wealthily in Padua"

Petruchio wants a wealthy wife. He is willing to forgo some other traits one might want from a wife in order to find one with a lot of money. If her eyes are crossed or if "she screams like a teething brat," Petruchio says he will marry her as long as she is wealthy, so he is considering the trade-offs. In general, when considering whom to date or marry, if someone has more of some good traits, one might be willing to forgive other not-so-desirable traits. Petruchio seems to take this to the extreme – willing to accept almost anything to have a wife with money.

Wealth does seem to matter for marriage. Recent research by Berkeley sociologist Daniel Schneider concluded "a steady job and a stable relationship are not enough – wealth must also precede marriage."[131] However, men usually enter into marriages with more wealth than women.[132]

Topics: Trade-offs

LA LA LAND

"Another Day of Sun"

The opening number of *La La Land* involves many people singing about living in Southern California. It's not all glamorous for the singers, but they sing that despite their struggles, at least it is sunny. When a place has a great climate, it should be more appealing, all else equal. That should cause an increase in demand for living in a beautiful area– and with it the prices for houses and land should also increase.

Topics: Supply and Demand, Housing Prices

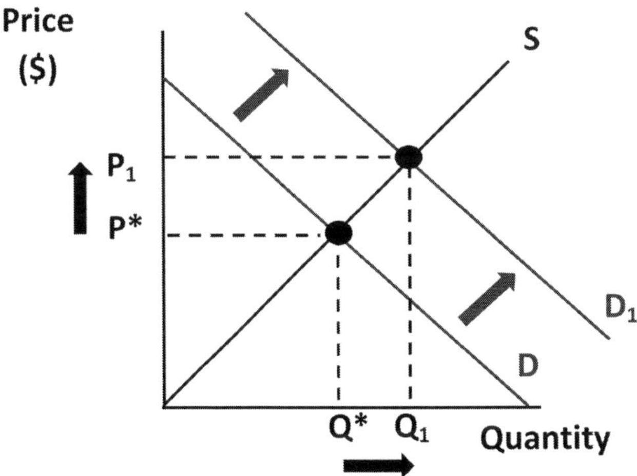

FIGURE 17

LEGALLY BLONDE

For a musical based on a 2001 movie comedy, *Legally Blonde* presents a surprising number of economic situations. The musical centers on Elle Woods' decision to win back her ex-boyfriend Warner by getting accepted to and attending Harvard Law School. Elle's decisions highlight trade-offs and opportunity costs, but there are several other economic gems found in this show, including examples of price discrimination and screening.

"Omigod You Guys"

In the opening number of *Legally Blonde*, we get introduced to Elle and learn that she might soon be engaged. To prepare, she goes to the mall to buy a dress. However, the sales clerk sees Elle and thinks because she is blonde she must be dumb and a big spender. She attempts to sell Elle an older dress for an exorbitant price. Elle realizes she is being duped and doesn't allow it.

This is a good example of attempted price discrimination. Price discrimination occurs when a firm sells the same product to different people for different prices when there are no cost differences driving their decision. In order to successfully price discriminate, a firm must have some pricing power therefore the market cannot be extremely competitive. Otherwise customers would just go to the next firm. The firm also needs to be able to identify those with higher willingness-to-pay and those with lower-willingness-to-pay.

In this store, the sales clerk apparently has the power to attempt to negotiate prices with each customer individually. By attempting to charge each customer a different price, the clerk is attempting first-degree price discrimination. This type of price discrimination also occurs at many auto dealerships, where car prices are negotiated on a person-by-person basis. Some private universities also engage in first-degree price discrimination, as they may have a "sticker" price but many students pay less based on aid received for academic ability and financial need.

Topics: Price Discrimination

"What You Want"

Near the beginning of the musical *Legally Blonde*, Elle Woods gets dumped by her boyfriend, Warner. Elle was expecting Warner to propose to her, but instead she finds out that he doesn't think Elle would make a good wife. In "What You Want," Elle sings about the effort she is willing to exert to win back Warner's affection. Her plan is simple. She will get accepted to Harvard Law School and then attend it. She thinks attending Harvard will convince Warner she's the kind of girl he should marry.

To do this, the opportunity cost is enormous. (Recall that the opportunity cost is what you give up to get something – it doesn't have to be solely monetary.) First, Elle Woods must give up the fun activities of her senior year at college to study for the law school entrance exam (LSAT) so she can do well enough to get into Harvard. Once that happens, she flies across the country, paying for her friends to join her, to meet the admissions committee to convince them to admit her.

The biggest costs are after that, however. Once admitted, she has to move from Southern California to Harvard and spend three years at Harvard Law School. That would mean thousands of hours spent – not to be a lawyer – but to win back Warner. She is giving up the opportunity to work at a job and earn money while simultaneously spending thousands of dollars in tuition. The opportunity cost of winning Warner's affection is enormous.

Topics: Opportunity Cost, Trade-offs.

"Blood in the Water"

To introduce the new students to Harvard Law School, Professor Callahan gives them a crash course on how they should behave – saying they should argue with each other viciously (like sharks with blood in the water). Callahan sings that "only spineless snobs will quarrel with the morally dubious jobs."

Professor Callahan runs a highly successful and profitable law firm. But his law firm is so profitable in part because he seems to be taking cases that he describes as "morally dubious." He describes cases in the song where he advocates defending a banker who defrauded a "kind old grandma" and a mafia member who killed a nun and puppies.

The students initially seem horrified – they want to use their law degree to make the world a better place. The song highlights that there are many career paths people could take, even for those who earn the same degree. Some career

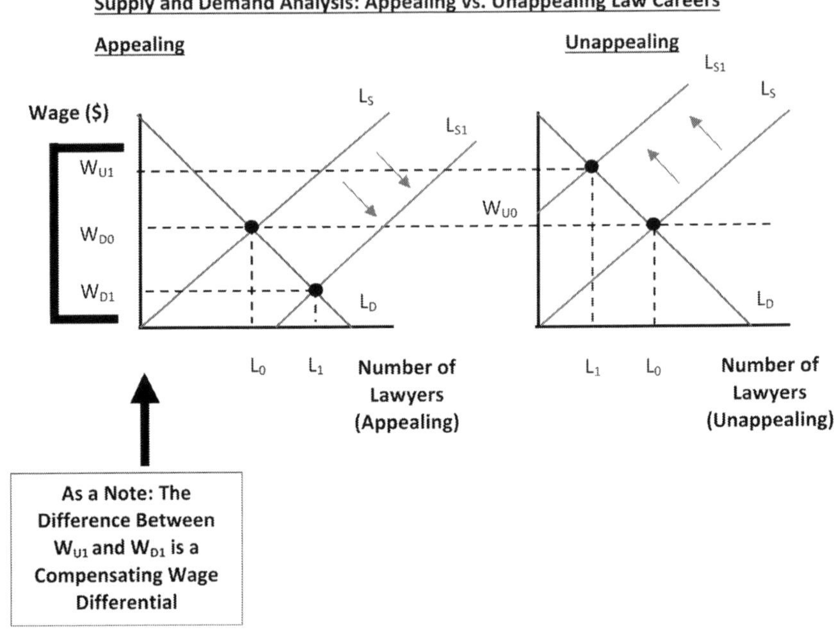

FIGURE 18

paths are more appealing and those who work in those careers feel their job is rewarding outside of the monetary compensation (economists call this non-pecuniary compensation). For example, consider a student who wishes to become an immigration lawyer. That job is appealing to some people in that they feel they will be helping others. Other lawyers might make their incomes by taking cases that are "morally dubious" and not as personally rewarding.

We would expect the supply of lawyers who wish to take the more rewarding jobs to be higher, which should push the wages down. Likewise, we'd expect fewer lawyers to want to take jobs to defend puppy killers and mafia hit-men, meaning those lawyers should earn higher wages.

Indeed, we see this play out when we look at the wages for attorneys with different specializations. The median salary for immigration lawyers is just over $60,000.[133] This is $20,000 to $40,000 per year less than what most other types of lawyers earn.[134]

Topics: Labor Economics, Compensating Wage Differentials

"There! Right! There!"

Elle and the lawyers at Mr. Callahan's law firm are trying to acquit Brooke Windham from the charge that she murdered her husband. The pool boy, Mikos, is on the stand, claiming he had an affair with Brooke, which is being used as the motive for her wanting to kill her husband. She didn't have the affair, but needs to convince the jury that this witness isn't credible.

Elle Woods realizes, however, that Mikos is well dressed. Really well dressed. So well dressed, in fact, that she is screening Mikos based on this information. Their legal team assumes that because Mikos is so well dressed, he must be either gay . . . or from Europe. While their song is a little silly (and perhaps offensive), it does relate to how people and firms make decisions based on screening. Loosely defined, screening is the process where the person who is doing the screening, "the screener," will exert effort or resources in an attempt to obtain useful information. In the song, the defense makes a plan to get Mikos to admit that he, indeed, is gay.

Some screening is relatively easy for people and firms, including screening based on how somebody is dressed. Employers will examine how a person dresses as a quick way to judge whether he or she will fit into the company.[135] Further, the classic phrase "dress for the job you want" refers to the idea that if you wish for a promotion, make sure your dress choices are appropriate for that job – not just the job you currently have. Etiquette experts still think this is sound advice for those seeking promotion.[136]

Topics: Screening, Signaling, Discrimination

LES MISERABLES

Victor Hugo's novel inspired one of the most well-known musicals of all time. The show also happens to have a number of interesting economic situations arise. These include a worker trying to earn a good income after prison, people engaging in illegal activities to earning money, and an example of perfectly inelastic preferences. These concepts make this a great show for those studying economics.

"Work Song"

After a hard day of work, Jean Valjean is paid less than the other workers because he is an ex-convict. One of his fellow co-workers thinks this is perfectly acceptable, as "honest" men like him deserve more. This raises an interesting economic question: is Valjean underpaid for his service? Economic theory can give us a bit of guidance. If there is a market setting with plenty of firms that need workers and criminals are just as productive as non-criminals for firms, Valjean should have no problems finding work for a better wage. The reason is that other firms would figure out that Valjean is just as productive as non-convicts but could be hired for a cheaper wage. Given the central assumption that firms want to maximize profits, if they could lure Valjean away from his current employer by paying him a bit more, albeit less than what non-convicts receive, they'd increase their profits! But Valjean's salary would also increase, as the demand for his services would be increasing and should keep increasing until his salary reflects his productivity. A market system, while not perfect, helps ensure that people are paid for their productivity – and firms usually attempt to exploit every opportunity to earn a profit by doing this.

However, it could be that while Valjean is a reformed criminal and a productive worker, ex-criminals are less productive in general, are more likely to steal from the firm, or perhaps require more supervision by their bosses. Under that situation, while Valjean is productive, ex-convicts are less productive or more expensive on average and since Valjean is an ex-convict, he is suffering from this. If this was the situation, Valjean would be a victim of what economists call "statistical discrimination." This occurs when a person in a group is discriminated against, not because the firm or other decision maker is inherently biased, but because statistics indicate facts about members of a group and the person is easily classified as a member of that group.

For example, a 17-year-old male who is the safest driver in the world will still have an incredibly high car insurance premium. Why? It isn't because insurance companies hate 17-year-old males, but because on average teenage men get into more accidents than members of any other demographic group. They are costlier for the insurance company to insure, hence the cost to obtain insurance for teenage males is higher.

Topics: Labor Economics, Statistical Discrimination

"At the End of the Day"

This early Act I song has the factory workers singing about the difficulties of their lives as part of the working poor in 1823 France. The singers discuss how difficult it is to get ahead and how they seem to have no money left over after making required purchases. Further, they are working long hours just to make ends meet.

Those reading this book in a first-world country would surely agree that these workers were in pretty bad shape. The national income in France in 1820 was about $1.3 billion (after adjusting for inflation). This worked out at an annual per-capita income of under $50 for every man, woman, and child. Thankfully, economic growth in France has meant that in 2014 the national income was $2.4 trillion, or over $35,000 for every man, woman, and child. The poorest citizens today in France - like in much of the world - are better off than many of the richest citizens 200 years ago.

Topics: Economic Growth, Poverty

"Lovely Ladies"

The prostitutes and their customers are singing. Prostitution is prohibited in many markets, but should it be? Economists might disagree over whether prostitution (and other banned activities) should be illegal, but their approach to thinking about the issue is different. When considering whether to ban a product or service, economists tend to ask different questions than politicians. Economists, unlike politicians, tend not to ask whether the product/service itself is good or bad. Economists instead ask whether the benefits from prohibiting the product or service outweigh the costs. For example, by prohibiting prostitution, you likely have fewer prostitutes, albeit at a higher price. But by prohibiting it, those who do engage in prostitution might be at higher risk for being victims of other criminal activities.[137] This is because it is tougher to go to the police when one has committed a crime against you when you are committing an illegal act yourself.

"Lovely Ladies" also highlights compensating wage differentials. Because prostitution is such an undesirable profession, higher wages are needed to induce people to choose prostitution as a career. Several economists have studied the wages paid to prostitutes. One theory is that because prostitutes damage their prospects on the marriage market, they must be paid much more than typical pay for jobs of similar effort.[138] This seems to hold to be true, as in 2014, the typical price for one hour with a prostitute was $265. That said, after adjusting for inflation, this is down over 20% from 2006.[139]

Topics: Economics of Crime, Prohibition, Prostitution, Compensating Wage Differentials

"Master of the House"

Monsieur and Madame Thenardier are innkeepers. In "Master of the House" they sing about their antics – putting water into wine and stealing their guests' items. They are looking to rob, con, and swindle from their guests. What makes this song instructive is when we ask: why don't most business owners behave this way?

Perhaps most business owners are not as sleazy as the Thenardiers. That likely is part of why we don't see this behavior – many people would find this behavior morally wrong. But game theory and the theory of repeated games can also explain good behavior by business owners. If an innkeeper was only going to see a person one time, then the way they treat or exploit a guest might not matter much, as long as they get paid! But most firms know the value of repeat customers and of word-of-mouth. So even if a shop owner wouldn't mind fleecing their customers, they might treat them well because the relationship between a firm and a customer could be thought of like a repeated game. Given that each customer might come back and spend money in the future, or might refer their friends to the business, ethical behavior often is more profitable in the long run than unethical behavior.

Topics: Game Theory, Repeated Games

"Stars"

Javert sings about the effort he will put in to find Jean Valjean. He says he "will never rest, till death." Javert clearly wants to find Valjean badly, as he sees Valjean as nothing but a fugitive who has escaped the law. In the song "Stars," Javert swears upon the stars that he will never yield, under any circumstance, in his quest to find Jean Valjean.

Javert provides a great example of inelastic demand. Demand is considered inelastic if a change in the price of obtaining the good does not cause a large charge in the quantity demanded. In "Stars," Javert is implying that he will pursue Valjean forever, regardless of the personal price. In fact, economists would say Javert has perfectly inelastic demand – as the price he will incur has zero effect on his willingness to find Jean Valjean.

Topics: Elasticity, Inelastic Demand

LITTLE SHOP OF HORRORS

"Dentist!"

Scrivello is a sadistic bully who as a child liked shooting "puppies with a BB gun" and to "poison guppies," among other things. So naturally his mom recommended that he become a dentist. She thought this would be the best way for him to do what he loved – inflict pain on other people. He did become a dentist and he clearly thinks he made the right choice.

Scrivello's enjoyment of dentistry allows us an opportunity to examine what would happen to wages for a job when many people find that job desirable. If there is a profession that provides external benefits, we would expect many people to wish to perform that job. When that happens, then we expect a large supply of workers to result in a decrease in the wage for workers in that profession – as we see in Figure 19.

However, most people don't wish to inflict pain on others or enjoy the other aspects of the dentistry, so the supply of dentists is not high. Because of that, dentists earn good salaries. The median salary for dentists in 2015 was about $158,000, well above the national average.[140] Even more, a job as a dentist has good job security, prompting Nassim Nicholas Talib to title one section of his book *Fooled by Randomness* as "Your Dentist is Rich, Very Rich."[141] He argues that dentists are so rich not only because they have good salaries, but also because almost everybody who becomes a dentist can be assured of a good career with a good income. While a musician who hits it big might have a fancier car and a bigger house than a dentist, "in expectation," the dentist is richer.[142] The reason is many musicians attempt to become a star, but end up poor – only the most successful ones become rich. This is in contrast to dentists, who are almost always assured of a good career with a good income.

Topics: Labor Economics, Probability, Compensating Wage Differentials.

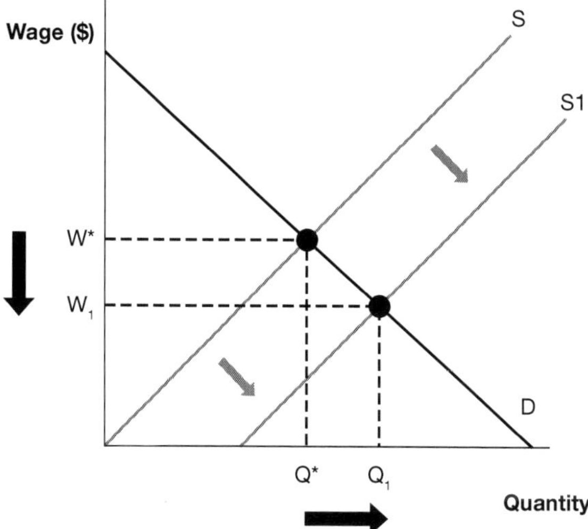

FIGURE 19

MADE IN DAGENHAM

"Everybody Out"

In a musical based on a true story, a strike is being called at a Ford Motors plant in Dagenham, U.K., which is a suburb of London. Female sewing machinists, however, were classified as working a category B job whereas men were paid as if it were a category C job – which paid 15% more.[143] There was a three-week strike until the issue was resolved. Assuming men and women were equally productive, this seems to be a clear case of economic discrimination.

Economic discrimination occurs when somebody is paid a different amount for producing the same output. While men and women are paid different amounts in the United States – the median woman's weekly wage is about 18% less than the median man's wage[144] – there are many reasons for this difference outside of discrimination. Harvard economist Claudia Goldin has done quite a bit of research about unequal wages between men and women. She found that non-linearity in compensation explains much of the gender wage gap and that a major difference in earnings comes from hours worked. When the hours worked is controlled for, she found in many professions that a person who works 50 hours a week makes more than 25% per hour more than their counterparts working 40 hours a week. This is a key finding, as those who put in very long weeks are rewarded with much higher hourly rates. Given that women work fewer hours than men on average, this explains a significant portion of the gap.[145]

There are other reasons why men earn more than women, at least in the United States. These include the level of danger in jobs (men are much more likely to be killed in the line of work and with that comes a wage premium[146]), the choice of job, time out of the labor force to raise children, and more.

Once controlling for all of these factors, there is little left that is credited to economic discrimination. Estimates from serious scholars vary from no wage gap at all[147] to up to 7%.[148] That's not to say there isn't any discrimination. Unfortunately, there will be. That said, the standard dialogue on wage discrimination is inadequate.

Many in the press will use the average wage differences between men and women to claim there is discrimination. This is poor analysis, but if a person wanted to stick by the claim that average wage differences meant discrimination, then he or she would also logically have to make other claims of discrimination. White Americans earn less than Asian Americans. When in their twenties, college-educated men earn less relative to college-educated women without children. These cases, like the overall gender wage gap, are mostly caused by factors other than discrimination. Simply looking at average pay differences is not an adequate way of measuring whether there is discrimination.

Economic discrimination – like they sing about in Dagenham – is actually pretty rare when markets are competitive. When markets aren't competitive or when the government plays a big role, discrimination could occur much more often. For a discussion of why this is true, see "Story of My Life" (from *Shrek the Musical*).

Topics: Wage Gaps, Discrimination

MAMMA MIA

"Money, Money, Money"

Donna isn't happy with her life. She thinks she is working too hard and earning too little. (Who doesn't?) And she thinks her life will be better if she could find a wealthy man. This song illustrates one aspect of the marriage market – as someone who is wealthier, all else equal, will be a more appealing potential partner for women.[149] That said, there is a gender difference on the impact of wealth on appeal: 78% of never-married women say it is "very important" that a husband holds a "steady job," compared to 48% of never-married men who say the same about women.[150]

The song also highlights the marginal utility of wealth. What would an extra $1,000 mean to Donna? Probably quite a bit. But to a "rich man" who owns a yacht? I'm sure he would rather have the extra $1,000, but it won't be nearly as important to him.

Topics: Diminishing Marginal Utility, Signaling, Marriage Market

"The Winner Takes it All"

When Donna is singing "The Winner Takes it All," she is implying that romantic relationships are a zero-sum game, that one person's gains are another person's losses. As long as a relationship is consensual, Donna's view is incorrect, as consenting relationships must provide benefits to both parties. (Otherwise the couple wouldn't be in the relationship.)

Taking Donna's notion of a zero-sum game beyond just romantic relationships, many people also incorrectly think that many economic situations are zero sum – like trade or income inequality. If trade were a zero-sum game, then the gains that one party received must result from equivalent losses to the other party. This is certainly not occurring, as trade is not zero sum. Trade between two parties only takes place if both parties gain. It occurs because of different levels of efficiency, and that is what allows the trade to benefit both parties. Similar to romantic relationships, a (trade) relationship would not occur if both parties were not better off because of the trade.

Many people also incorrectly associate the notion of a zero-sum game to income inequality. These individuals would see that there is a total amount of income earned throughout society. The thought process would be that one person earning a large income must mean that others are missing out on that equivalent amount of money. But this ignores the fact that economic progress is not a zero-sum game. A person with a high income is usually earning it by providing goods or services to society that are incredibly valuable.

To make incomes more equal (i.e., decrease income inequality), you generally must impose higher taxes on those with higher incomes or create other rules that stifle highly productive individuals. That reduces the incomes that the wealthiest and most productive workers can obtain. This decreases their incentives to produce new products and more efficient production methods that increase the overall well-being of society. This is why Bill Clinton's former economic advisor Alan Blinder wrote that "equality is bought at a price. Thus, like any commodity, we must decide rationally how much to purchase. We will probably want to spend some of our potential income on (income) equality, but not all of it."[151]

Topics: Game Theory, International Trade, Gains from Trade, Income Inequality, Zero-Sum Games

MARY POPPINS

"Fidelity Fiduciary Bank"

"Fidelity Fiduciary Bank" provides a couple of economic lessons. First, for each dollar invested, there must be a dollar saved. The song states that by saving they will help provide funds to invest in "all manner of private enterprise: shipyards, the mercantile, collieries, tanneries." The funding for these items often comes from savers, and the song illustrates how lending and saving go hand in hand and how that leads to economic growth. The principle that savings equals investment is taught in principles of macroeconomics courses, and is illustrated here.

"Fidelity Fiduciary Bank" also helps illustrate bank's preferences to lend out the money they receive in deposits. Banks receive deposits for which they pay little or no interest and earn money by lending out those deposits to customers for higher interest rates. Because they earn money by lending their deposits, when banks receive deposits they will try to lend most of their deposits instead of holding them as cash reserves (which earn no interest).

The U.S. and most other countries have laws in place regarding the minimum amount banks must hold in reserves, which is called the required reserve ratio. In the United States, the required reserve ratio is 10%, meaning that banks must hold at least 10% of all deposits on hand, but are allowed to lend up to 90% of deposits to earn money from interest. As long as banks find profitable places to lend out their money, they have an incentive to only keep the minimum amount required by law.

The lending behavior of banks has an impact on the money supply. Suppose a bank lends out 85% of the amount it receives in a deposit, which means it keeps the required 10% plus an additional 5%. On a $1,000 deposit, that means the bank would lend out $850. However, customers generally redeposit the borrowed money into a bank account, so the bank would then lend out 85% of the $850 deposit or an additional $722.50. Again, most often that money gets redeposited again, so the bank would again lend out 85% of that $722.50 deposit for an additional $614.12 entering the money supply, and so on.

The fact that banks can lend out most of a deposit, and that money keeps getting redeposited into banks leads to what economists call the "money multiplier." When some new amount of money is deposited into a bank – the addition to the money supply will greatly exceed the amount that the bank has received.

To compute the money multiplier, compute one divided by required reserve ratio. So if $1 is deposited in a bank – and the required reserve ratio is 0.1 (and the bank lends out the maximum allowed by law), the money multiplier is 10 and the money supply will increase by $1 * (1/0.1) = $10. The money multiplier led to a $10 increase in the money supply from a $1 increase in deposits. Based on our example where banks hold 15% of funds, the multiplier would be (1/0.15=) 6.67. This would mean that a $1 deposit would lead to a $6.67 increase in the money supply.

Topics: Banking, Required Reserve Ratio, Money Multiplier, Money Supply

MATILDA

"Bruce"

The sadistic principal, Miss Trunchbull, discovers that Bruce stole a piece of her cake. As punishment, she wants Bruce to eat an entire cake. Bruce really enjoyed the first piece of cake but is full and apprehensive about eating more. A second piece – he'd probably enjoy that as well, but it wouldn't be as tasty. But after two pieces of cake, he could actually get sick. That means additional consumption of the cake actually negatively affects Bruce's well-being.

This song beautifully illustrates the law of diminishing marginal utility. Recall that the law of diminishing marginal utility says that as a person consumes more of a product, each subsequent unit consumed is less valuable than the one before. In other words, the marginal utility – in this case, it is Bruce's marginal utility from consuming an additional piece of cake – is always declining.

In fact, given that too much cake could make Bruce sick, as Miss Honey notes early in the song, marginal utility eventually can be negative. Meaning that each extra piece of cake that Bruce eats makes him worse off.

For almost all products, the law of diminishing marginal utility holds. Think about the size of a house (or apartment, dorm room, etc.). Would an extra 100 square feet have value? For most people – of course! But think about for whom that extra 100 square feet would be most valuable? Would it mean more to somebody crammed into a 350-square-foot studio apartment? To someone who has a 900-square-foot place? Or someone with a house that has 2,500 square feet of living space? While the extra space likely has value for everybody, it will mean the most to – and therefore give the most utility to – the person who currently lives in the smallest place. The importance of 100 additional square feet diminishes as the size of the home gets bigger. If you looked at two mansions and one had 10,000 square feet and the other had 10,100 – would you even notice?

Topics: Utility, Marginal Utility, Diminishing Marginal Utility

"My House"

Miss Honey sings that although she has a small house, it provides what she needs and it is hers. This song highlights the importance of property rights. Property rights, as defined by Arman Alchian are "the exclusive authority to determine how a resource is used, whether that resource is owned by government or by individuals."[152] Hoover Institution Fellows Terry Anderson and Laura Huggins have researched property rights extensively and define property rights as "the rules of the game that determine who gets to do what and who must compensate whom if damages occur."[153] While the idea of property rights might seem like they only matter for those who are rich – they are crucial to have a well-functioning economy.

For a simple example, if you buy a ticket to a Broadway show, why are you allowed to sit in a certain seat for a few hours to watch the show? It is because of property rights. The theatre owns the property and they transferred the property rights to use the seat for a few hours. Without property rights, these transactions wouldn't happen.

Private property rights help ensure that one's property cannot be taken by other citizens or expropriated (outright seizure) by the government. Strong property rights are to crucial to a successful society. Research by MIT economists Daron Acemoglu and Simon Johnson (2005) published in the prestigious *Journal of Political Economy* found that property rights were key to long-run economic growth, investment, and financial development.[154]

It should be clear why this is true. With weak or non-existent property rights, any investment a person makes could be seized by others. If that is the case, people will invest less in themselves, their businesses, and their communities. Weak property rights ensure an economy has almost no chance of growing, whereas strong property rights give people an opportunity to reap rewards from their investments.

Strong property rights also help in an area many wouldn't expect – minimizing pollution. With strong property rights, you have the right to unpolluted air, or at least you know what your rights are regarding how polluted your air could be. Historically, countries with lower regard for property rights, like the former Soviet Union, have had far worse records on environmental quality than countries with stronger property rights like the United States and many Western European Countries.[155]

For example, the former Soviet Union eroded the Black Sea coast by 50% between 1920 and 1960, with hotels, hospitals, and even a military sanitarium collapsing into the sea as the shoreline gave way.[156] Sand, gravel, and trees of the Black Sea's coast were used as construction materials to comply with the Soviet Union's five-year plans for housing. Since the concept of "private property" did not exist, "no value [was] attached to the gravel along the seashore. Since, in effect, it is free, the contractors haul[ed] it away."[157] Mines, oil wells, and ships freely dumped waste into available bodies of water – killing most of the fish in the

Oka River in 1965.[158] Moreover, the Aral and Caspian seas are significantly polluted with untreated sewage and are gradually disappearing as water is diverted for irrigation.[159]

Other countries with weak property rights have also had issues with environmental quality. In the 1990s in the Chinese city of Chongqing, a paper mill factory was noted for its excessive pollution (Stroup 2016). The factory was supposed to be shut down due to its "oppressive smoke" pollution as well as gas explosions.[160] Furthermore, the same city's 4,500-acre forest has been reduced by half due to the air pollution and acid rain continuously causes massive crop loss.[161] Yet the mill kept running.

Economist Seth Norton's research has confirmed that countries that protected and valued property rights have greater access to safe drinking water and sewage treatment and longer life expectancies.[162]

Topics: Property Rights

MOANA

"Where You Are"

On the island of Motunui, the fish are becoming tougher to catch and the edible plants are dying. The island is struggling to produce enough food. Moana wants to go to the sea to find more food, but Chief Tui, Moana's dad, doesn't want Moana to leave the island.

This song gives us an opportunity to explore a couple concepts. Chief Tui sings "the village of Motunui is all you need . . . we share everything we make." By saying they share everything they make, it sounds like there are not very well-defined property rights in Motunui. Further, the idea that each person produces according to their ability and consumes based on their needs is the founding belief of communism. That could be part of why the people of Motunui are struggling to find food. When a person doesn't have the right to keep the fruits of her labor, she'll be less likely to work hard.

The hypothetical island of Motunui joins a list of real world countries that have experienced failures of communism. A few examples of these failures are worth noting. In the late 1950s and early 1960s, millions of Chinese citizens starved in part because of communist policies that discouraged work. (The estimates range between 15 and 45 million![163]) In the former Soviet Union, the average person spent over an hour a day standing in lines to buy needed products.[164] The lines existed because without market-based prices and incentives, there were often shortages of food, shoes, clothing, and other essential products. The U.S.S.R. eventually collapsed, due in large part to the inability to sustain economic growth. This is not surprising when so much time was spent not on productive activities, but simply waiting in line.

A second concept that "Where You Are" illustrates is benefits from trade. Chief Tui didn't want to go beyond Motunui, but it was likely that other countries were better at producing food, and that the citizens of Motunui could have traded some other product for food to make both countries better off.

Topics: Property Rights, Communism, International Trade, Gains from Trade

NEWSIES

"Santa Fe (Prologue)" and "Santa Fe"

In both the prologue and the reprise of "Sante Fe," Jack sings about the clean air in Sante Fe, New Mexico. Clean air is what economists call a public good, which is a product that satisfies two properties. First, the quality of a public good doesn't diminish when an additional person consumes it. Second, it is difficult (or impossible) to exclude people from consuming a public good, even if that person is unwilling to pay for it.[165]

Clean air satisfies both of these qualities. If an area has clean air, people cannot be restricted from consuming it. Further, allowing an extra person to consume clean air doesn't decrease the quality. (Technically, each human inhales oxygen and exhales carbon dioxide, so there is a very minimal reduction in quality – but it is small enough that we can ignore that quality reduction in this analysis.)

Another example of a public good is a strong military. A person in the United States cannot "opt-out" of being protected by the military, even if he/she doesn't wish to pay for it and one extra person living in the United States does not diminish the quality of the military's service.

The two properties of public goods cause a market failure. Without government intervention, a free market will tend to under-produce public goods. This is because of the free-rider effect. Each person will have an incentive to not pay for the public good – or buy less than they would otherwise – and attempt to free-ride off of what others are consuming. To get to the amount that maximizes well-being, you often need a governmental or quasi-governmental entity to get involved. For the military, governments collect tax revenues and produce the output. For clean air, governments tax pollution, create cap-and-trade markets, and mandate and enforce certain standards.

Topics: Public Goods, Free-rider Problem, Market Failure

"The Bottom Line"

Joseph Pulitzer and his colleagues discuss how to make more money from selling their newspapers. At the start of the song, the company's system has the newspaper carriers (newsies) sell the papers to customers for a penny each, or $1.00 per hundred copies. The company sells 100 papers to the newsies for $0.50 – so the newsies will earn $0.50 per 100 papers sold. To increase profits, they decide to increase the price the newsies pay to $0.60 per 100 papers. For every 100 papers sold, the newsies will now earn only $0.40, $0.10 less than before, while the company will earn $0.10 more. Pulitzer concludes that if they charge the newsies this higher price, the newsies would have to work harder just to earn the same amount of money.

"The Bottom Line" provides an opportunity to think about the law of supply as it applies to labor markets. The newsies are supplying their labor – and basic supply curve analysis would indicate that as the price people could receive by delivering newspapers drops, the quantity of papers they would deliver would also drop, as we see in Figure 20.

Supply curve analysis seems to contradict Pulitzer's logic. However, the supply of labor is often driven by the idea of how much leisure time somebody wants to purchase. That is influenced by two effects: the income effect and the substitution effect. The substitution effect indicates that as the price somebody is paid drops, that person would consume more leisure and work fewer hours – resulting in a labor supply curve like we see above. However, the income effect indicates that as people make less money, they cannot afford to purchase as much leisure time, and they'd actually work more – which is what Pulitzer claims.

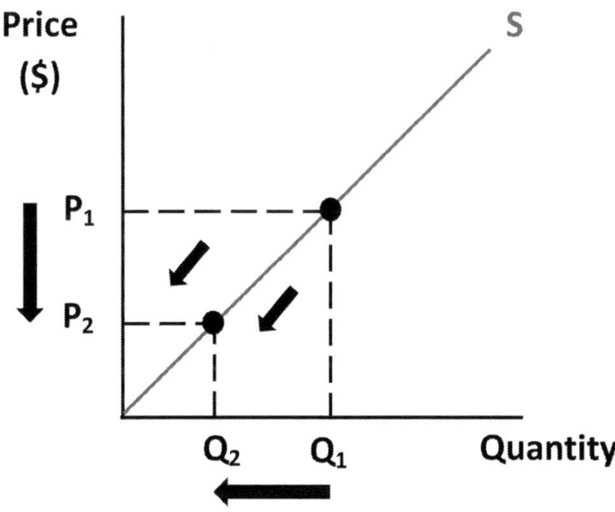

FIGURE 20

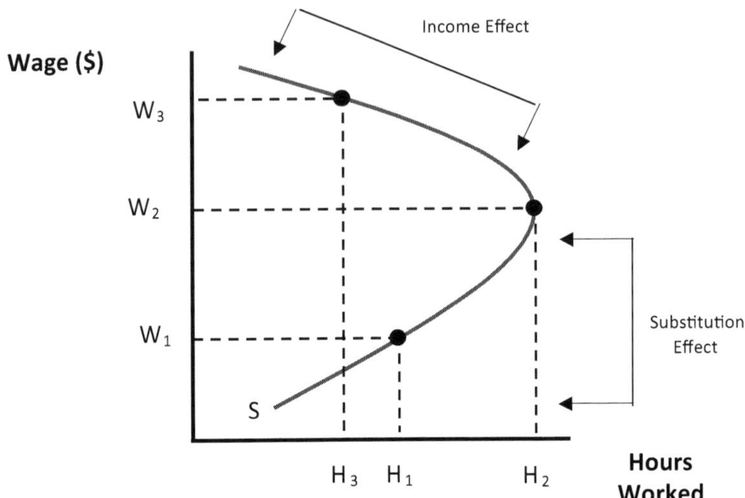

FIGURE 21

This results in what economists call the backward bending labor supply curve. However, it is usually thought of as "backward bending" because for those earning low wages, the supply curve increases before it eventually bends backwards. Therefore, it appears that Pulitzer was indeed using faulty economic logic when he thought a lower wage would induce the newsies to work more hours.

Topics: Supply Curve, Labor Economics, Backward Bending Labor Supply Curve

"The World Will Know"

Outraged after Joseph Pulitzer increases the cost of newspapers for the newsies by ten cents per 100 papers, newsie Jack Kelly organizes a union and ultimately a strike. This strike is known in history as the Newsboys' Strike of 1899. The goal of this strike, like most strikes, was to get higher wages for workers.

Jack sings about "stopping the scabbers." A scab is a derogatory term used by unions to describe a strikebreaker – somebody who works for a company despite the fact that the union is striking against them. Strikebreakers hurt unions mainly because the firm will still have access to workers and be able to produce their product(s). Part of the union's goal of striking is to halt production to force the firm to bargain with the union. Strikebreakers weaken the union's bargaining position as the firm can continue production.

Laws on hiring strikebreakers differ across countries.[166] In some countries it is not allowed. In the United States, hiring strikebreakers is allowed under certain situations[167] and companies hiring them can hurt unions beyond just allowing the company to resume production. Strikebreakers are allowed to be hired as permanent replacements for striking workers and often stay employed after the strike ends,[168] further weakening a union that decided to strike. Throughout history, there have been many cases of violence both against union members and against those crossing the picket line to work as strikebreakers.[169]

Topics: Unions, Labor Economics, Strikes, Strikebreakers

OLIVER!

"You've Got to Pick a Pocket or Two"

Fagan is helping everybody to pick pockets and convincing them that it is OK to steal from others. Even if legal to pick pockets, it is an activity that adds no value to society. This is different from most jobs. Most jobs, in addition to the person earning money, add value to society. Anybody who works for a grocery store, for example, has a job that is valuable to society. Regardless of what task a person has, they are helping ensure the public has a place where they can buy groceries. A person who makes his or her living painting also enhances peoples' lives with their art. Actors provide value for everybody who watches their performance(s), and teachers are helping to educate people. Most jobs contribute to society in addition to providing income to the worker.

But not all jobs are valuable to society and anything that involves stealing certainly would not. On a personal note, I used to earn some of my income from playing poker (semi-) professionally. That didn't produce anything of value and didn't help society. (Although it was a fun hobby.) As Nobel Prize-winning economist Paul Samuelson wrote, professional gambling "subtracts from the national income."[170] It subtracts from national income when a person gambles instead of producing something that has value. Another example of a job that wouldn't add value would be when lawyers expend resources competing with other lawyers to find clients for a class-action lawsuit. That adds no value to society as nothing new is produced or created. But lawyers in general have value, as they help maintain a stable rule of law for a country.

Topics: Labor Economics

Surplus

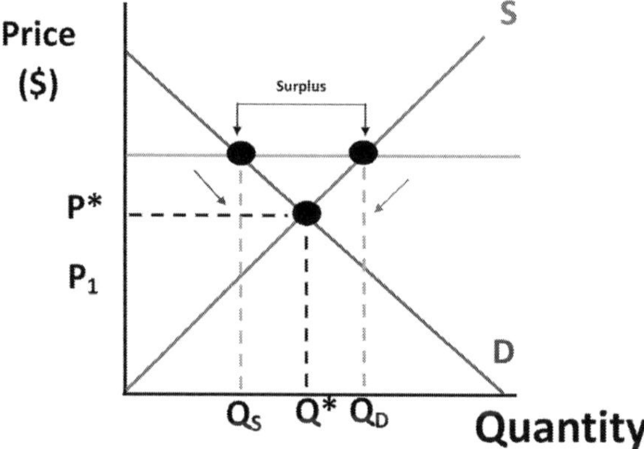

FIGURE 22

Shortage

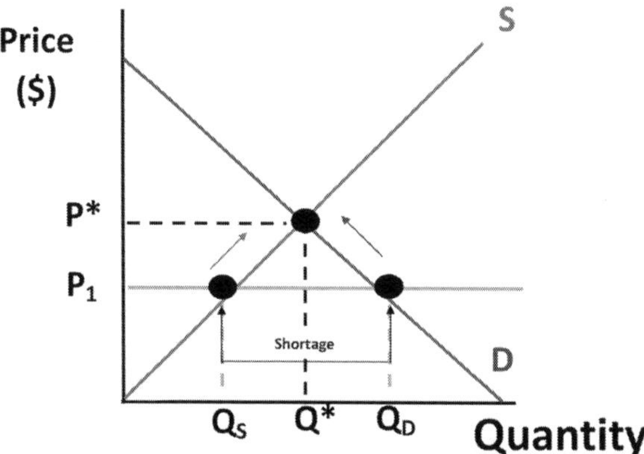

FIGURE 23

"Who Will Buy?"

People at the market are wondering who will buy their products. But this is a worry that they need not have. In fact, this issue was addressed by the founder of modern economics, Adam Smith. Smith marveled at the fact that every day in markets, people did not leave the market wanting more products nor did sellers have excess inventory at the end of the day. When you think about this, it does seem odd. Surely there should be some days where sellers bring too much, right? Then they would have extra inventory. Or there should be days where there are more buyers who want products than products available for sale. That would lead to a shortage. Yet neither shortage nor surplus happened.

The reason for neither shortages nor surpluses is that price changes will equilibrate the quantity demanded and quantity supplied. If too much of a product has been brought to a market – we would initially see a surplus of the product available. (See Figure 22.) But with too much of the product available, in order to sell their products, you'd see the sellers dropping their price. The price would fall until the quantity demanded equals the quantity supplied and there is no shortage.

If there is too little of a product available, a shortage, we would expect some consumers who can't obtain the product would be willing to pay more. We would also expect sellers to realize they could get more for their products – pushing the price up until the quantity demand exactly equals the quantity supplied and there is no shortage.

So while the sellers at the market are concerned about who will buy the product, they have the wrong worry. In markets, they will be able to sell their product. But if there are too many sellers or not enough buyers, they should be worried about whether they will receive a low price for their products.

Topics: Demand and Supply, Shortages, Surpluses

ON THE TWENTIETH CENTURY

"Five Zeroes"

Mrs. Primrose has decided to give Oscar, Owen, and Oliver a check for $200,000. This check is to help fund a Broadway show. Broadway shows as an investment are interesting since a majority of shows lose significant amounts of money.[171] However, a small subset of shows produce enormous returns. For example, people who invested in the musical *Wicked* received a 250% profit on their initial investment annually for many years![172]

This is an incredibly risky investment strategy. In fact, the state of New York actually requires all large investors to be vetted, ensuring they can afford to lose their entire investment in case a show flops.[173]

Topics: Investing

ONCE ON THIS ISLAND

"Mama Will Provide"

The Goddess Asaka sings to Ti Moune that "Whatever you need, mama will provide." In the show, the context is that the earth will provide everything that Ti Moune needs for her journey. This will allow Ti Moune to go about life without worrying about having life's necessities. But instead of thinking about the earth, we could also think about the government. Economists, much like the population at large, debate how much of a safety net the government should provide. What can't be debated is that the size of the safety net in the United States and many other countries has increased dramatically over the past century.

In the United States, there was a five-year period in which government spending increased dramatically. As Milton Friedman notes in his book, *Free to Choose*,

> Before 1929, federal government spending typically amounted to 3 percent of less of the national income. Since 1933, government spending has never been less than 20 percent of the national income . . . and two-thirds of that is spending by the federal government.[174]

As far as how much of this spending goes towards the poor, nobody knows for sure, but there are several estimates. Edward Conard estimates that the poorest 20% of households received an average of $15,200 in transfer payments from the federal government in 2006.[175] These are from cash payments, near-cash payments (like food stamps), and payments for health care. It is worth noting that Conard's estimates contain payments to both the poor and the "almost-poor," as the U.S. poverty rate has been between 12 and 16% for most of the past 50 years and he estimated the amount paid to the poorest 20% of households. So the amount of spending per poor family would likely be higher than Conard's estimates. Michael

Tanner writes that our federal spending on the poor averages more than $14,800 for "every poor man, woman, and child in this country."[176] Both Conard's and Tanner's estimates are for federal government spending only and do not consider spending by state or local government agencies. If "mama" is the government, then in the United States the title of the song is correct: mama will provide.

Topics: Government Spending, Fiscal Policy

ONE MAN, TWO GUVNORS

"Bangers and Mash"

Everybody is surprised by what's happening – the ugly man has a "6-foot stunner who is on him like a rash." But the mystery seems to be solved, as someone witnesses the ugly man handing her an envelope "stuffed full of cash." It seems like he simply hired a prostitute, or at the very least an escort, to be by his side.

We also hear about "a politician with a smug little face" who was involved in a scandal that left him in disgrace. But then he gets knighted by the Queen, again, after apparently bribing an official. Bribery and other forms of corruption – which is defined as the abuse of public or private office for personal gain[177] – are incredibly costly. The Organisation for Economic Co-operation and Development (OECD) estimates that over $1 trillion in bribes are paid annually. The cost to society is much more than that, however, as bribes cause public officials to engage in inefficient actions that they otherwise would avoid. The OECD estimates the cost of corruption to society at 5% of world GDP, $2.6 trillion, annually.[178]

Topics: Markets, Bribery, Corruption

"IOU"

A debtor sings that he owes "a fortune and a fortune I ain't got." One could ask how somebody who owes a fortune and doesn't have the means to pay it back was lent the fortune in the first place. Usually when investors are examining prospective customers for lending their money, they will look closely at the ability of the person (or firm, government entity, etc.) to pay back the money. If somebody is too high of a risk, a lender often will choose not to lend the money at all.

But sometimes lenders will loan money to people who have a higher risk of defaulting. Bonds, which are IOUs from companies, governments, or other agencies, are rated based on how likely it is that the lender will not get paid back. The top rating, indicating the safest places to invest, is AAA. This includes (as of early 2017) Microsoft and Johnson & Johnson.[179]

There are several other bond ratings and each rating has a different average interest rate that is paid out on their bonds. The following table shows a few of these ratings and the average annual interest rates paid for ten-year treasury bonds:

TABLE 2

S&P rating	*Grade*	*Average Interest Rate*
AAA	Prime	2.98%
AA	High	3.27%
A	Upper Medium	3.79%
BBB	Lower Medium	5.61%

Notice that as the risk goes up, the interest rate goes up. (Note, interest rates are as of December 2016.)[180] The reason the interest rates are higher for lower-graded bonds is that lower-graded bonds are more likely to fail, and investors need extra compensation in order to take on the additional risk.

Topics: Borrowing, Lending, Money Market

PACIFIC OVERTURES

"Welcome to Kanagawa"

A madam is discussing her business and sings "I own a small commercial venture with a modest clientele in Kanagawa." She runs a brothel and has new workers whom she has to train. This song is interesting because we see that the madam has the same issues running a brothel as many business owners have in their more normal businesses. The new workers she has to train aren't as experienced as other workers.

Work experience is a key factor that helps lead to higher wages. Workers with little or no experience often have to be trained – which is costly for the firm. Because of this, workers with little experience should expect lower salaries.

Topics: Markets

PHANTOM OF THE OPERA

"Notes"

Firmin and Andre discuss the business of the theatre. They have been threatened by the Phantom to replace Carlotta with Christine, but Firmin just seems to be concerned with sales, as he says "at least the seats get sold" and "half your cast disappears but the crowd still cheers." While Andre is upset that people are walking out, Firmin tells him they should just be happy about the free publicity.

The live theatre industry in most cities could be thought of as an oligopoly. There are a few sellers, all are relatively big players in the market, and the actions of one theatre affect another. For oligopolies, advertising can be important as it could increase the demand for a product – allowing a company to both sell more and charge a higher price, as we see below.

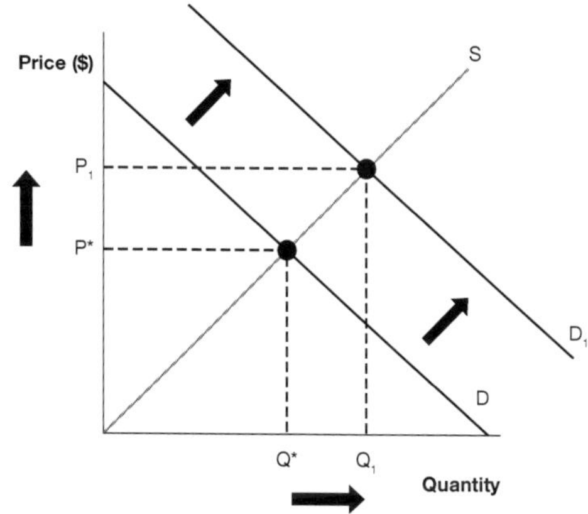

FIGURE 24

In "Notes," we hear how excited Firmin is about getting free advertising. While they way they are getting free advertising is a bit grotesque, he certainly does see the economic value.

Topics: Marketing, Advertising, Oligopoly

PIPPIN

"Simple Joys"

The game "Would you rather?" has been played by millions of people. It is simple – a person is asked to decide between two (usually, but not always unpleasant) options. The game illustrates trade-offs nicely, as the person is usually deciding between two things, and taking one means giving up the other. "Simple Joys" from Pippin describes several unpleasant "Would you rather?" scenarios as likely being better than "a man who never learns how to be free" including a "crab on a slab" and a "newt on a root."

There is another economic issue worth exploring from "Simple Joys." Early in the song we learn that Pippin is unhappy despite having everything he wants, including wealth and fame. This is a good passage to introduce the question of whether money buys happiness. Nobel Prize-winning economists Daniel Kahneman and Angus Deaton examined over 450,000 survey responses to the Gallup-Healthways Well-Being Index and found that higher incomes improve emotional well-being, but only up to about $75,000 per year. They conclude that higher levels of income will bring great "life satisfaction" as they get higher. (Life satisfaction is measured from a self-reported response about how satisfied someone is with their life.) But they also find that incomes higher than $75,000 do not buy happiness.[181]

This seems to conflict with research done by Betsey Stevenson and Justin Wolfers. They found no evidence that happiness drops off after a certain income level.[182] Other studies have shown that how one spends and earns money also affects happiness. Recent research has shown that money spent on experiences makes people happier than money spent on items.[183]

Topics: Trade-offs, Marginal Utility, Utility, Happiness

RAGTIME

Set at the turn of the 20th century, *Ragtime* has a beautiful score and a powerful message. Many of the songs directly relate to economic issues, including opportunities to immigrants, the impact of discrimination, the reaction of unions to productivity increases that cost people jobs in the short term, how entrepreneurs shape the economy, and differing views of the merits of wealthy entrepreneurs.

"Prologue"

The prologue introduces us to many of the characters. Father is well off because he has a business creating fireworks that has been very successful. This is in contract to Mother, who has a traditional mother's role – doing housework and keeping the home in order. Back in the early 1900s, it was much more common for men to be part of the workforce and for women to work at home. In fact only 19% of women were in the workforce in the early 20th century.[184] The percentage of women in the workforce has increased dramatically over the past 115 years in the United States. In 2015, well over 50% of women aged 18 and above were in the workforce.[185]

Grandfather is retired and living with Mother and Father. That Grandfather isn't living on his own but instead is living with his child and their family is worth exploring. This type of family arrangement was much more common in the United States in 1900 than it is today. Today, in the U.S., with higher overall incomes than in the early 1900s and social security payments to most retirees, fewer elderly people live in intergenerational homes. In 2010, only about 20% of people over 65 lived in a multigenerational household (i.e., live with their children or other younger family members). In 1900, 57% of those aged 65 and above lived in intergenerational households.[186]

We hear other stories as well. Tateh, an immigrant from Latvia, came to the U.S. dreaming of a more prosperous world. J.P. Morgan and Henry Ford, two of the wealthiest people in the world, enjoy a conversation. J.P. Morgan earned his income from many businesses, including the United States Steel Corporation, railroad companies, and from financial investments.[187] Henry Ford earned his income from the car company he founded, Ford Motor Company.

Not everybody liked Morgan and Ford, including Emma Goldman, who fought against capitalism, believing that it was harming immigrants. Later in her life the actual Emma Goldman lived in communist Russia and wrote about her realization that communism was a repressive system.[188]

Topics: Immigration, Entrepreneurship, Labor Economics, Capitalism, Communism, Socialism

"Success"

Tateh, a new immigrant to America from Latvia, is singing about the promise of the American dream. Both historically and today, many immigrants come to the United States seeking a better life. Today, most immigrants (documented or otherwise) in the United States are from Mexico. In Mexico, the median income was about $14,000 for a family of four in 2017.[189] That is much lower than one could receive in almost any job in the U.S. If someone worked 40 hours a week in the U.S. for the federal minimum wage of $7.25 for 50 weeks in the year, he or she would earn $14,500. Those who immigrate, of course, often are earning well below the median income in Mexico and many find jobs that pay more than the minimum wage – meaning the move to the United States results in dramatically better living standards for almost all immigrants.

But looking beyond just the incomes, Tateh sings: "Here in America anyone at all can succeed." There was a lot of truth to that statement in early 1900s America, and there is still a lot of truth to that statement today. That is because there is a lot of income mobility, which refers to the ability from somebody who is currently in one income quintile (for example, the poorest 20% of Americans) to later move into a different income quintile (for example, have an income that is in the 60–80% percentile). Several organizations and economists studying income mobility have concluded that incomes in the United States are incredibly mobile, and have been consistent over time.[190] One item of concern, however, is that there is less income mobility among African American families – meaning that African American children born into the poorest 20% of households are more likely to remain poor than poor children of other races.[191]

Topics: Immigration, Labor Economics, Income Mobility

"Henry Ford"

Henry Ford was one of the greatest entrepreneurs of all time. Much of his success was due to the use of the assembly line. In 1913, Ford oversaw the first moving assembly line, and it decreased the time it took to build a car from 12 hours to 2½.[192] Why did it work so well? He had people at each step of the assembly line perform the same tasks repeatedly. In the song, Ford sings "even people who ain't too clever, can learn to tighten a nut forever." The assembly line helped lead to over 10 million model T cars being produced. Ford's innovations not only made him rich, but helped make cars cheaper. This helped improve the lives of millions of Americans.

Today the cost of producing many products, including automobiles, are decreasing not because of assembly lines, but because firms are replacing workers with machines. Between 1979 to 2016, U.S. manufacturing output more than doubled – it increased by 167%. However, during this time the number of U.S. manufacturing jobs actually decreased by 37%.[193] This is great for society in the long term, as costs decrease and workers are now available to perform other useful tasks. In fact, this is exactly the type of progress that causes economic growth. In the short term, however, some people are worse off because they lose their jobs. Jobs lost due to automation provides another example of structural unemployment, where people lose their jobs and don't have the skills to match the available jobs.

Topics: Entrepreneurship, Production, Unemployment, Economic Growth

"The Night That Goldman Spoke at Union Square"

Younger brother stumbles into Union Square just hoping to warm up on a cold night. But instead he finds himself at a protest rally where Emma Goldman is discussing why unions should strike. A strike is one way that unions seek to achieve higher wages for their workers. By striking, the workers choose collectively to stop working. This means the workers are earning no income, but the business owners go without production and income as well – which often forces a negotiation.

Another way that unions could increase wages is by increasing the demand for domestic labor – which often could occur if laws are passed that restrict international trade or laws. Unions have also sought to increase demand for union products and services relative to non-union products and services – like with the "Look for the union label" ads. By using one of these methods to increase the demand for labor, wages for union workers would increase as shown in Figure 25.

Another alternative to increase wages is for a union to decrease the supply of workers. (See Figure 26.) The supply of labor could be decreased by requiring certifications, increasing the cost of acquiring training and capital, raising union fees, or other means. This would also cause an increase in the equilibrium wage.

Topics: Unions, Labor Economics

Increase in Demand for Union Products/Services

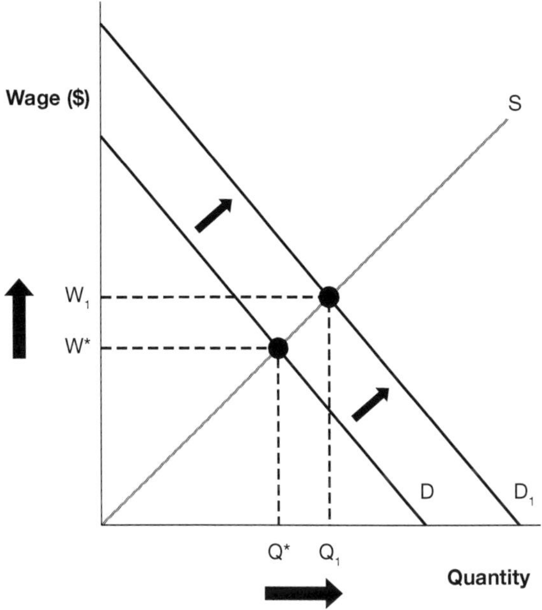

FIGURE 25

Decrease in Supply of Workers

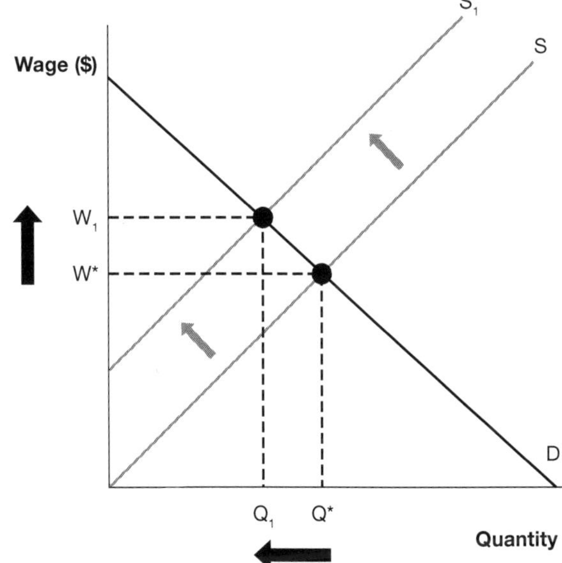

FIGURE 26

"Buffalo Nickel Photoplay, Inc."

Tateh initially had drawings that simulated movement and later went on to invent a projector to make movies. With these innovations, Tateh became wealthy. His story isn't unique. Throughout history, thousands, or even millions of entrepreneurs have earned considerable amounts of money by making slight improvements in existing products and then offering them to the public. What is even better from a societal point of view is that while Tateh was becoming rich, he was doing so by offering products that people valued. This means that he was also making the world a better place!

Topics: Entrepreneurship, Innovation, Product Differentiation

RENT

"Santa Fe"

Angel and Collins sing about their desire to open a restaurant in Sante Fe, New Mexico. This song shows one of the benefits that free markets provide – the ability for workers to sort themselves into the tasks they most enjoy. The right to choose one's own occupation may seem like a fundamental human right to people who have always had this option, but it is a right that has not always existed throughout history. For example, the government of the former Soviet Union often assigned workers to specific jobs. Worse still, sometimes these jobs were far from a worker's home, forcing them to relocate. This lack of freedom wasn't just restricted to workers, as students were often assigned to a school based on the government's future job expectations for that student (Grolier Multimedia Encyclopedia 2015; Federation of American Scientists 2000).

In addition to taking away a person's freedoms, restricting individuals' freedom to choose jobs is not an efficient way for an economy to be set up. Being able to choose one's job ensures the person has a job that best matches his or her passions and skills, and will usually lead to a productive workforce. This freedom also allows the opportunity for people to start their own businesses. Entrepreneurs creating new and more efficient products and processes have been a primary cause of the increase in well-being we've seen worldwide over the past 200+ years.

Topics: Entrepreneurship, Economic Freedom, Economic Growth

"Seasons of Love"

"Seasons of Love" asks the question "How do you measure a year?" of someone's life. But the question of how to make accurate measurements has many applications for economics. Recall that a country's gross domestic product (GDP) is defined as the market value of all final goods and services produced in a country in a given time period. That definition is very precise and means that only market transactions count – not any non-market transactions like housework or do-it-yourself construction. Also, only transactions through legal markets count – so illegal markets in drugs, gambling, and prostitution won't add to GDP. Further, some commentators like Nobel Prize-winner Joseph Stiglitz have criticized GDP for not containing any impact on the environment in their measurement[194] while recent economics research has examined alternative measurements that could be used instead of GDP that also examine quality-of-life measures like lifespan and leisure time.[195]

Another measurement that is sometimes controversial is the unemployment rate. The definition of how the unemployment rate is calculated is straightforward – the number of unemployed people divided by the number of people in the labor force (those who are employed plus those who are unemployed). But to be classified as unemployed in the U.S., you have to be out of work and have searched for work within the past four weeks. If you aren't searching for work, you are considered out of the labor force, and won't count as unemployed. Likewise, if you are working part-time and would rather work full-time, you aren't factored in to these statistics. There is nothing wrong with the unemployment rate statistic per se, but many think it underrepresents the problems in the labor market.[196]

Topics: Measurement Issues, GDP, Unemployment

"Voice Mail #4"

Alexi Darling is offering Mark Cohen a job in a voice mail message. In the offer, she says "you know you need money . . . don't be afraid of kerching kerching." Mark doesn't want take the job, but Alexi reminds him that he needs money. Throughout the show, it's pretty clear Mark isn't too interested in the work Alexi has to offer. He views this as "selling out" and certainly as less desirable than working on his own projects. Therefore, to induce Mark to take the job, Alexi has to offer him a higher wage. Economists refer to the higher wages people receive to work in undesirable jobs as compensating wage differentials.

Topics: Labor Economics, Compensating Wage Differentials

SCHOOL OF ROCK

"Here at Horace Green"

Rosalie, the principal, is describing the value of an education at Horace Green Prep School. She sings "we rule the rankings . . . test right off the chart. Greatness is routine." It is clear that Rosalie thinks that there is enormous value to attending Horace Green Elementary. Given that parents pay significant amounts of money to send their kids there, many parents must agree.

There are two main reasons that a person might find value in going to a prestigious school. The first is if the school provides a better education. If the school provides a better education it will provide people with more human capital. Then the school's graduates will be better prepared for their future studies and other worldly endeavors. This could make Horace Green a good investment.

A second reason a prestigious school could be valuable is not that it provides students with human capital, but that graduating from one sends a strong signal of quality. If a school is prestigious and everybody knows it, it will be tough to get into the school. Employers can use the fact that somebody got into Horace Green as a sign that he or she must be an exceptional student. This would be very valuable and result in future opportunities.

Nobel Prize-winning economist Michael Spence helped develop the economic theory that showed what was needed for a signal to be effective.[197] First, the person or firm seeing the signal must recognize it as a signal. Second, the activity that generates the signal should be costly, but less costly to those who are talented. Getting an education certainly sends a signal of quality.

For example, a college degree is a good signal of a person's ability to perform many jobs – it isn't cheap to complete (both in terms of money and effort) but it is much tougher to complete for those with lower intellectual skills. Even among those who attain a college degree, there are opportunities to send signals of higher ability to employers. Earning top grades while in school could be an effective signal. Once again – it is difficult to earn top grades, but more difficult for those with lesser skills. Other possible activities that could signal talent include the college from which a person graduated, a person's activities and leadership roles, the major a person chose, or just about any activity that is would be difficult for a person with lesser skill levels to achieve.

So why is a degree valuable? Is it because the schooling adds human capital (skills) to the graduate, or was the person already skilled and the degree just signals to the world that the person has a high level of skills. Economist debate about how much a degree increases a person's human capital versus just providing a signal. The argument that education is primarily a signal says that the person has some underlying level of talent but needs to earn a degree so employers know they have that talent. The alternative view, is that an education provides skills that help the student later in life.

I certainly believe that education has value beyond a signal (that is part of why I became an educator). A good education can help someone gain job-specific skills, improve critical thinking, and more. That said, one also sends a positive signal when getting a degree.

Topics: Education, Human Capital, Signaling

SHE LOVES ME

She Loves Me follows the story of Amalia and Georg, who dislike each other in real life. They are both writing letters to an anonymous person of the opposite sex. They haven't met their letter-writing counterpart in person yet, but both Amalia and Georg are slowly falling in love. What they don't know is that they are actually writing letters to each other. If the storyline sounds familiar, perhaps you saw the movie *You've Got Mail*, which was based on the same book.[198]

She Loves Me is set in a store – a perfumery to be precise – and several songs relate to economic concepts from the store setting. These songs address human capital acquisition, customer retention, and more. But the blossoming romance between Amalia and Georg also gives us an opportunity to examine the economics of signaling.

"Thank You Madam"

The workers of the store sing "Thank you, madam. Please call again. Do call again, Madam." With a total of only ten words, "Thank You Madam" is easily the shortest song covered in this book. The store workers in the musical *She Loves Me* sing to their customers every time they leave the store. They run a perfumery, which is in a monopolistically competitive industry. Recall that a monopolistically competitive industry is characterized by many small sellers, a market that is relatively easy for firms to enter and exit, and products that are differentiated. When a firm operates in a monopolistically competitive market, differentiation is valuable. If a firm can differentiate themselves from competitors, then they have more power to charge higher prices and earn higher profits.

The workers at the store sing a song to each customer as they depart, making them feel special. This would likely go a long way to keeping customers happy and retaining them and could be a smart business move. Most businesses and

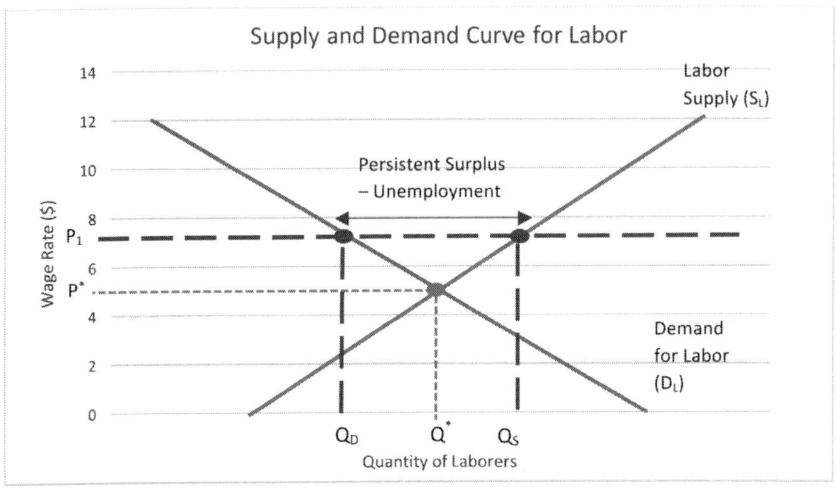

FIGURE 27

FIGURE 28

From: Organisation for Economic Co-Operation and Development (2017). *Short-Term Labour Market Statistics*. Retrieved January 6, 2017, from OCED.Stat: http://stats.oecd.org/index.aspx?queryid=36499#

business experts insist that it far less expensive to keep current customers than it is to attract new customers.[199] By singing as each customer leaves, the firm is incurring extra costs in terms of wages paid to workers (singing takes time). But if singing to customers keeps them coming back, that is an inexpensive way to ensure future business.

Topics: Markets, Competition, Monopolistic Competition

"Try Me"

In "Try Me," delivery boy Arpad Laszlo is pleading with his boss for a promotion. He has been a delivery boy for Maraczek's Parfumerie for the past two years, but has also taken every opportunity to learn about sales. After two years of self-training to prepare himself for a potential new job as a clerk, Arpad is trying to convince his boss to give him a chance. His pleading involves him discussing what he has learned, and he sings "I know every item in the store. Every tube, jar, box, bottle, carton and container."

"Try Me" highlights the idea of human capital. Human capital is the skill set an employee acquires that allows him or her to earn more money. It is similar to the idea of physical capital (plants, machinery, equipment, etc.) in that they are items that can help produce more output, but human capital is referring to a person's skills. Arpad is highlighting the human capital he has acquired via on-the-job training at Maraczek's Parfumerie, and that's why he thinks he could handle the new tasks (and earn higher wages). He sings that he knows "every item in the store" and that by hiring him the boss would get "first class clerking and conscientious working."

"Try Me" also gives us the opportunity to think about the potential costs of high minimum wages – as the boss would be far less likely to pay low-skilled Arpad a higher, government-imposed minimum wage. When a minimum wage is in place and has an impact it does a couple of things. First, more people are willing to work for the new, higher wage. Second, firms will hire fewer workers. As we see from this demand-and-supply diagram (Figure 27), that means we'll see a surplus of workers. When there are more people willing to work than jobs available, there will be higher unemployment rates among workers competing for jobs that pay the minimum wage.

This is standard economic theory and shows that minimum wages should result in unemployment among the least-skilled workers. The empirical evidence confirms that minimum wages do seem to matter and we can see that when we look at unemployment by age in the United States. Teenagers, with less experience and lower skill levels, are the most likely to bump into problems with the minimum wage when looking for jobs. When looking at the U.S. unemployment rates among teenagers vs. others, we see strong evidence that minimum wages cause unemployment.

As the graph shows, the teenage unemployment rate is consistently more than double the unemployment rate is for adults.[200] This higher unemployment rate is incredibly costly, as those who are unemployed are neither earning money nor obtaining the skills, like Arpad gained, to move into the next higher-paying job.

Topics: Human Capital, Labor Economics, Income Inequality, Mobility

"Vanilla Ice Cream"

Amalia is writing a letter to a man. She has been writing to this man for the past several months and likes him, but hasn't actually met him yet. As she is trying to write, Amalia gets distracted because her co-worker Georg just delivered ice cream to her house.

By bringing Amalia ice cream, Georg is sending a signal to her that he is a good person and perhaps could be a suitable partner. Like with Georg and Amalia, a person could try to signal to somebody else that he/she would make a good romantic partner. However, there are also many economic applications. Potential employees can try to signal to firms that they are a good person to hire.

When a person has a particular talent and thinks he or she could be a good fit for an employer, the person will want to make sure the firm knows it. However, if that talent is valuable, other people will want to claim that they also have that talent – even if they don't. (Some might claim they have that talent and be lying. Others might genuinely, albeit incorrectly, think they have a particular talent.)

For a signal to be successful at indicating skill or talent, it must be costly to obtain. However, it must be less costly for a skillful person to obtain, so it is worthwhile for the skillful person to obtain it, but not others. Amalia might think anybody *could* bring ice cream, but who is more likely to bring it? Most likely a person who has the traits needed in a good partner.

Topics: Signaling, Game Theory

SHREK THE MUSICAL

"Story of My Life"

"Story of My Life" from *Shrek the Musical* features Pinocchio, the Three Little Pigs, and many other fairytale creatures who live in DuLoc. Unfortunately, these creatures are discriminated against by the government and banished to a swamp. The government of DuLoc is opposed to these creatures, and any non-conformist, so it has banished them.

One reason this can occur without much consequence to the person doing the discriminating is that government agents do not pay a cost for discriminating (Becker 2010). This is in stark contrast with what occurs with market systems, as markets impose a cost on those who discriminate because of the profit motive. Let's think through the logic of why. Suppose you have two groups of people: those with green hair and those with purple hair. The people are otherwise identical, except for their hair. And those with green hair are just as productive as those with purple hair, but are being paid less money for doing the exact same work. Using supply and demand diagrams, Figure 30 shows the market with discrimination.

We see the lower demand leads to a lower wage for those with green hair. But discrimination in a market system against those with green hair isn't sustainable. Why? Well suppose those with green hair are paid less than those with purple hair despite the fact that these folks are identical other than their hair color. If this happened and a firm had the chance to hire a worker, any profit-maximizing firms will want to hire the cheaper worker – the people with green hair. But by hiring people from the group that are being paid less, the demand for people in that group goes up, which helps make the wages equal and eradicates discrimination.

Graphically we can see how this works. The demand for the green-haired workers increases as firms hire more of them – while the demand for those with

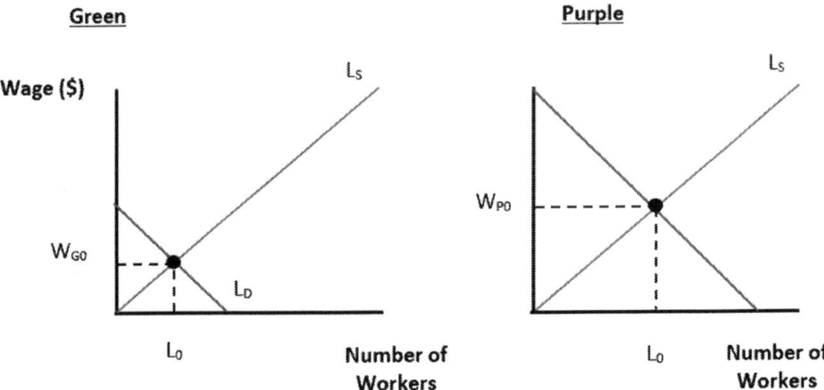

FIGURE 29

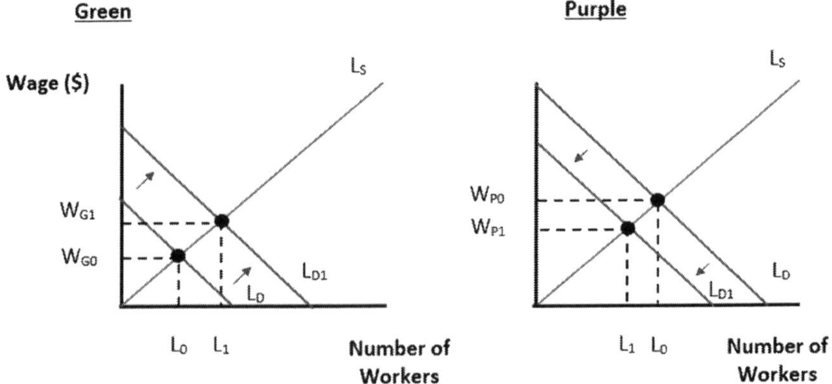

FIGURE 30

purple hair would decrease. This would push the wages for green-haired workers higher and for purple-haired workers lower – so the wages become more similar. Firms would keep hiring the cheaper workers until the wages equalized.

Firms that maximize profits will take advantage of every opportunity to increase profits, including hiring cheaper workers when possible. But, ironically, this willingness to exploit a difference in wages is precisely the reason we won't see differences in wages for workers with the same skill levels in the long run – at least in a market system.

But governments don't face these same incentives. If an official in a government position wants to discriminate – that government office might not be as productive, but it won't impact profits, and therefore the official faces almost no consequences. "Story of My Life" illustrates this. It is worth noting here that throughout history, governments have been the worst discriminators, supporting slavery, apartheid, mass executions, and other forms of discrimination.[201]

Topics: Discrimination

SOMETHING ROTTEN

How would you like to be a writer when your main competition is William Shakespeare? In *Something Rotten* we learn about the Bottom brothers, who are struggling to produce their plays when competing against the greatest playwright of all time. We also learn about the innovations that helped lead to economic growth and an innovation that could help the Bottom brothers differentiate their plays in a competitive market. *Something Rotten* – set in 1590s England – provides several economic lessons.

"Welcome to the Renaissance"

"Welcome to the Renaissance" is the opening number and introduces the audience to the time period – 1590s England. The song also brilliantly illustrates how society benefits from innovation and entrepreneurship, as people were benefiting from some great innovations. They sing "here we've made advances in the sciences, we have the latest gadgets and appliances." The song also describes new innovations such as the printing press and tobacco, along with research that studied how freezing preserves food products[202] and the writings of Shakespeare and others.

Market economies can provide monetary rewards to firms that create and market innovative products. Firms such as Apple, Facebook, and Google are current examples of innovative firms that are worth billions because of their new products. These firms also provide enormous benefits to the public at large by producing products that people want. Some estimates indicate that firms creating innovative products capture as little as 5% of the value of that product.[203] The public at large collects the rest of the value. "Welcome to the Renaissance" is a great song to illustrate this. After all: the printing press was amazingly important for the evolution of society. While Gutenberg, the inventor, earned money, the public benefited enormously from its proliferation.

Topics: Innovation, Economic Growth

"A Musical"

The Bottom brothers are playwrights competing with William Shakespeare in the 1590s. Shakespeare is brilliant, of course, so these brothers need to figure out the next innovation for their business to be successful. What is the innovation they need? A musical, of course.

This song is a great introduction to the benefits that society gains from innovation and entrepreneurship. In the song, it is clear that musicals offer many advantages over conventional plays. If the Bottom brothers are correct, audiences will enjoy this new product and will choose to spend their money attending musicals. Given that Shakespeare and the Bottom Brothers are competing playwrights, by offering an innovative product, the Bottom Brothers might get additional business and earn more money.

Topics: Entrepreneurship, Product Differentiation

SUNDAY IN THE PARK WITH GEORGE

"Putting it Together"

George is an artist. He is comfortable making art, but is not comfortable selling it. But he sings about how he needs money to buy a new machine. George discusses several things that seem unpleasant about selling, including that he considers himself "up on the trapeze" and that he is "just a dab of politician."

George is clearly considering the trade-offs of his work. To earn the money to do the things he really enjoys, he must endure the social scene and kiss up to the rich donors. Alternatively, he could live poorer and avoid this social scene. Because he chooses to sell his work, we can conclude that he views the income he'll receive as worth the hassle.

Topics: Labor Economics, Trade-offs

SUNNY AFTERNOON

"The Moneygoround"

In "The Moneygoround," the band is singing about how their money keeps getting split up before it reaches them. They sing "Robert owes half to Grenville, who in turn gave half to Larry, who adored my instrumentals, and so he gave half to a foreign publisher." While the band is (understandably) not happy about what is happening to their money, this song provides an opportunity to examine what economists call the multiplier.

The multiplier shows us the amount that economic activity increases when there is an injection of money. An injection of money increases economic activity by more than the initial injection, because the money gets spent and respent by each person receiving it. The value of the multiplier depends on what economists call the marginal propensity to consume – which is just a fancy phrase indicating how much out of each dollar a person decides to spend. The formula for the multiplier is 1/(1-marginal propensity to consume).

In this song, we see the band's managers getting a payment, which then gets split many times. The group of people related to the band is financially better off. We hear that each person who receives money pays half to somebody else. By each person giving half of the amount they receive to the next person, the marginal propensity to consume in this song is 0.5 – which means the money multiplier is 2. So for every $1,000 the band receives, there would be an increase of $2,000 in economic activity.

Multipliers are used by governments and other agencies to estimate how much an economic activity will increase economic output.

Topic: Multiplier

SUNSET BOULEVARD

Sunset Boulevard presents the story of Norma Desmond. She was a famous silent movie actress, but when talking movies were created, Norma's skill set was no longer in demand. This is a classic case of creative destruction, where a new innovative good, talking movies, replaced an inferior one. This made the world better off, as customers much preferred talking movies to silent movies. With that change, however, the silent film industry was destroyed. Many careers were also destoryed, including Norma Desmond's.

"With One Look"

"With one look" Norma Desmond was able to play any role, at least when movies were silent. Ms. Desmond claims that "No words can tell the stories my eyes tell, watch me when I frown, you can't write that down." Ms. Desmond was fantastically talented – the biggest star there was. But when the talking movies came along, her skill set was no longer in demand. Norma Desmond is unemployed – and economists would say she is structurally unemployed. Structural unemployment occurs when an individual's skill set doesn't match up to the available jobs. Many who are structurally unemployed have lost manufacturing jobs that became more automated. In Ms. Desmond's case, she has the skills to act in silent movies but not in talking movies.

Topics: Structural Unemployment, Creative Destruction

"The Lady's Paying"

Norma Desmond is rich, and she wants to treat Joe to new clothing on his birthday. Expensive clothing. Norma has the workers from "the best men's shop in town . . . close it down for a day." But Joe is clearly reluctant, turning down the opportunities to be dressed in the expensive outfits and telling Norma that, as a writer, his clothing choices don't matter much. After an argument, Norma prevails and ends up buying the expensive clothing for Joe.

Norma spends an exorbitant amount of money to buy clothing for Joe – but Joe clearly doesn't think these purchases are that valuable. It seems obvious from the song that Joe would have been much better off had Norma just given him the equivalent amount of money. The difference in well-being from Joe being given the clothing instead of just being given the equivalent amount of cash is the deadweight loss of the presents.

Topics: Deadweight Loss

"Eternal Youth is Worth a Little Suffering"

The trainers sing "I need three more weeks to get these thighs in shape. No more carbohydrates, don't be naughty." These words illustrate what Norma Desmond should expect to endure over the next few weeks. Ms. Desmond wants to look younger, and is willing to endure significant pain to reach her goal. This is a great song to illustrate both trade-offs and opportunity cost. The trade-offs here are clear – to look younger and better, Norma Desmond has to give up proteins, carbohydrates, and fats. In short, she has to endure "a little suffering." This song illustrates opportunity costs. Norma Desmond pays the beauty consultants who are providing her with advice, but she is so rich that her monetary payments likely do not matter to her. The non-monetary costs of looking younger are large, however. The opportunity cost of beauty, in her case includes forgoing carbohydrates and dealing with injections.

Topics: Opportunity Costs, Trade-offs

IS THERE A DEADWEIGHT LOSS FROM CHRISTMAS?

Economists have debated whether there is a deadweight loss from Christmas. The most notable debate came with several scholarly articles in the top economics journal – *The American Economic Review*. The initial article, by Joel Waldfogel, found that Christmas gift giving resulted in an enormous deadweight loss. He conducted a survey and found that people's willingness-to-pay for the set of presents they received was much lower than the price that was paid for them – indicating that people would have been much better off simply receiving cash instead of gifts.[204]

But Waldfogel's analysis used only college students, and Solnick and Hemenway argued that the limited age range might have produced misleading results.[205] So Solnick and Hemenway implemented a survey with graduate students and staff at the Harvard School of Public Health. They find results opposite of Waldfogel, that the median gift recipient valued the gift at 11% more than the store price – indicting that Christmas didn't cause inefficiency because the sentimental value of receiving something as a gift meant Christmas gifts were more valuable than just receiving cash.[206]

So how could one reconcile the large differences in value between the two surveys? This was the goal of a subsequent paper written by John List and Jason Shogren.[207] As experimental economists, they argue that surveys have biases, and that purchasing experiments where people are offered money to sell their Christmas gifts back would be better. List and Shogren first ran a survey that was similar to the surveys conducted by the other authors. Their survey results found that participants actually valued the gifts at about 98% of the store price – so in between the results of the other papers. List and Shogren then ran an auction where they paid cash to purchase the presents people received back from them. They found that people needed between 21 and 35% *more than* the store price to sell back their Christmas presents – indicating that by receiving a product as a present, the product was much more valuable than an equivalent product that could be purchased at the retail price.[208]

So should we just give cash to everybody instead of buying Christmas (or birthday, or Chanukah) presents? Many economists contend that this would be more efficient. And if we were all heartless robots, then yes, cash would be better! But because we are human beings, we place a sentimental value on presents that increases the value of presents to beyond the store price.[209] The sentimental value people attach to presents indicates that gift giving increases well-being.

TENDERLOIN

"How the Money Changes Hands"

In this song we hear money cycles through the economy from the landlord to the farmer to the grocer to the banker. They sing "everybody's happy . . . just as long as the money changes hands." With the money changing hands, it gives us another opportunity to discuss the multiplier effect. When an infusion of money is made into an economy, the gains go beyond the initial cash payment.

For example, suppose that a person in a small town discovers $80,000 buried in her backyard. She is $80,000 better off, but what about the economy of the town? Well, the others in the town will also likely be better off. If the person who discovered the gold spends $60,000 of the $80,000 in the town, the town has now benefited from an extra $60,000 in economic activity. But the gains won't stop there. The recipients of that $60,000, who could be local restaurants, home contractors, or other businesses now have more money than they would otherwise. They would spend a portion of that $60,000 – creating still more economic activity!

The multiplier effect has been the subject of attention among economists and politicians. Charles J. Whalen and Felix Reichling from the Congressional Budget Office write that "the Great Recession sparked wide interest in the economic effects of fiscal policy." This includes debates over the size of the multiplier, since the size of the multiplier will directly affect the impact of increases in government spending or decreases in taxes have on the economy.[210]

Topics: Multiplier, Fiscal Policy

THE ADDAMS FAMILY

"Pulled"

Wednesday Addams is discussing the things that make her happy which include "Unicorns with dancing mice, sunrise in wide open spaces" and Disney World. These are not the things she expected to enjoy – and she is confused (pulled) about it. Economists describe the happiness somebody gets from a product or service as their utility. Wednesday now gets utility from "unicorns with dancing mice," "puppy dogs with droopy faces," and butterflies, among other things. She never used to gain utility from these things before, which is part of why she's so puzzled.

One possible explanation for her new preferences is the law of diminishing marginal utility, which indicates that as you acquire more of an item, each additional unit becomes less valuable. Conversely, if you have very little of an item, the first (and often second) unit of an item is much more valuable. The Addams Family had not previously valued – and therefore does not have – puppy dogs, string quartets, or Chia Pets. Therefore, Wednesday may be enjoying these products or experiences for the first time, giving her higher marginal utility than she gets from her usual products (like coffins and crossbows).

Topics: Utility, Diminishing Marginal Utility

"Secrets"

Morticia Addams doesn't like secrets. She says that secrets are "the enemies of passion" and that by avoiding secrets "your marriage'll be healthier by far." She also says she would divorce her husband Gomez if he ever lied once. She clearly views any possible benefits of keeping secrets (and/or lying) as being much lower than costs of keeping secrets.

Topics: Benefit–Cost Analysis

THE BRIDGES OF MADISON COUNTY

"Almost Real"

Are wars good? Of course not. But do wars help the economy? The answer to this is also no. But could a war improve a country's Gross Domestic Product? Well, yes. Gross Domestic Product (GDP) is one of the main measures of economic well-being and is the value of the new goods and services produced in a country within a year. So in wars, GDP will often rise. But GDP is limited in terms of thinking about well-being because it does not account for destruction. Naturally, in wars, much is destroyed.

In "Almost Real," Francesca describes the conditions in Italy during World War II. She says "the streets [were] rubble" and "the water was filthy." She also claims that people could not get either cigarettes or haircuts. World War II, which some people credit as being the boost that finally helped the United States recover from the Great Depression, did indeed cause an increase in gross domestic product (GDP), but it absolutely did not cause an increase in well-being. Thinking about Americans, many were abroad and poor while fighting (not to mention that many died), and those at home had to endure a rationing system that limited the amounts of many products that they could obtain, including gasoline, sugar, tires, and meat.[211]

War does not make society better off, and wars present an opportunity to remind people that a country's GDP is an imperfect measure of economic well-being. The flaw comes from what is known as "the broken window fallacy." If something is destroyed and a government pays people to rebuild it, it will appear like there were economic gains. But at the end of the day, all that is there is what was originally in place. GDP does not account for things that are destroyed. GDP also does not account for which type of products is produced. So if an economy increases military purchases and decreases food purchases by the same amount, GDP will stay the same even if people are hungry.

Topics: Trade-offs, GDP, War

THE FIX

"America's Son"

Cal is running for office. His advisors don't have a favorable view of voters, telling Cal to restrict his campaign to talking about three things – "the economy, crime, taxes."

There are a couple ways one could look at this. Perhaps Cal and his team are in favor of smaller governments. Their claims of wanting less government spending and lower tax rates would seem to indicate this. Another possible explanation is that Cal and his team simply will say anything to get elected. This would be consistent with public choice theory, which assumes that politicians and bureaucrats don't necessarily do what's best for society, but instead choose the options that make election (or re-election) most likely.

Topics: Public Choice Theory

THE FULL MONTY

If you only hear the name or see the posters, you might think *The Full Monty* is a lewd musical. I found it nothing of the sort. It is uplifting and shows the power of the entrepreneurial spirit. Just as wonderful – it has many economic themes woven throughout. The men featured in the show have lost their jobs at the factory and are unemployed. They are depressed and desperate, and their unemployment is causing financial stress that is affecting their lives and the lives of their families.

From this desperation, an idea to earn money arises – they'll strip and go "the full monty." By doing this, they become entrepreneurs. The show highlights the effort they put into their endeavors along with the rewards received, both financial and personal.

"Scrap"

The factory in Buffalo shut down, and many men are now unemployed. Jerry, Dave, Malcolm, and the others are singing about their lives without jobs. Instead of working they are watching porn, cleaning the refrigerator, and being "a loser that still lives at home with his mother."

The plant shutting down gives a good opportunity to talk about several topics. The first is the different types of unemployment. It is possible that the plant shut down because the tasks became more automated or because the firm moved their plant to a lower-cost area of the world. If this is why the plant closed, the men are suffering from structural unemployment, which occurs when there is a mismatch between the skills of workers and the available jobs.

Structural unemployment can be quite painful, as it often involves either taking a reduction in salary or training to gain new job skills. But it has been part of our society for hundreds of years. For example, in 1800, over 90% of the workforce worked in agriculture while today it is under 5%.[212] This has been a good change for society, as the decrease in farm labor has meant a drop in food prices and the ability for our society to produce many other goods. A similar change has been occurring with a shift from manufacturing to service jobs. The reduction in the resources to produce products has made us richer, but the transitions have been painful for many as the skills learned aren't as applicable in today's job market.

In addition to highlighting structural unemployment, "Scrap" also reveals the personal costs unemployment can have on individuals. Many people gain significant self-worth from their jobs[213] and being unemployed, in addition to causing financial harm, can be painful in non-financial ways. For example, a 2013 Gallup Poll found that those who were unemployed were more than twice as likely to be depressed as those who were working full time (11.4% depression rates vs. 5.6%). Being out of labor force, which means not working but also not looking for a job, had a 16.6% rate of depression.[214]

Topics: Unemployment

"Man"

Unemployed and desperate for a way to earn a little extra money, Jerry has an idea – he and his friends could become strippers! Jerry thinks this could be a good business and he and his friends would therefore be entrepreneurs.

Jerry sings about the ways in which he and his friends would make good strippers. Whether it is because they have hairy backs or they "smell scary," these men would be different than those who normally strip – i.e., each one would be a "man"! This is an example of product differentiation. The market for strippers could be classified as monopolistically competitive, which occurs when there are very low barriers to entering a market, there are many firms each with a small part of the overall market share, and each product is similar, but not exactly identical.

In a market that is large enough, each stripper (or team of strippers, in this case) could be thought of as a monopolistic competitor, as nobody is identical, there aren't many barriers to a new person stripping, and there are many other strippers for customers to choose among.

Topics: Entrepreneurship, Product Differentiation, Monopolistic Competition

THE LAST FIVE YEARS

"The Schmuel Song"

Before he will give Cathy her Christmas present, Jamie wants to tell her the story of Schmuel, the "tailor of Klimovich." Schmuel works long hours every day just to keep up with the day-to-day operations of his business. He has a dream of producing a fantastic dress that will fire "the mad desires" of women everywhere. But he is too busy. That is, until a talking clock convinces him that if he starts to produce the dress, the time will appear – which it magically does! The clock says "Oh Schmuel, you'll get to be happy . . . I give you unlimited time." With this time, Schmuel goes after his dream, produces the dress, and it turns out to be as fantastic and life-changing as he was hoping.

"The Schmuel Song" song does a great job at illustrating short run vs. long run trade-offs. Schmuel had a long-term dream, but the day-to-day operations of his business prevented him from pursuing it. Likewise, Jamie thinks Cathy is so caught up in day-to-day details that her short-term behavior is getting in the way of her long-term goals. Jamie gives her a watch, but the watch is only symbolic to the bigger gift he wants to give her: time to pursue her dreams. Jamie convinces Cathy that they can make ends meet if she quits her job – so she should pursue her dreams of an acting career.

The conflict between short-run satisfaction and long-run planning plays out with many economic decisions. For example, the decision to save, and how much to save, is an economic dilemma that pits the two against each other. Likewise, the decision to attain more education is costly: it costs money to go to college (at least in the U.S. and many other countries), and it also takes time that could have been spent earning money instead of in school. But for most people, getting a college degree is a valuable investment.

There is another economic lesson from "The Schmuel Song." It shows the impact of a resource – in this case, time – on Schmuel's ability to produce.

A business's ability to produce is related to the resources – land, labor, and capital – at its disposal. Given these limitations in the beginning of the song, Schmuel does not have the time to create the beautiful dress in his dreams. But with the magic clock in the song giving him "unlimited time," he has more of a key resource and is able to sew that dress.

Topics: Production Possibilities Frontier, Short Run vs. Long Run, Time Horizons

"A Summer in Ohio"

What could possibly be better than a summer in Ohio? Well, lots of things if you're Cathy from the musical *The Last Five Years*. Cathy is now an actress, and the summer, according to her, is not going well. This is because she is sharing a room with a former stripper and her snake; the best role she can find is opposite a midget named Karl; and she is suffering from a lack of hot water and cable TV. Yet, she is enduring these hardships to pursue her dream of being an actor.

This song does a great job illustrating the trade-offs Cathy incurs for pursuing her dream. "A Summer in Ohio" is a letter that Cathy is writing to her husband, Jamie. While Cathy is clearly sad to miss the summer with her husband and is not happy with the conditions she must endure, she is willing to persevere because it is a trade-off she is willing to make. Her passion for building an acting career is worth the miserable conditions and time away from her husband.

The opportunity cost of any activity is the next best alternative that is given up. In this case, Cathy's opportunity cost of pursuing her dream to act means living away from her husband. The fact that she is willing to live away from her husband and act with a gay midget, room with a former stripper and her snake, and live in a place without hot water or Vietnamese food illustrates that there are many costs she incurs and that trade-offs are not always pleasant.

Topics: Opportunity Cost, Trade-offs

THE LAST SHIP

"Shipyard"

The musical *The Last Ship* is set in Wallsend, England. In Wallsend, there is one shipyard and it will close in the near future. With the closing of the shipyard, the workers will be unemployed. What's worse, as shipbuilders in a town that soon won't have a shipyard, their skills likely won't translate easily into another industry. These individuals would be considered structurally unemployed. Structural unemployment occurs when the skills of the workers don't match the skills that are needed by employers.

Structural unemployment is often difficult for those who are unemployed. If a similar job cannot be attained there are a few options. First, the person could take a different job, usually for lower pay. Second, the person could go into a retraining program to learn a new skill that might be a better match for the available jobs. A third option is the person could simply drop out of the labor market altogether and stop working. There are other economic lessons from "Shipyard."

Tommy Thompson sings that "Das Kapital's me bible." *Das Kapital* by Karl Marx claims that capitalism depends on the exploitation of labor. He also wants the workers to "become the rightful owners of this shipyard." Marx's writings have been highly influential – but no country that has attempted to use any version of communism has ever been able to sustain economic growth. Many, like Cuba and North Korea, have remained impoverished for years while nearby countries that embrace markets have thrived.

Peggy White is a nurse and sings about fixing "busted arms and busted heads; broken backs and broken legs." She also sings about radiation and the poisonous fumes. In short, the shipyard she's describing is a dangerous place. Because of that, the shipyard workers are likely being paid more than if they worked a job that required the same skills but was safe. This increased payment for working a dangerous job is called a compensating wage differential.

Topics: Unemployment, Structural Unemployment, Unions, Labor Economics, Communism, Capitalism, Compensating Wage Differential

THE LION KING

"I Just Can't Wait to be King"

Simba can't wait for the future, as he might be king. Instead of being willing to forgo future privileges, he is not patient at all. This indicates that that Simba is "discounting" the future. This means that consumption in the future is viewed as less valuable than consumption now. Many people share Simba's attitude and value the present more than the future. The amount in which a person values the present over the future is the subject of much economic research and has implications.

Research shows that people discount the future at very high rates. When asked between receiving a sum of money now and an equivalent sum of money in a year, most will need significantly more to wait a year. Several studies find that adults have a discount rate between 0.28 and 0.30.[215] That would indicate that, on average, adults would view receiving $71 right now as about as good as receiving $100 a year from now. Research by University of Pittsburgh economist David Huffman and his co-authors found that older people have a higher discount rate, 0.54, and that those with severe ailments were likely to discount the future even more.[216] This should seem logical, as living for extra years (or being healthy in future years) will be less likely when one is older or has a severe ailment.

Discounting is important when governments attempt to think through policies that have a long-lasting impact. For example, if people discount the future dramatically, a government policy that has an impact 20, 50, or 100 years from now will be less important to policy makers.

Topics: Time Preferences, Discounting

THE LITTLE MERMAID

"I Want the Good Times Back"

Ursula, the sea witch, is singing about her dreams and desires. In doing so, we learn that she is not a very good person. What's more, we also learn a bit about her unusual preferences. Ursula is already incredibly wealthy as her dad "divvied up the kingdom into two" and Ursula got half. But she desperately wants more, including "disgusting wealth" and "wild soirees." Ursula seems different from most people (or in her case, sea-creatures), as most people exhibit a diminishing marginal utility of wealth. That means that once a person becomes wealthy enough, more money still is better, but any extra amount of money won't mean as much. But Ursula doesn't seem to follow the convention as she seems like she will only be happy when she has unlimited power.

In addition to knowing a bit about her preferences, we also see that Ursula seems to be thinking like a game theorist. She sings "I want the little girl, and boys, I want her bad. I want her sitting here to lure her dear devoted dad. I want my goody-goody brother to come rescue her, the sap." Her path to happiness gets quite complicated but she does have a plan. First, she wants unlimited power and thinks the key is to get King Triton to agree to give her his trident – his weapon that has magical abilities. Second, to induce King Triton to give up his trident, Ursula realizes that her best hope is to ransom off Ariel, King Triton's daughter. Third, to be able to ransom Ariel, Ursula first has to trick her into signing away her soul. Finally, to get Arial to sign her soul away, Ursula must come up with a great plan. Ursula thinks backwards to what needs to be done to accomplish her goals.

Ursula's approach for thinking through how to capture the trident is similar to how game theorists examine sequential games. A game theorist starts by looking at the choices that are made at the end of the game and works backwards, examining what each logical move should be at every step of the game. A game theorist solves for each correct move at each step of the game, until they have solved the entire game. So it appears Ursula could be a game theorist! (Except she's quite mean, whereas most game theorists are lovely and huggable.)

Topics: Utility, Marginal Utility, Marginal Utility of Wealth, Game Theory, Backward Induction, Sequential Games

"Poor Unfortunate Souls"

Ariel wants legs so she can pursue Prince Eric. But getting legs comes at a cost. A big cost. She will be forced to give her voice to Ursula. And if she doesn't kiss Prince Eric within three days, she also will be forced to spend eternity in Ursula's "watery hell-soaked lair." Yikes! Despite these costs, Ariel enters into the agreement, thinking that the chance to win her true love outweighs the significant costs of not having a voice and a possibility of being an eternal slave. The opportunity cost was severe, but in the moment Ariel thought the trade-offs – giving up her voice and risking her soul – were worth it to try to woo Prince Eric.[217]

Combining Ariel's desperation and the contract she entered, an analogy could be made to payday lending firms that charge incredibly high interest rates. (Or pawn shops that borrow money at high rates with items as collateral.) Ariel is desperate and is willing to enter a contract where she endures highly unfavorable terms.

Topics: Trade-offs, Opportunity Costs

THE MUSIC MAN

"Wells Fargo Wagon"

The Iowa town of River City – which is fictitious but based on Mason City, Iowa – is excited when the Wells Fargo wagon comes to town. And why not! The Wells Fargo Wagon was an efficient way to get products in 1912. This song helps illustrate the benefits of new innovations. The newly emerging transportation system in the 20th century helped create new ways for products to be delivered. In 1912 Iowa, this meant receiving products delivered – which was more convenient than previous methods of obtaining products.

This song provides a nice lesson in economic history. Throughout the past century, the U.S. went from selling many items via catalog, to having large shopping centers, then to shopping via television (e.g., the Home Shopping Network), and to online shopping today. The "Wells Fargo Wagon" is a great song to introduce the fact that American businesses are always seeking more efficient ways to get products to consumers. The companies that helped bring those methods to the mainstream, like Wells Fargo, Sears (with their catalog), shopping mall owners, and Amazon.com all enjoyed success. But society at large also gained from more efficient delivery of products. Maybe you don't sing each time a package is delivered from Amazon – but perhaps you should!

Topics: Innovation, Entrepreneurship, Economic History

THE PAJAMA GAME

"7½ Cents"

An hourly wage of 7½ cents? It "doesn't mean a thing" according to the singers. But as Prez says "give it to me every hour, forty hours every week, and that's enough for me to be living like a king!" Seven-and-a-half cents an hour is incredibly low, lower than wages that are paid to workers in developing countries. The song goes on to highlight, however, that if those wages are saved over five, ten, or 20 years, it could add up. In fact, over 20 years, Prez tells us that a person could have $3,411.96 if they don't spend any of their money. While they are talking about saving 100% of their money, this would actually serve as a good guide to others: if any person saved just 7½ cents of their hourly wages and worked full time with a few hours of overtime now and then, that person could also save over $3,400 after 20 years. This is especially staggering when considering estimates that about 60% of American households have less than $1,000 in savings.[218]

But the singers actually make a pretty crucial error when calculating how much they could save: they ignore the fact that they could earn interest on their savings. And the interest that is earned then would also earn interest. When a deposit earns interest in one period and that interest stays invested and also earns interest, we call this compound interest. If a person saved $171 each year (about what they estimate in the song) and earned interest on their savings, they would have much more than $3,400 at the end of 20 years.[219]

With an interest rate of 3%, which could be obtained pretty easily by investing in bonds, that person would have about $4,700 after 20 years. With an interest rate of 6%, which is less than the average rate of return in the stock market over the past 90 years, the person would have $6,500 after 20 years. This is because the interest earned in a previous period also then earns interest in each subsequent period – or compounds.

Some great figures in history have talked about the power of compound interest. Billionaire Warren Buffett said "My wealth has come from a combination of living in America, some lucky genes, and compound interest."[220] Economist John Maynard Keynes wrote that "every £1 which Drake brought home in 1580 has now become £100,000. Such is the power of compound interest!"[221] And Roger Babson wrote "the world's greatest invention was six per-cent compound interest, which goes on twenty-four hours a day, seven days a week, and fifty-two weeks a year."[222]

With the power of compound interest, a person who was willing to save $1/hour of his or her earnings could easily have over $100,000 at the end of 25 years. The power of compound interest is a reason that many financial experts stress that it is crucial for people to start saving at a young age[223] as you don't have to save much in order to end up with a significant amount if you start saving when young.

Topics: Savings, Compound Interest

THE PRODUCERS

"I Wanna be a Producer"

> "I spend my life accounting, with figures and such.
> To what is my life amounting, it figures, not much."

Leo Bloom and his fellow accountants are unhappy. Very unhappy, actually. They are singing in the beginning of the song and make it clear that they do not like their jobs. That fits the impression many people have – that accounting is a boring job.[224] The fact that many think accounting is boring along with the fact that there is a high demand for accountants is a key reason that accountants generally earn high salaries. New college graduates with accounting degrees often earn starting salaries of $50,000 a year or more.[225]

This premium for working in a boring job is called a compensating wage differential. A compensating wage differential can work in reverse, as those in enjoyable jobs sometimes earn less than those with similar skill-sets working in more enjoyable jobs. In the song, Leo discusses his dreams of working in theatre. Working in theatre is often seen as glamorous, appealing, or fulfilling and therefore many seek jobs in the theatre industry. But the supply of theatre majors is greater than the jobs that are available, resulting in lower salaries for new graduates (often under $30,000 per year) and higher unemployment rates.[226]

Topic: Labor Economics, Compensating Wage Differentials

THE ROTHSCHILDS

"Bonds"

In "Bonds," peace bonds are being sold (in contrast to war bonds). The peace bonds that were sold in Europe in the early 1800s, by the famous financier Nathan Rothschild and others, were coupon bonds – where the bond pays some amount of interest each year. Today's coupon bonds tend to pay some amount of money annually for a certain number of years, and then at the end of the set period of time (ten years or 30 years, for example) the person receives back their initial investment. The bonds in the early 1800s offered interest payments in perpetuity (i.e., forever).[227] At the beginning of the song – the bonds are selling for 23, then drops to 22, and keeps dropping all the way to 5.

In "Bonds," the price of the bond keeps dropping throughout the song. The price of a bond and the interest rate one receives for that bond are inversely related so as one increases, the other decreases. This is because the bond pays the same amount of money with each coupon payment regardless of the price that is paid, the interest rate keeps getting larger. The bond price is dropping in the song which means the interest rate is increasing.

Another common type of bond is a zero-coupon bond. Zero-coupon bonds pay no interest payments during the life of the bond and simply pay some amount of money after a set period of time. In the U.S., zero-coupon bonds are often redeemed for $1,000. Therefore, if somebody paid $980 for a U.S. zero-coupon bond that could be redeemed for $1,000 in a year – she would earn an interest rate of 2.04% (which we find by taking the profit of $20 and dividing by the price paid of $980). If the person paid $960 for a bond that redeemed for $1,000, she would earn interest of 4.17%. Similar to coupon bonds, zero-coupon bond prices and interest rates have an inverse relationship.

Topics: Bonds, Interest Rates

THE SOUND OF MUSIC

"My Favorite Things"

What are your favorite things? Are they "brown paper packages tied up with strings" along with "bright copper kettles and warm woolen mittens." They probably are not, but they were Maria's favorite things. The song provides a good example that different people get utility from different items. Some people will place a greater value on experiences, some on physical products, and some on products or services that help others. One of the central assumptions of economics, however, is that each person maximizes his or her own utility subject to their budget constraint.

Topics: Utility

"How Can Love Survive?"

Elsa sings and her friend Max is consoling her after she informs him that Captain Von Trapp isn't marrying her yet. Elsa and Max are under the impression that poorer people have an easier time falling in love. Elsa illustrates this when she sings "how can I show what I feel for him, I cannot go out and steal for him."

This song illustrates a couple of points. First, while money can purchase many things through markets – there are plenty of things that cannot be purchased through a market, like love. But love, like sunsets, clean air and other items, have tremendous value, even if they can't be purchased with money.

Second, Max and Elsa also discuss their ability to have a successful marriage based on their income. In the United States, the Bureau of Labor Statistics has found that an increased ability to earn income increases the probability of marriage and decreases the probability of divorce for young men, but decreases the probability of marriage for young women.[228]

They found that earning capacity had no effect on the probability of a woman getting a divorce.

Topics: Markets, Non-Market Valuation

THE WEDDING SINGER

"All About the Green"

Glen gives Robbie some advice about the future. Glen says that "If you wanna be somebody, it's all about the green." Robbie and Glen seem to have different values. Glen and his friends think the main goal of life should be to earn a large income. Robbie seems to think differently and wants a career that's more meaningful. Many professions that people think are more fun or meaningful – like teaching, social work, and acting – have lower salaries. The reason is that an increased supply of people wish to get into those professions, pushing the wages lower.

The Wedding Singer is set in the early 1980s and "All About the Green" makes several references to economic events and people in that time period, including mentioning Lee Iacocca (Chrysler executive), Michael Milken (known as the Junk Bond King), savings and loan deregulation, and Ronald Reagan's economic policies. We also find out that Glen isn't great at predicting the future – as he sees huge success for New Coke but can't imagine how any coffee shop could expand nationally, since "nobody's ever gonna pay three bucks for a cup of coffee."

Topics: Economic History, Utility, Compensating Wage Differentials, Labor Economics

THOROUGHLY MODERN MILLIE

"How the Other Half Lives"

Millie Dillmount and Miss Dorothy meet at a hotel, and they have had different lives to this point. Millie grew up poor but wants to be rich. Miss Dorothy grew up rich but wants to see what life is like for the poor. The song highlights income inequality. Millie is dreaming of the life that Miss Dorothy has, including shopping

TABLE 3 Gini Coefficients (Disposable Income, Post Taxes and Transfers) by Country – 2013/2014

Country	*Gini Coefficient*
Iceland	0.244
Norway	0.252
Denmark	0.254
Finland	0.257
Sweden	0.281
Germany	0.292
France	0.294
Korea	0.302
Canada	0.322
Italy	0.325
Japan	0.330
Australia	0.337
Spain	0.346
United Kingdom	0.358
Israel	0.365
Turkey	0.393
United States	0.394
Mexico	0.459

at Saks Fifth Avenue and Bergdorf Goodman (luxury retailers). Miss Dorothy wants to try out life where she has to clip coupons and sings she wants to "brown bag all my lunches" and use "layaway to buy my clothes."

Economists have multiple measures of income inequality, but the most frequently used one is the Gini coefficient. The Gini coefficient is a ratio – between zero and one – that attempts to express how much income inequality there is within a country. A larger number represents more inequality, a smaller number means incomes are more equal across citizens.

Table 3 presents the Gini coefficients for several different countries. One thing that jumps out is that the United States has a high Gini coefficient – indicating a large level of income inequality. In fact, incomes in the United States are more unequal than any other developed country in the world.[229]

Topics: Income Inequality, Gini Coefficient

"The Speed Test"

Millie Dillmount is interviewing for a job with Mr. Graydon. During the interview Mr. Graydon first has Millie Dillmount dictate his spoken words, then requires her to type up the letter. And Millie must complete these tasks in a limited amount of time. Mr. Graydon sings "If you can make sense of my unintelligible patter, then the job is yours and Hudson's Floor Wax really doesn't matter." As we learn in the song, Millie Dillmount is successful – so she gets the job!

The test Mr. Graydon made Millie Dillmount take is a form of screening, which occurs when somebody attempts to filter out false information from another party. Firms often screen potential employees. Many people who apply for jobs might not be qualified, but by screening, the employer could help to distinguish between those who can do tasks and those who cannot.

For example, the federal government requires some workers to take a civil service exam – and the worker must pass the exam to be considered for the position. These positions include workers in air traffic control, law enforcement, and the postal service.[230] The idea of exams to work in a profession isn't limited to the government, however. Many firms will only want to hire a Certified Public Accountant (CPA) for their accounting needs, and to become a CPA one must pass the CPA exam. And many government and non-government jobs required applicants to take drug tests to screen for drug users. Other methods of screening include using internet and social media searches of the candidate and FBI background checks.

Topic: Labor Economics, Screening

TOVARICH

"A Small Cartel"

According the singers, "There's nothing nicer than a small cartel." A cartel is a group of firms that collude to keep the price higher and the production lower in order to earn higher profits. The idea is to emulate the pricing of a monopolist and share in the higher profits instead of competing. While it may be great for the firms, it is terrible for consumers.

For the most part, colluding to form a cartel is illegal in the United States and most other developed countries.[231] But that doesn't mean cartels don't exist. The most famous cartel is the Organization of Oil Exporting Countries (OPEC), which helps regulate the supply of oil to keep the price high. By keeping the supply lower, they are able to keep the price higher.

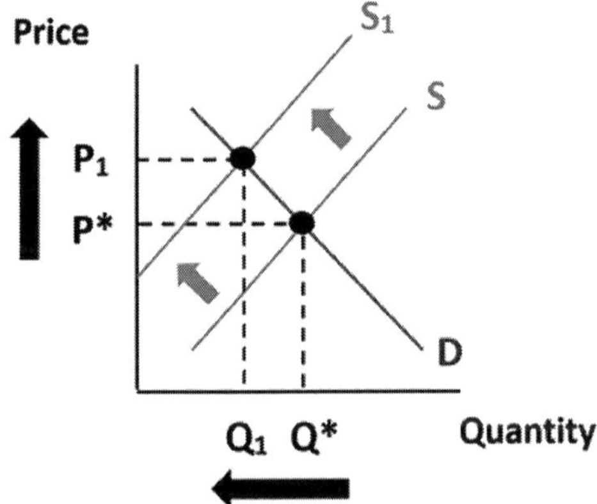

FIGURE 31

OPEC isn't the only cartel most Americans would know. Another example of a cartel is the National Collegiate Athletic Association (NCAA). The NCAA acts as a cartel in terms of buying a product – an athlete's labor – not selling it, but the idea is the same. Top basketball and football players are worth a considerable amount to the university. A top athlete could help increase ticket sales, TV ad revenue, donations to the university, and bring in other sources of revenue.

Sports economists Stephen A. Bergman and Trevon D. Logan from The Ohio State University estimated that a top football recruit (called a five-star recruit) is worth more than $150,000 in expected bowl game proceeds and more than $500,000 per year to a university.[232] Economist Richard Borghesi found that a five-star recruit for basketball is worth about $625,000 annually.[233]

If there was no cartel and schools just competed for athletes by paying them, top athletes would be paid salaries – large ones. However, because there is a cartel, schools are not allowed to pay an athlete more than a scholarship even though each top athlete has enormous value to them. This restriction has consequences. In order to entice the top athletes, some programs may simply decide to offer illegal (under-the-table) cash payments. Several universities in recent years have been caught providing illegal payments, including the University of Southern California and the University of Michigan.[234] The NCAA cartel also causes other issues. Because they cannot legally pay athletes, schools will want to do everything possible to entice the top athletes to attend. This will include employing the best coaches. College football and basketball coaches in America often earn more annually the presidents of those institutions.[235] Part of the reason is that a top coach helps to recruit top athletes who are worth significant amounts of money for his or her university. Schools also may spend significant amounts of money on equipment and facilities.[236] These are side effects of the NCAA's decision to prohibit paying student athletes.

Topics: Collusion, Cartels, Game Theory

URINETOWN

"Privilege to Pee"

The musical Urinetown presents a businessperson who deals with a water shortage by instituting a toilet tax. The lyrics go "I run the only toilet in this part of town, you see. So, if you've got to go you've got to go through me." If someone doesn't pay the toilet tax, he or she is banished, hence the "Privilege to Pee." This song allows us to examine the diamond–water paradox. The paradox is that water is essential for life, while diamonds are unnecessary. Because of this, demand for water is much greater than the demand for diamonds. But water is free (or close to free), while diamonds are quite expensive. The paradox is solved by examining both the demand curve and supply curve. The supply of water is so large, at least in most of the developed world, that the price for water is essentially zero. The supply of diamonds is quite limited which is why the price for diamonds is high.

The diamond–water paradox has been alluded to since at least 384 BC by Plato,[237] but was treated with more formal economic analysis by Adam Smith. As he writes in *The Wealth of Nations*,

> Nothing is more useful than water: but it will purchase scarce anything; scarce anything can be had in exchange for it. A diamond, on the contrary, has scarce any use-value; but a very great quantity of other goods may frequently be had in exchange for it.[238]

Urinetown presents a case where water no longer is free – and we start to see market prices associated with water. While the developed world generally has access to clean water, unfortunately this is not the case worldwide. In 2015, over 600 million people in the world did not have access to reliable water sources.[239]

Topics: Demand and Supply, Diamond–Water Paradox

WORKING

The musical *Working* contains songs where different people sing about their work. As could be expected, much of the content relates to economics. The content isn't limited to labor economics topics, although labor economics topics are well represented. Singers also illustrate utility, trade-offs, opportunity costs, and more.

"All the Livelong Day"

"All the Livelong Day," which is the opening song of *Working*, has many people describe their jobs and tasks. Among those singing are a fireman, a waitress, and a mason. The song highlights a diversity of jobs among the characters of the show, which parallels the wide range of jobs available in society.

During the song, Mike Dillard sings that he wants to get paid $1 million to turn his life into a TV documentary so he can quit his job at the store. This raises a question – how many people would quit their jobs if they received a large windfall? In the U.S., according to a 2013 Gallup poll, most would continue working. Gallup found that only 31% of Americans said they would stop working if they won $10 million in the lottery.[240] They did find an age divide – as only 18% of workers aged 18–34 said they'd stop working, while 49% of those 55 or older said they would stop working. However, many of those who were between 18–34 said they would look for a different job.[241]

Topics: Labor Economics

"Traffic Jam"

Several workers are unhappy about the traffic they have to endure simply to get to work. At one part of the song they sing "Well I left my job about 5 o'clock. It took fifteen minutes go three blocks." However, the fact that the workers can drive to work has been a big contributor to economic growth. For example, in Chicago in 1850, almost everybody lived within two miles of their workplace.[242] But transportation improvements (first trains, then automobiles) allow people to live much farther away. This is important, as the fact that people don't have to live so close to their employer gives more choices for jobs. People have a greater chance to work at a job that is a good match for their skills and interests. The ability for workers to sort into the jobs for which they are best suited means a more productive workforce and more economic growth. In addition, better transportation allows people to live in different neighborhoods and bigger homes than they'd otherwise enjoy.[243]

"Traffic Jam" also highlights the negative impact of a commute on job satisfaction. Several studies in public health journals have highlighted the negative effects of commuting, which include increased stress and higher risk of a heart attack.[244] Researchers have found that a long commute decreases life satisfaction by so much that the average person earning $100,000 per year with an hour-long commute would be as happy earning $60,000 per year with no commute.[245]

Topics: Utility, Economic Growth

"I'm Just Movin'"

> I still love it though the work is hard
> You see these part-time girls work slow all week
> Then Friday night go dancin' for their kicks
> But here is where I'm dancin'

In "I'm Just Movin'," Babe sings about the skills she has acquired to be a checkout person at a grocery store. She also sings that she doesn't like to take too much time off because she wants to keep working. Babe's love for her job and the hard work she is putting in means she is accumulating human capital – the skills and knowledge that are acquired through working, education, training, and other experiences.

Putting a lot of effort into a job is a good way to gain additional human capital. Hard work early in one's work life can help a person develop the human capital to get higher paying jobs later in life. Working more hours leads to higher pay. This is obvious when the person is working hourly – but research shows those who work longer hours in salaried jobs earn more as well.[246]

Topics: Human Capital, Labor Economics, Income Inequality

"Neat to be a Newsboy"

An 11-year-old sings about having a job as a "newsboy." Much of the song focuses on his favorite part – throwing the paper into the bushes – not exactly indicating this is a reliable worker.

That said, by having a job at age 11, the newsboy is likely to acquire many of the skills required by employers, including showing up to work every day even when he does not want to work, understanding the importance of showing up on time, and understanding how to deal with bosses.

One reason many economists (myself included) have reservations about minimum wage laws is that teenagers are disproportionally affected – and are unemployed in much higher numbers as a result. For example, in the fourth quarter of 2016, the unemployment rate for workers aged 25–64 was only 3.9%, while the unemployment rate for teenagers was 12.9%. For African American teenagers, a group that is more likely to be in poor-performing inner-city schools and more likely to be raised by a single parent, the percentage was even higher, at 24.8%. These higher unemployment rates are exactly what economic theory predicts would occur with minimum wages.

The high unemployment rates mean that some teenagers who want jobs don't have them. Teenagers without a job now aren't acquiring the types of soft skills from working that are incredibly valuable. The lack of these initial jobs could mean a lifetime of lower wages for millions of individuals.

Topics: Minimum Wage, Human Capital

"Just a Housewife"

"Just a Housewife" features housewife Kate Rushton singing about how society does not perceive her as intelligent due to her choice to be a stay-at-home mom. She discusses her responsibilities: doing the laundry, cleaning, shopping for groceries, and other tasks one might expect from a stay-at-home mom. Her feelings of incompetence and expendability increase when she realizes that her work and skills are not viewed as valuable in society – specifically from an economic standpoint.

This song highlights a key factor about how Gross Domestic Product (GDP) is calculated. When calculating GDP, non-market work doesn't count. This means that Kate's work would not count towards a country's GDP, since it isn't being purchased through a market. However, if somebody is hired to perform the duties discussed in the song – like cleaning the house, watching children, or cooking dinner – that would be included when calculating GDP. In order for something to be included in GDP, there must be a transaction through a legal market. Housework, do-it-yourself home repairs, and transactions occurring through illegal markets do not count towards a country's GDP.

In the end, Kate recognizes that while her work may not be seen as valuable to many, she feels it is important. While not as quantifiable or included in the GDP, stay-at-home parents like Kate contribute to the overall well-being of society and utility of their families.

Topics: GDP, Labor Economics

"If I Could've Been"

People are reflecting on their lives and what they "could've been." They look back at all the dreams they had and realize they didn't accomplish their goals. Some of the reasons include "then I got married" and "then my dad took sick."

Life presents a series of trade-offs. For some, getting married is worth forgoing other options. For others getting married is not worth it. Many of life's trade-offs involve a comparison of short-run satisfaction vs. long-run goals. How much a person chooses to discount the future will play a role. If a person places a greater weight on future consumption or goals, he or she will be more likely to forgo current consumption. With lesser preference placed on the future, a person will choose to consume more now.

Topics: Trade-offs, Time Preferences, Discounting

FIVE TIPS TO PREPARE FOR THE LONG TERM

1 **Save** – especially if you get a matching contribution from your employer. And start saving early. I don't think anybody knows how much money they will need to save for the future. But if you make a mistake and save too much, is that really going to cause you stress and heartache in the future?

2 **Learn to be happy with what you have.** For those reading this in a developed country, you are incredibly rich. You probably live in a bigger house or apartment, eat more food, have more free time, and have more material items available to you than your grandparents and great-grandparents could have ever imagined. If you can learn to be happy with what you have, it makes saving a lot easier – and will make you a happier person.

3 **Find a job you love – but understand the financial consequences of any choice you make.** You work too many hours in life to pursue a job you hate. But if there are three or four different careers you think you might be passionate about– take a look at the money differences. That doesn't mean you shouldn't take the low-paying job, but don't be ignorant of the choice you're making.

4 **Gain the human capital you need.** Reading this book is a good start! Education is quite valuable, especially in the United States. Different jobs and careers require different levels of education and training. Once you know the career you'd like, invest in yourself!

5 **Avoid credit card debt.** High interest rates from credit cards can create a crippling debt spiral. With interest rates that are almost always over 10% (and sometimes much higher), a small amount of credit card debt can be very costly. If you use credit cards, I recommend you only use them because they are convenient and pay them off at the end of each month.

"Brother Trucker"

Frank Decker is singing about his life as a trucker. Frank sings about several topics related to his work, including that he's not part of a union and that truck driving often means a lot of time away from home. One part of the song seems inaccurate, at least based on U.S. laws. Frank sings about how he only got "four hours sleep in the last two nights." In the U.S., truck drivers are only allowed to drive a maximum of 11 hours per day and must take a 30-minute break every eight hours.[247] So if Frank only got four hours sleep over two nights because of his job, he'd actually be breaking the law.

Jobs available for truck drivers have increased dramatically over the past 40 years.[248] In many ways, the increase in trucking industry jobs has helped offset the decrease in manufacturing jobs. It is a job that requires a specialized driver's license and sometimes even extra endorsements depending on what is being shipped (e.g., hazardous materials), but the barriers to a truck-driving job are relatively low.[249] Truck drivers also earn reasonable incomes. The median income a truck driver earned in 2015 was $40,260,[250] which not too far from the median *household* income of about $55,000 in the United States.[251]

One innovation in the economy should concern truck drivers, however. If self-driving vehicles become widespread, truck driving as a profession could become obsolete. This would be another example of creative destruction: a new innovation that is creative and valuable can cause significant temporary job losses.

Topics: Truck Driving, Manufacturing, Creative Destruction

"It's an Art"

Delores Dante sings about her job as a waitress and how she works for tips, which is quite typical in the United States. In the United States, tips often range between 15 and 20% of the price of a meal.[252] Tips are a main component of earnings for most waiters and waitresses[253] and can help lead to a nice income.

That said, some have argued for an end to tipping. The arguments vary, but include that it can be confusing to guests, misleading to customers about the true price of products, and that it leads to discrimination (because people may tip differently based on race or other characteristics).[254]

Topics: Tipping

YOU'RE A GOOD MAN CHARLIE BROWN

"Happiness"

Towards the end of *You're a Good Man Charlie Brown*, the Peanuts gang sing about what makes them happy. Similar to the real world, each member of the Peanuts gang has a different idea of what would bring them utility. Some items are material items like Linus who wants "5 different crayons" or Snoopy who, unsurprisingly, wants "pizza with sausage."

But others sing about the items that would bring them happiness that do not come from markets. This should seem perfectly normal – many of the best things in life aren't sold in markets, like a beautiful sunset, good health, and friendships. While these items aren't sold in markets, there are hundreds of economists who research non-market valuation – valuing items that aren't sold in markets. Economists have used non-market valuation techniques to estimate the value of clean lakes, clean air, a shorter commute, visibility at the Grand Canyon, and more.[255]

Economists have even created estimates for the value of a human life. It sounds gruesome, but when examining policies that might cost or save human lives, policy makers need some way to determine how much weight to place on each human life saved or lost. The method economists frequently use to measure the value of a human life is the prices people are paid to take a higher probability of death. For example, if someone was willing to be paid \$10 to accept a one in a million chance of dying, the estimate for the value of life the person placed on themselves is \$10 million (which we find by taking \$10 and dividing by the increased probability of death). Usually people aren't presented with a case where they are explicitly offered a one in million chance of death for a payment. But many people take more dangerous jobs, which have higher risks of death, to receive higher salaries. This is a payment for a higher probability of death. Others choose not to drive the safest cars, saving money in the process. The saved money is also a payment one takes for facing a higher probability of death.

While morbid, estimated values of the value of a life are useful for public policies, and many government agencies will use them if a particular policy or regulation will either save or cost lives. The U.S. Department of Transportation, U.S. Environmental Protection Agency, and U.S. Food and Drug Administration estimate the value of a life at between $9.3 and $9.7 million.[256]

Topics: Non-Market Valuation, Value of a Life

NOTES

1 O'Roark (2012)
2 The World Bank Group (2016)
3 Occupational Employment and Wages (2016)
4 Kuhn and Lozano (2008); Conard (2016); Francis (2006); Gould (2016)
5 Voth (2001)
6 *The Economist* (2014b)
7 Whaples (2001)
8 Alexander (2012)
9 Ibid.
10 Andreoni (1990)
11 Leonhardt (2008)
12 Murphy (2009)
13 See Keynes (2003 [1936]) and Simpson (2010)
14 Krugman (2012)
15 Friedman and Schwartz (1971)
16 United States History (2017)
17 Krugman (2011)
18 Ibid.
19 Powell (2003) and Murphy (2009)
20 Ibid.
21 Powell (2003)
22 Hubbard and O'Brien (2016)
23 Jacobson and Wogan (2012)
24 Schakowsky.House.Gov (2017)
25 Carnevale, Rose, and Cheah (2011)
26 Adams (2015)
27 Schiavone (2013) and National Center for Education Statistics (2015)
28 See Jenkins (2009); Early (2000); National Multifamily Housing Council (2017)
29 The World Bank Group (2017)
30 Ibid.
31 Ibid.
32 Ibid.
33 Howe (2014), Percentage of Students With Internship Experience Climbs (2015)

34 Sally and Jones (2006). Excerpt: "John Nash developed his beautiful bargaining solution by making 'certain idealizations' about negotiations . . . Nash translated these idealizations into simple mathematics . . . each bargainer has a threat point, the outcome if no deal occurs – in current negotiation parlance, the best alternative to a negotiated agreement, BATNA, and $BATNA_2$."
35 Ibid.
36 Travis (2013)
37 Clark (2013) and Travis (2013)
38 Data points provided by the following sources: The Bureau of Labor Statistics (2017a); The U.S. Bureau of the Census (1981, 1982, 1987, 1991, 1993); The U.S. Department of Labor (2001, 2010); Nearing (1911)
39 The World Bank Group (2016); CIA (2016)
40 Goldstein (2008)
41 Facing History and Ourselves (2017)
42 C. R. (2013)
43 Ibid.
44 See Palairet (2000); Brewer (2016), Boduszyński (2010); Doder (1993); *Hyperinflation in Zimbabwe* (2011); Dugger (2010); Bomberger and Makinen (1983); Makinen (1981)
45 Hewitt (2016)
46 See Fleming (1973); Knox and Schacht (2007)
47 Killewald et al. (2017)
48 Greenwood et al. (2014); *The Economist* (2014a)
49 See Coppock and Mateer (2014), p. 46
50 Ibid., p. 47
51 Ramsey (2017)
52 A Chicken in Every Pot (1928)
53 Wilde (2015)
54 Coleman-Jensen et al. (2016)
55 Ogden et al. (2015)
56 Finkelstein et al. (2009)
57 McElroy (2014); Ross and Mirowsky (1999)
58 Ross and Mirowsky (1999)
59 Schramm (2006)
60 The College Board (2017)
61 Table 303.10 (2015)
62 Smith-Barrow (2016); Payscale (2016). Please note: I calculated the average MBA mid-career pay for all schools by transferring Payscale's mid-career pay data into Microsoft Excel.
63 Forex Capital Markets (2017)
64 Wall Street Oasis (2013)
65 Mateer and Coppock (2014)
66 McGinty and Mullins (2012)
67 IBDB (2017)
68 Rousu (2015); Smith (2012)
69 Hutton (2001)
70 Statistic Brain (2016)
71 Wollan (2015)
72 Chao (2006)
73 Nafziger and Lindert (2012); OECD (2017)
74 A Better Way (2010)
75 Mankiw (2011)
76 Weiss and Gaffney (2015)
77 For more discussion of this, I recommend the chapter "Survival Jobs" in Wienir and Langel (2004)
78 Fabian (2016)

79 Teachout (2015)
80 See Caulfield (2016) and Billboard (2017), listing when *Hamilton* peaked at #3 on the Billboard 200 and #1 on Billboard's Rap Album Charts, respectively.
81 Caulfield (2015)
82 Tony Awards (2016)
83 Playbill (2016)
84 Mankiw (2016)
85 Chernow (2004)
86 U.S. Department of the Treasury (2010)
87 Ibid. and PBS (2000)
88 Chernow (2005)
89 See Butler et al. (2008); Ratner (2008); Kaufmann and Kraay (2002)
90 Military Advantage (2017)
91 U.S. Army (2017a, 2017b)
92 Piketty (2014), Chapter 4
93 Stringham (2015), Chapter 7
94 Stringham (2015)
95 Boland (2014)
96 Richardson (2015)
97 Ellis (2000), Chapter 2
98 Ibid.
99 Fabian (2010)
100 Ibid.
101 Carey (2013)
102 See Chernow (2005), pp. 680–94
103 Cadena and Kovak (2013); Guo (2014); Holzer (2011)
104 For example, The University of California, Berkeley's Center for Latin American Studies
105 Cortes (2008)
106 See tables and charts from *The Economist* (2014c)
107 Ibid.
108 Ibid.
109 Cunningham and Kendall (2016)
110 Galley (2014); Wright and Rogers (2009)
111 See The Bureau of Labor Statistics (2000); The U.S. Department of Labor (2015)
112 See Adamy (2016); Aguirre et al. (2012); Elborgh-Woytek et al. (2013); Woetzel et al. (2015)
113 U.S. Centers for Medicare and Medicaid Services (2017)
114 Jacobs (2011); Szurmak (2017)
115 Callahan and Ikeda (2003)
116 Department of the Treasury with the Department of Education (2012)
117 Lino (2014)
118 Fox (2015)
119 *Historical Timeline = Farmers & the Land* (2014); Hertz (2016)
120 *Employment in Agriculture* (2016)
121 Carnevale et al. (2011)
122 Smith-Barrow (2016)
123 Brickman et al. (1978)
124 Adams (2012)
125 Ibid.
126 Friedman (1977); Matos-Rodriguez and Hernandez (2001)
127 The United States Census Bureau (2017)
128 Ibid.
129 Coppock and Mateer (2014)
130 Pannell et al. (2013)

131 Schneider (2011)
132 Chang (2010)
133 Payscale (2017)
134 Kane (2017)
135 Green (2013)
136 Fisher (2015)
137 Koster (2017)
138 Edlund and Korn (2002)
139 *The Economist* (2014c)
140 Dentists (2015)
141 Taleb (2005)
142 Ibid.
143 Goodley (2013)
144 Usual Weekly Earnings (2017)
145 Goldin (1993, 2015)
146 Perry (2015)
147 The U.S. Department of Labor (2009); Perry (2016)
148 Sommers (2017)
149 *The Economist* (2014d)
150 Ibid.
151 Baumol and Blinder (1998), p. 418
152 Alchian (2008)
153 Anderson and Huggins (2009); The Hoover Institution (2017)
154 Acemoglu and Johnson (2005)
155 DiLorenzo (2016); Stroup (2016)
156 DiLorenzo (2016)
157 Ibid.
158 Ibid.
159 Ibid.
160 Hertsgaard (1999)
161 DiLorenzo (2016)
162 Norton (1998)
163 For example, see Akbar (2010); Dikötter (2010); Mirsky (2012)
164 See Smith (2012); Cowen and Tabarrok (2009)
165 Because consumers cannot be easily charged to experience, observe, use, etc. a public good, the demand for such a good can be more than is (typically) supplied. Due to this greater-than-anticipated demand for public goods and free-rider problem (i.e., someone receives a benefit without having to pay for it), a market economy may underproduce public goods. For more, see Mateer and Coppock (2014), pp. 222–224
166 The Government of Quebec (2017); Ornstein et al. (2003); Full Fact Team (2011); Warneck (2007)
167 Kohler and Getman (2005)
168 Ibid.
169 Gartner (1990); Smith (2003); Norwood (2002); Gall (2003)
170 Samuelson (1976)
171 Weiss and Gaffney (2015)
172 Ibid.
173 Ibid., p. 108
174 Friedman and Friedman (1990)
175 Conard (2016), p. 263
176 Tanner (2012)
177 CleanGovBiz (2014)
178 Ibid.
179 Linnane (2016)
180 CleanGovBiz (2014); *Fixed Income, Bonds & CDs* (2017)

181 Kahneman and Deaton (2010)
182 Stevenson and Wolfers (2008)
183 Cassano (2015)
184 Discovery Communications, LLC. (2015)
185 See The Bureau of Labor Statistics (2000); The U.S. Department of Labor (2015)
186 Pew Research Center (2010)
187 History.com (2009b); Wilson (2013)
188 Goldman (1923)
189 www.oecdbetterlifeindex.org/countries/mexico/
190 E.g., see Conard (2016)
191 Reeves (2014); Conard (2016)
192 History.com (2009a)
193 Jeffrey (2015)
194 Stiglitz et al. (2010)
195 Jones and Klenow (2016)
196 Fox (2016); Matthews (2012)
197 Spence (1973)
198 Both were based on *Parfumerie* by Miklós László.
199 For example, Daly (2002, p. 85) writes that "Conventional business wisdom contends that it costs 10 times as much to obtain a new customer as it does to retain an existing customer." Gillen (2005, p. 89) writes that "Attracting a new customer can cost as much as 15 times more than retaining an existing customer."
200 Without a minimum wage it would make sense to see a lower unemployment rate among teenagers than the rest of the public. This is true because most teenagers are just entering the workforce and could work in a wide variety of lower-skilled jobs. Contrast this with adults, who often gain skills relevant for certain jobs or industries. Adults often have fewer options and might be unemployed longer, whereas teenagers would have a wider variety of available options.
201 Massey and Denton (1993)
202 Rastogi (2014); Singh and Heldman (2001)
203 Conard (2016), p. 195
204 Waldfogel (1993)
205 Solnick and Hemenway (1996)
206 Ibid.
207 List and Shogren (1998)
208 Ibid.
209 The book *Nudge* by Richard Thaler and Cass Sunstein refers to this as a difference between "econs" – those who behave perfectly according to economic theory, and "humans" – who don't.
210 Whalen and Reichling (2015)
211 The National WWII Museum (2016)
212 Coppock and Mateer (2014), p. 211
213 Fryers (2006); Linn et al. (1985)
214 Brown and McGeeney (2013)
215 See Goda et al. (2015); Harrison et al. (2002); Dohmen et al. (2012)
216 Huffman et al. (2016)
217 I like Disney stories as much as the next person, but can we agree that Ariel is, in the words of Lin-Manuel Miranda, inventing "a new kind of stupid"?
218 Fottrell (2015)
219 This can be easily estimated using an online Compound Interest Calculator (n.d.).
220 Buffett (2010)
221 Keynes (1963 [1930])
222 Babson (1935)
223 Davidson (2012)
224 Hall (2005); Melby (2011)

225 Bramwell (2013); Mateer and Coppock (2014)
226 JP (2012); Weiss and Gaffney (2015)
227 Goetzmann and Rouwenhorst (2005); Ritholtz (2013)
228 Aughinbaugh et al. (2013)
229 Fisher and Smeeding (2016); Sherman (2015)
230 Bookhaven Press LLC (2017)
231 Fox (1997); European Commission (2016); Haucap et al. (2010)
232 Bergman and Logan (2013); Elliott (2016)
233 Borghesi (2015)
234 The Week Staff (2011); Auerbach (2013)
235 Newman (2014); Camera (2016)
236 Desrochers (2013); Hobson and Rich (2015)
237 Smith (1776) quotes Plato as writing: "If you are wise, you will also bid your disciples discourse with no man but you and themselves. For only what is rare is valuable; and 'water,' which, as Pindar says, is the 'best of all things,' is also the cheapest."
238 Smith (1776), pp. 31–32
239 World Health Organization and UNICEF Joint Monitoring Programme (2015)
240 Newport (2013)
241 Ibid.
242 Conzen (2016)
243 Kain (1965)
244 Morin (2014)
245 National Public Radio (2011); Stutzer and Frey (2004)
246 Goldin (1993, 2015)
247 Laing (2011)
248 Parming (2013)
249 Washington State Department of Licensing (2017)
250 The Bureau of Labor Statistics (2017b)
251 Posey (2016)
252 Rane (2015)
253 Lam (2015)
254 Lechtenberg (2013); The Wall Street Journal (2016); Stuart (2014)
255 Batalhone et al. (2002); Haab and McConnell (2002); Hanemann (2005); Schulze et al. (1985); Smith et al. (1997); Swärdh (2009); Ridker (1967); Wegge et al. (1996)
256 McGinty (2016)

SONG REFERENCE TABLE

Topic	*Songs*
Absolute Advantage	1. Anything You Can Do (Annie Get Your Gun) 2. Gaston (Beauty and the Beast)
Advertising	1. Notes (Phantom of the Opera)
Assortative Mating	1. Make Our Garden Grow (Candide)
Backward Bending Labor Supply Curve	1. The Bottom Line (Newsies)
Backward Induction	1. I Want the Good Times Back (The Little Mermaid)
Banking	1. Fidelity Fiduciary Bank (Mary Poppins)
Bargaining	1. Solidarity (Billy Elliot)
Bartering	1. Money (Cabaret)
Benefit–Cost Analysis	1. Secrets (The Addams Family)
Bonds	1. Bonds (The Rothschilds)
Borrowing	1. IOU (One Man, Two Guvnors)
Bribery	1. Bangers and Mash (One Man, Two Guvnors)
Business of Broadway	1. Broadway Baby (Follies)
Capital	1. When Children are Asleep (Carousel) 2. Dear Sweet Sewing Machine (Fiddler on the Roof) 3. 96,000 (In the Heights)
Capitalism	1. What was Good Enough for You (Bonnie and Clyde) 2. Tradition (Fiddler on the Roof) 3. Prologue (Ragtime) 4. Shipyard (The Last Ship)
Cartels	1. A Small Cartel (Tovarich)
Charitable Giving	1. Lady Hyacinth Abroad (A Gentleman's Guide to Love and Murder) 2. Money Song (Avenue Q)
Collusion	1. A Small Cartel (Tovarich)

continued . . .

Continued

Topic	*Songs*
Communism	1. What was Good Enough for You (Bonnie and Clyde) 2. Tradition (Fiddler on the Roof) 3. Where You Are (Moana) 4. Prologue (Ragtime) 5. Shipyard (The Last Ship)
Comparative Advantage	1. Anything You Can Do (Annie Get Your Gun) 2. Gaston (Beauty and the Beast) 3. Rhode Island is Famous for You (Inside U.S.A.)
Compensating Wage Differential(s)	1. What Kind of Man (Curtains the Musical) 2. Right Hand Man (Hamilton) 3. Blood in the Water (Legally Blonde) 4. Lovely Ladies (Les Misérables) 5. Dentist! (Little Shop of Horrors) 6. Voice Mail #4 (Rent) 7. Shipyard (The Last Ship) 8. I Wanna be a Producer (The Producers) 9. All About the Green (The Wedding Singer)
Competition	1. Giving Them What They Want (Dirty Rotten Scoundrels) 2. Thank You Madam (She Loves Me)
Compound Interest	1. 7½ Cents (The Pajama Game)
Corruption	1. Bangers and Mash (One Man, Two Guvnors)
Costs	1. Let it Go (Frozen)
Creative Destruction	1. Used to Be (Hands on a Hardbody) 2. With One Look (Sunset Boulevard) 3. Brother Trucker (Working)
Deadweight Loss	1. The Lady's Paying (Sunset Boulevard)
Demand	1. When Children are Asleep (Carousel) 2. Piragua (Reprise) (In the Heights)
Demand and Supply	1. Who Will Buy? (Oliver!) 2. Privilege to Pee (Urinetown)
Diamond–Water Paradox	1. Privilege to Pee (Urinetown)
Diminishing Marginal Utility	1. Better with a Man (A Gentleman's Guide to Love and Murder) 2. Money, Money, Money (Mamma Mia) 3. Bruce (Matilda) 4. Pulled (The Addams Family)
Discount Rate	1. Say No to This (Hamilton)
Discounting	1. I Just Can't Wait to be King (The Lion King) 2. If I Could've Been (Working)
Discrimination	1. Life Story (Closer than Ever) 2. There! Right! There! (Legally Blonde) 3. Everybody Out (Made in Dagenham) 4. Story of My Life (Shrek the Musical)

continued . . .

Continued

Topic	*Songs*
Economic Cycles	1. Pharaoh's Dreams Explained (Joseph and the Amazing Technicolor Dreamcoat)
Economic Freedom	1. My Shot (Hamilton)
	2. Santa Fe (Rent)
Economic Growth	1. What was Good Enough for You (Bonnie and Clyde)
	2. Real Nice Clambake (Carousel)
	3. If I Were a Rich Man (Fiddler on the Roof)
	4. Dear Sweet Sewing Machine (Fiddler on the Roof)
	5. Used to Be (Hands on a Hardbody)
	6. Inutil (In the Heights)
	7. At the End of the Day (Les Misérables)
	8. Henry Ford (Ragtime)
	9. Santa Fe (Rent)
	10. Welcome to the Renaissance (Something Rotten)
	11. Traffic Jam (Working)
Economic History	1. Merry Christmas Maggie Thatcher (Billy Elliot)
	2. Real Nice Clambake (Carousel)
	3. Wells Fargo Wagon (The Music Man)
	4. All About the Green (The Wedding Singer)
Economic Planning	1. A Map of New York (If/Then)
Economic Systems	1. Tradition (Fiddler on the Roof)
Economics of Crime	1. Lovely Ladies (Les Misérables)
Economics of Prostitution	1. Sugar Daddy (Hedwig and the Angry Inch)
Education	1. What Do You Do with a BA in English? (Avenue Q)
	2. Life Story (Closer than Ever)
	3. Beauty School Dropout (Grease)
	4. Inutil (In the Heights)
	5. Here at Horace Green (School of Rock)
Elasticity	1. I Don't Need a Roof (Big Fish)
	2. Guns and Ships (Hamilton)
	3. Stars (Les Misérables)
Entrepreneurship	1. Come to the Fun Home (Fun Home)
	2. Prologue (Ragtime)
	3. Henry Ford (Ragtime)
	4. Buffalo Nickel Photoplay, Inc. (Ragtime)
	5. Santa Fe (Rent)
	6. A Musical (Something Rotten)
	7. Man (The Full Monty)
	8. Wells Fargo Wagon (The Music Man)
Exchange Rates	1. Money (Cabaret)
Externalities	1. The Spring of Next Year (Dear World)
Factors of Production	1. Dear Sweet Sewing Machine (Fiddler on the Roof)
Federal Reserve	1. Cabinet Battle #1 (Hamilton)
Financial Markets	1. Wall Street (Dames at Sea)

continued . . .

Continued

Topic	*Songs*
Fiscal Policy	1. A New Deal for Christmas (Annie) 2. Money Song (Avenue Q) 3. And the Money Kept Rolling In (Evita) 4. Pharaoh's Dreams Explained (Joseph and the Amazing Technicolor Dreamcoat) 5. Mama Will Provide (Once on This Island) 6. How the Money Changes Hands (Tenderloin)
Free-rider Problem	1. Santa Fe (Prologue) / Santa Fe (Newsies)
Frictional Unemployment	1. Right Hand Man (Hamilton)
Gains from Trade	1. Molasses to Rum (1776) 2. Gaston (Beauty and the Beast) 3. Rhode Island is Famous for You (Inside U.S.A.) 4. The Winner Takes it All (Mamma Mia) 5. Where You Are (Moana)
Game Theory	1. Solidarity (Billy Elliot) 2. Matchmaker (Fiddler on the Roof) 3. Master of the House (Les Misérables) 4. The Winner Takes it All (Mamma Mia) 5. Vanilla Ice Cream (She Loves Me) 6. I Want the Good Times Back (The Little Mermaid) 7. A Small Cartel (Tovarich)
Gentrification	1. Bilbao Song (Happy End) 2. In the Heights (In the Heights)
Gini Coefficient	1. How the Other Half Lives (Thoroughly Modern Millie)
Government Failure	1. Human Drama Kind of Thing / If I Had this Truck (Hands on a Hardbody)
Government Spending	1. Mama Will Provide (Once on This Island)
Great Depression	1. We'd Like to Thank You Herbert Hoover (Annie) 2. A New Deal for Christmas (Annie)
Gross Domestic Product (GDP)	1. Everybody Ought to Have a Maid (A Funny Thing Happened on the Way to the Forum) 2. Seasons of Love (Rent) 3. Almost Real (The Bridges of Madison County) 4. Just a Housewife (Working)
Happiness	1. Simple Joys (Pippin)
Health Care	1. I'm Not a Well Man (I Can Get it For You Wholesale)
Housing Prices	1. Another Day of Sun (La La Land)
Human Capital	1. Life Story (Closer than Ever) 2. Beauty School Dropout (Grease) 3. You Gotta Get a Gimmick (Gypsy) 4. My Shot (Hamilton) 5. In the Heights (In the Heights) 6. 96,000 (In the Heights) 7. Here at Horace Green (School of Rock) 8. Try Me (She Loves Me)

continued . . .

Continued

Topic	*Songs*
	9. I'm Just Movin' (Working)
	10. Neat to be a Newsboy (Working)
Immigration	1. Born in Laredo (Hands on a Hardbody)
	2. Pacienca y Fe (In the Heights)
	3. Prologue (Ragtime)
	4. Success (Ragtime)
Income Inequality	1. Make Our Garden Grow (Candide)
	2. If I Were a Rich Man (Fiddler on the Roof)
	3. The Winner Takes it All (Mamma Mia)
	4. Try Me (She Loves Me)
	5. How the Other Half Lives (Thoroughly Modern Millie)
	6. I'm Just Movin' (Working)
Income Mobility	1. Alexander Hamilton (Hamilton)
	2. Success (Ragtime)
Inelastic Demand	1. Stars (Les Misérables)
Inequality	1. I Don't Understand the Poor (A Gentleman's Guide to Love and Murder)
Innovation	1. Come to the Fun Home (Fun Home)
	2. Buffalo Nickel Photoplay, Inc. (Ragtime)
	3. Welcome to the Renaissance (Something Rotten)
	4. Wells Fargo Wagon (The Music Man)
Institutions	1. Ten Duel Commandments (Hamilton)
Interest Rates	1. Bonds (The Rothschilds)
International Trade	1. Molasses to Rum (1776)
	2. Gaston (Beauty and the Beast)
	3. Rhode Island is Famous for You (Inside U.S.A.)
	4. The Winner Takes it All (Mamma Mia)
	5. Where You Are (Moana)
Internships	1. Closer to Her (Big Fish)
Investing	1. Five Zeroes (On the Twentieth Century)
Investment	1. When Children are Asleep (Carousel)
John Nash	1. Solidarity (Billy Elliot)
Labor Economics	1. What Do You Do with a BA in English? (Avenue Q)
	2. Closer to Her (Big Fish)
	3. Life Story (Closer than Ever)
	4. What Kind of Man (Curtains the Musical)
	5. A New Argentina (Evita)
	6. Beauty School Dropout (Grease)
	7. Take a Break (Hamilton)
	8. I'm Gone (Hands on a Hardbody)
	9. Just Leave Everything to Me (Hello Dolly)
	10. Happy to Keep his Dinner Warm (How to Succeed in Business without Really Trying)
	11. The Company Way (How to Succeed in Business without Really Trying)

continued . . .

Continued

Topic	*Songs*
	12. Blood in the Water (Legally Blonde)
	13. Work Song (Les Misérables)
	14. Dentist! (Little Shop of Horrors)
	15. The Bottom Line (Newsies)
	16. The World Will Know (Newsies)
	17. You've Got to Pick a Pocket or Two (Oliver!)
	18. Prologue (Ragtime)
	19. Success (Ragtime)
	20. The Night that Goldman Spoke at Union Square (Ragtime)
	21. Voice Mail #4 (Rent)
	22. Try Me (She Loves Me)
	23. Putting it Together (Sunday in the Park with George)
	24. Shipyard (The Last Ship)
	25. I Wanna be a Producer (The Producers)
	26. All About the Green (The Wedding Singer)
	27. The Speed Test (Thoroughly Modern Millie)
	28. All the Livelong Day (Working)
	29. I'm Just Movin' (Working)
	30. Just a Housewife (Working)
Labor Force	1. I'm Gone (Hands on a Hardbody)
Labor-Leisure Trade-Off	1. Take a Break (Hamilton)
Lending	1. IOU (One Man, Two Guvnors)
Lottery	1. 96,000 (In the Heights)
Luxury Goods	1. Everybody Ought to Have a Maid (A Funny Thing Happened on the Way to the Forum)
Manufacturing	1. Brother Trucker (Working)
Marginal Utility	1. Great Big Stuff (Dirty Rotten Scoundrels)
	2. Bruce (Matilda)
	3. Simple Joys (Pippin)
	4. I Want the Good Times Back (The Little Mermaid)
Marginal Utility of Wealth	1. I Want the Good Times Back (The Little Mermaid)
Market Design	1. Matchmaker (Fiddler on the Roof)
Market Economy	1. Tradition (Fiddler on the Roof)
Market Failure	1. Human Drama Kind of Thing / If I Had This Truck (Hands on a Hardbody)
	2. Santa Fe (Prologue) / Santa Fe (Newsies)
Market Structure	1. Come to the Fun Home (Fun Home)
Markets	1. Giving Them What They Want (Dirty Rotten Scoundrels)
	2. Sugar Daddy (Hedwig and the Angry Inch)
	3. Bangers and Mash (One Man, Two Guvnors)
	4. Welcome to Kanagawa (Pacific Overtures)
	5. Thank You Madam (She Loves Me)
	6. How Can Love Survive (The Sound of Music)

continued . . .

Continued

Topic	*Songs*
Marketing	1. Notes (Phantom of the Opera)
Marriage Market	1. Money, Money, Money (Mamma Mia)
Measurement Issues	1. Seasons of Love (Rent)
Minimum Wage	1. Closer to Her (Big Fish)
	2. Neat to be a Newsboy (Working)
Mobility	1. Try Me (She Loves Me)
Monetary Policy	1. Pharaoh's Dreams Explained (Joseph and the Amazing Technicolor Dreamcoat)
Money	1. Money (Cabaret)
Money Market	1. IOU (One Man, Two Guvnors)
Money Multiplier	1. Fidelity Fiduciary Bank (Mary Poppins)
Money Supply	1. Fidelity Fiduciary Bank (Mary Poppins)
Monopolistic Competition	1. Come to the Fun Home (Fun Home)
	2. You Gotta Get a Gimmick (Gypsy)
	3. In the Heights (In the Heights)
	4. Thank You Madam (She Loves Me)
	5. Man (The Full Monty)
Multiplier	1. The Moneygoround (Sunny Afternoon)
	2. How the Money Changes Hands (Tenderloin)
National Debt	1. Cabinet Battle #1 (Hamilton)
Non-Market Valuation	1. How Can Love Survive? (The Sound of Music)
	2. Happiness (You're a Good Man Charlie Brown)
Oligopoly	1. Everybody Say Yeah (Kinky Boots)
Opportunity Cost(s)	1. Molasses to Rum (1776)
	2. You'll be Back (Hamilton)
	3. Satisfied (Hamilton)
	4. Your Obedient Servant (Hamilton)
	5. What You Want (Legally Blonde)
	6. Eternal Youth is Worth a Little Suffering (Sunset Boulevard)
	7. A Summer in Ohio (The Last Five Years)
	8. Poor Unfortunate Souls (The Little Mermaid)
Pollution	1. The Spring of Next Year (Dear World)
Poverty	1. I Don't Understand the Poor (A Gentleman's Guide to Love and Murder)
	2. If I Were a Rich Man (Fiddler on the Roof)
	3. At the End of the Day (Les Misérables)
Preferences	1. I Don't Need a Roof (Big Fish)
Price Ceiling	1. It Sucks to be Me (Avenue Q)
Price Discrimination	1. Bargaining (Do I Hear a Waltz?)
	2. Airport Song (Honeymoon in Vegas)
	3. Omigod You Guys (Legally Blonde)
Probability	1. Dentist! (Little Shop of Horrors)
Producer Surplus	1. So What (Cabaret)

continued . . .

Continued

Topic	*Songs*
Product Differentiation	1. You Gotta Get a Gimmick (Gypsy) 2. In the Heights (In the Heights) 3. Everybody Say Yeah (Kinky Boots) 4. Buffalo Nickel Photoplay, Inc. (Ragtime) 5. A Musical (Something Rotten) 6. Man (The Full Monty)
Production	1. Henry Ford (Ragtime)
Production Possibilities Frontier	1. Impossible / It's Possible (Cinderella) 2. Dear Sweet Sewing Machine (Fiddler on the Roof) 3. The Schmuel Song (The Last Five Years)
Prohibition	1. Lovely Ladies (Les Misérables)
Property Rights	1. My House (Matilda) 2. Where You Are (Moana)
Prostitution	1. Lovely Ladies (Les Misérables)
Public Choice Theory	1. Me and My Town (Anyone Can Whistle) 2. A New Argentina (Evita) 3. Ten Duel Commandments (Hamilton) 4. The Room Where it Happens (Hamilton) 5. Cabinet Battle #1 (Hamilton) 6. America's Son (The Fix)
Public Goods	1. Santa Fe (Prologue) / Santa Fe (Newsies)
Recessions	1. We'd Like to Thank You Herbert Hoover (Annie)
Rent Control	1. It Sucks to be Me (Avenue Q)
Rent Seeking	1. Human Drama Kind of Thing / If I Had this Truck (Hands on a Hardbody)
Repeated Games	1. When You're Good to Mama (Chicago) 2. Master of the House (Les Misérables)
Required Reserve Ratio	1. Fidelity Fiduciary Bank (Mary Poppins)
Savings	1. When Children are Asleep (Carousel) 2. 7½ Cents (The Pajama Game)
Screening	1. There! Right! There! (Legally Blonde) 2. The Speed Test (Thoroughly Modern Millie)
Sequential Games	1. I Want the Good Times Back (The Little Mermaid)
Service Sector Jobs	1. Just Leave Everything to Me (Hello Dolly)
Signaling	1. There! Right! There! (Legally Blonde) 2. Money, Money, Money (Mamma Mia) 3. Here at Horace Green (School of Rock) 4. Vanilla Ice Cream (She Loves Me)
Size of Government	1. And the Money Kept Rolling In (Evita)
Short Run vs. Long Run	1. Say No to This (Hamilton) 2. The Schmuel Song (The Last Five Years)
Shortages	1. Who Will Buy? (Oliver!)
Slavery	1. Molasses to Rum (1776) 2. My Shot (Hamilton) 3. Cabinet Battle #1 (Hamilton)

continued . . .

Continued

Topic	*Songs*
Socialism	1. Prologue (Ragtime)
Statistical Discrimination	1. Work Song (Les Misérables)
Strikebreakers	1. The World Will Know (Newsies)
Strikes	1. The World Will Know (Newsies)
Structural Unemployment	1. With One Look (Sunset Boulevard) 2. Shipyard (The Last Ship)
Sunk Costs	1. Let it Go (Frozen)
Supply	1. So What (Cabaret) 2. When Children are Asleep (Carousel)
Supply and Demand	1. Piragua (Reprise) (In the Heights) 2. Another Day of Sun (La La Land)
Supply Curve	1. The Bottom Line (Newsies)
Surpluses	1. Who Will Buy? (Oliver!)
Taxes	1. My Shot (Hamilton)
Time Horizons	1. The Schmuel Song (The Last Five Years)
Time Preferences	1. When Children are Asleep (Carousel) 2. I Just Can't Wait to be King (The Lion King) 3. If I Could've Been (Working)
Tipping	1. It's an Art (Working)
Tit-for-Tat Strategy	1. When You're Good to Mama (Chicago)
Trade	1. Anything You Can Do (Annie Get Your Gun)
Trade-offs	1. Life Story (Closer than Ever) 2. Broadway Baby (Follies) 3. You'll be Back (Hamilton) 4. Satisfied (Hamilton) 5. Say No to This (Hamilton) 6. Your Obedient Servant (Hamilton) 7. Candy Store (Heathers the Musical) 8. Pacienca y Fe (In the Heights) 9. I've Come to Wive it Wealthily in Padua (Kiss Me Kate) 10. What You Want (Legally Blonde) 11. Simple Joys (Pippin) 12. Putting it Together (Sunday in the Park with George) 13. Eternal Youth is Worth a Little Suffering (Sunset Boulevard) 14. Almost Real (The Bridges of Madison County) 15. A Summer in Ohio (The Last Five Years) 16. Poor Unfortunate Souls (The Little Mermaid) 17. If I Could've Been (Working)
Traditional Economy	1. Tradition (Fiddler on The Roof)
Truck Driving	1. Brother Trucker (Working)
Unemployment	1. We'd Like to Thank You Herbert Hoover (Annie) 2. It Sucks to be Me (Avenue Q) 3. Right Hand Man (Hamilton) 4. I'm Gone (Hands on a Hardbody)

continued . . .

Continued

Topic	*Songs*
	5. Henry Ford (Ragtime)
	6. Seasons of Love (Rent)
	7. Scrap (The Full Monty)
	8. Shipyard (The Last Ship)
Unions	1. Solidarity (Billy Elliot)
	2. Merry Christmas Maggie Thatcher (Billy Elliot)
	3. A New Argentina (Evita)
	4. The World Will Know (Newsies)
	5. The Night That Goldman Spoke at Union Square (Ragtime)
	6. Shipyard (The Last Ship)
Utility	1. Better with a Man (A Gentleman's Guide to Love and Murder)
	2. Lady Hyacinth Abroad (A Gentleman's Guide to Love and Murder)
	3. Great Big Stuff (Dirty Rotten Scoundrels)
	4. Candy Store (Heathers the Musical)
	5. Bruce (Matilda)
	6. Simple Joys (Pippin)
	7. Pulled (The Addams Family)
	8. I Want the Good Times Back (The Little Mermaid)
	9. My Favorite Things (The Sound of Music)
	10. All About the Green (The Wedding Singer)
	11. Traffic Jam (Working)
Value of a Life	1. Happiness (You're a Good Man Charlie Brown)
Wage Gaps	1. Everybody Out (Made in Dagenham)
War	1. Almost Real (The Bridges of Madison County)
Wealth	1. 96,000 (In the Heights)
Women in the Workforce	1. Happy to Keep his Dinner Warm (How to Succeed in Business without Really Trying)
Zero-Sum Games	1. The Winner Takes it All (Mamma Mia)

REFERENCES

A Better Way. (2010). Retrieved from *The Economist* online: http://www.economist.com/node/17173919

A Chicken in Every Pot. (1928). Retrieved from National Archives Catalog: https://research.archives.gov/id/187095

Acemoglu, D., and Johnson, S. (2005). Unbundling Institutions. *Journal of Political Economy*, 113(5), 949–995.

Adams, S. (2012). Why Winning Powerball Won't Make You Happy. November 28. Retrieved from *Forbes* online: https://www.forbes.com/sites/susanadams/2012/11/28/why-winning-powerball-wont-make-you-happy/#20c36c6593a1

Adams, S. (2015). The College Majors With the Highest Starting Salaries. July 2. Retrieved from *Forbes* online: https://www.forbes.com/sites/susanadams/2015/07/02/the-college-majors-with-the-highest-starting-salaries/#5a7187b35024

Adamy, J. (2016). How to Boost U.S. GDP by $2.1 Trillion: More Women in the Workforce. Retrieved from *The Wall Street Journal* online: https://blogs.wsj.com/economics/2016/04/07/how-to-boost-u-s-gdp-by-2–1-trillion-more-women-in-the-workforce/

Aguirre, D., Hoteit, L., Rupp, C., and Sabbagh, K. (2012). Empowering the Third Billion and Women and the World of Work in 2012. Retrieved from Booz and Company: http://www.strategyand.pwc.com/media/file/Strategyand_Empowering-the-Third-Billion_Full-Report.pdf

Akbar, A. (2010). Mao's Great Leap Forward "Killed 45 Million in Four Years." Retrieved from *The Independent* online: http://www.independent.co.uk/arts-entertainment/books/news/maos-great-leap-forward-killed-45-million-in-four-years-2081630.html (September 20).

Alchian, A. A. (2008). Property Rights. Retrieved from *The Concise Encyclopedia of Economics* online: http://www.econlib.org/library/Enc/PropertyRights.html

Anderson, T., and Huggins, L. (2009). *Property Rights: A Practical Guide to Freedom and Prosperity*. Retrieved from Hoover Institution: http://www.hoover.org/research/property-rights-practical-guide-freedom-and-prosperity

Andreoni, J. (1990). Impure Altruism and Donations to Public Goods: A Theory of Warm-Glow Giving. *The Economic Journal*, 100(401), 464–477.

Auerbach, N. (2013). Michigan's 10-Year Disassociation with Chris Webber Ends. Retrieved from *USA Today* online: https://www.usatoday.com/story/sports/ncaab/2013/05/08/10-years-removed-from-violations-michigan-reveals-new-face/2144023 (May 8).

Aughinbaugh, A., Robles, O., and Sun, H. (2013). Marriage and Divorce: Patterns by Gender, Race, and Educational Attainment. *Monthly Labor Review*, U.S. Bureau of Labor Statistics, October. Retrieved from: https://doi.org/10.21916/mlr.2013.32

Babson, R. W. (1935). *Actions and Reactions: An Autobiography of Roger W. Babson*. New York: Harper and Brothers. Retrieved from: https://books.google.com/books/about/Actions_and_reactions.html?id=MLUSAQAAMAAJ

Batalhone, S., Nogueira, J., and Mueller, B. (2002). Economics of Air Pollution: Hedonic Price Model and Smell Consequences of Sewage Treatment Plants in Urban Areas. *University of Brasilla: Department of Economics Working Paper 234*. Retrieved from: http://www.ceemaunb.com/jmn/publicacoes/EconomyUrbanAirPollution.pdf

Baumol, W. J., and Blinder, A. S. (1998). *Economics: Principles and Policy*. San Diego: Harcourt Brace and Company.

Bergman, S. A., and Logan, T. D. (2013). The Effect of Recruit Quality on College Football Team Performance. Retrieved from *Journal of Sports Economics* online: http://www.econ.ohio-state.edu/trevon/pdf/Bergmen_Logan.pdf

Billboard. (2017). Chart History: Hamilton: An American Musical. Retrieved from Billboard: http://www.billboard.com/artist/317230/Original+Broadway+Cast/chart?f=335

Boduszyński, M. (2010). *Regime Change in the Yugoslav Successor States: Divergent Paths Towards a New Europe*. Baltimore, MD: The Johns Hopkins University Press.

Boland, B. (2014). Who Read 1,582-Page $1.1T Spending Bill? Congressman: "Nobody Did." Retrieved from CNSNews.com: http://www.cnsnews.com/news/article/barbara-boland/who-read-1582-page-11t-spending-bill-congressman-nobody-did

Bomberger, W., and Makinen, G. (1983). The Hungarian Hyperinflation and Stabilization of 1945–1946. *Journal of Political Economy*, 91(983), 801–824.

Bookhaven Press LLC. (2017). *Civil Service Exams*. Retrieved from Federal Government Jobs: http://www.federaljobs.net/exams.htm (May 23).

Borghesi, R. (2015). The Financial and Competitive Value of NCAA Basketball Recruits. Retrieved from *Journal of Sports Economics* online: https://www.researchgate.net/publication/286477289_The_Financial_and_Competitive_Value_of_NCAA_Basketball_Recruits

Bramwell, J. (2013). $53,300: The Average Starting Salary for New Accounting Grads. Retrieved from Accounting Web: http://www.accountingweb.com/aa/auditing/53300-the-average-starting-salary-for-new-accounting-grads (May 1).

Brewer, D. (2016). *Greece, the Decade of War: Occupation, Resistance and Civil War*. London/New York: I. B. Tauris.

Brickman, P., Coates, D., and Janoff-Bulman, R. (1978). Lottery Winners and Accident Victims: Is Happiness Relative? *Journal of Personality and Social Psychology*, 36(8), 917–927.

Brown, A., and McGeeney, K. (2013). In U.S., Employment Most Linked to Being Depression-Free. Retrieved from Gallup: http://www.gallup.com/poll/164090/employment-linked-depression-free.aspx (August 23).

Buffett, W. (2010). My Philanthropic Pledge. Retrieved from *Fortune* online: http://archive.fortune.com/2010/06/15/news/newsmakers/Warren_Buffett_Pledge_Letter.fortune/index.htm (June 16).

Butler, S. M., Beach, W. W., and Winfree, P. L. (2008). *Pathways to Economic Mobility: Key Indicators*. Philadelphia, PA: Economic Mobility Project.

Cadena, B. C., and Kovak, B. K. (2013). Immigrants Equilibrate Local Labor Markets: Evidence from the Great Recession. Retrieved from The National Bureau of Economic Research: http://www.nber.org/papers/w19272

Callahan, G., and Ikeda, S. (2003). Jane Jacobs, The Anti-Planner. Retrieved from Mises Institute: https://mises.org/library/jane-jacobs-anti-planner (June 20).

Camera, L. (2016). Survey: Coach's Salary Shouldn't Best President's. Retrieved from U.S. News and World Report: https://www.usnews.com/news/articles/2016-03-15/new-survey-college-coaches-shouldnt-make-more-than-college-presidents

Carey, B. (2013). Here's What the "Cornhusker Kickback" Did to Health Care in Nebraska. Retrieved from: https://downtrend.com/brian-carey/heres-what-the-cornhusker-kickback-did-to-health-care-in-nebraska (August 31).

Carnevale, A., Rose, S., and Cheah, B. (2011). The College Payoff: Education, Occupations, Lifetime Earnings. Retrieved from Georgetown University, Center on Education and the Workforce: https://cew.georgetown.edu/cew-reports/the-college-payoff/

Cassano, J. (2015). The Science of Why You Should Spend Your Money on Experiences, Not Things. Retrieved from Fast Company: https://www.fastcompany.com/3043858/the-science-of-why-you-should-spend-your-money-on-experiences-not-thing (March 30).

Caulfield, K. (2015). "Hamilton's" Historic Chart Debut: By the Numbers. Retrieved from Billboard: http://www.billboard.com/articles/columns/chart-beat/6722015/hamilton-cast-album-billboard-200

Caulfield, K. (2016). Nick Jonas Debuts at No. 2 on Billboard 200 Albums Chart, Drake's "Views" Steady at No. 1. Retrieved from Billboard: http://www.billboard.com/articles/columns/chart-beat/7408958/nick-jonas-last-year-was-complicated-no-2-billboard-200-albums-chart-drake-views (June 19).

Chang, M. (2010). *Fact Sheet: Women and Wealth in the United States*. Retrieved from Sociologists for Women in Society: https://www.socwomen.org/wp-content/uploads/2010/05/fact_2-2010-wealth.pdf

Chao, E. L. (2006). *100 Years of U.S. Consumer Spending: Data for the Nation, New York City, and Boston*. Washington, D.C.: The U.S. Department of Labor.

Chernow, R. (2005). *Alexander Hamilton*. New York: Penguin.

CIA. (2016). The World Factbook: North Korea. Retrieved from CIA online: https://www.cia.gov/library/publications/the-world-factbook/geos/kn.html

Civil Service Exams. (2017). Retrieved from Federal Government Jobs: http://www.federaljobs.net/exams.htm (March 9).

Clark, T. (2013). Opinion on Margaret Thatcher Remains Divided After Her Death, Poll Finds. Retrieved from *The Guardian* online: https://www.theguardian.com/politics/2013/apr/09/opinion-sharply-divide-margaret-thatcher (April 9).

CleanGovBiz. (2014). Retrieved from OECD: https://www.oecd.org/cleangovbiz/49693613.pdf

Coleman-Jensen, A., Rabbitt, M., Gregory, C., and Singh, A. (2016). Household Food Security in the United States in 2015. Retrieved from Economic Research Service: https://www.ers.usda.gov/publications/pub-details/?pubid=79760

Compound Interest Calculator. (n.d.). Retrieved from Moneychimp: http://www.moneychimp.com/calculator/compound_interest_calculator.htm

Compound Interest Calculator. (n.d.). Retrieved from Investor.gov: https://www.investor.gov/additional-resources/free-financial-planning-tools/compound-interest-calculator

Conard, E. (2016). *The Upside of Inequality: How Good Intentions Undermine the Middle Class*. New York: Penguin.

Conzen, M. P. (2016). *Commuting*. Retrieved from The Electronic Encyclopedia of Chicago: http://www.encyclopedia.chicagohistory.org/pages/323.html (November 23).

Coppock, L., and Mateer, D. (2014). *Principles of Macroeconomics*. New York: W. W. Norton and Company, Inc.

Cortes, P. (2008). The Effect of Low-skilled Immigration on US Prices: Evidence from CPI Data. *Journal of Political Economy*, 116(3), 381–422. Retrieved from: http://www.journals.uchicago.edu/doi/abs/10.1086/589756

Cowen, T., and Tabarrok, A. (2009). *Modern Principles of Economics*. London: Worth Publishers.

C. R. (2013). Germany's Hyperinflation-Phobia. Retrieved from *The Economist* online: http://www.economist.com/blogs/freeexchange/2013/11/economic-history-1 (November 15).

Cunningham, S., and Kendall, T. D. (2016). Prostitution, Hours, Job Amenities and Education. Retrieved from http://scunning.com/reho-2.pdf (December 14).

Cypher, J. (2013). Mexico: Prosperous, Competitive, Undergoing an Economic Renaissance? Retrieved from NACLA: https://nacla.org/article/mexico-prosperous-competitive-undergoing-economic-renaissance

Daly, J. L. (2002). *Pricing for Profitability: Activity–Based Pricing for Competitive Advantage*. New York: John Wiley and Sons.

Davidson, L. (2012, July 25). What Young People Need to Know About Retirement. Retrieved from *Forbes* online: https://www.forbes.com/sites/financialfinesse/2012/07/25/what-young-people-need-to-know-about-retirement/2/#27cfa3b54fd1

Dentists. (2015). Retrieved from Bureau of Labor Statistics: https://www.bls.gov/ooh/healthcare/dentists.htm#tab-5

Department of the Treasury with the Department of Education. (2012). *The Economics of Higher Education with the Department of Education*. Retrieved from https://www.treasury.gov/connect/blog/Documents/20121212_Economics%20of%20Higher%20Ed_vFINAL.pdf

Desrochers, D. M. (2013). Academic Spending Versus Athletic Spending: Who Wins? *Delta Cost Project at American Institutes for Research*, 1–15. Retrieved from: http://www.deltacostproject.org/sites/default/files/products/DeltaCostAIR_AthleticAcademic_Spending_IssueBrief.pdf

Dikötter, F. (2010). *Mao's Great Famine: The History of China's Most Devastating Catastrophe, 1958–62*. London: Bloomsbury Publishing.

DiLorenzo, T. (2016). Why Socialism Causes Pollution. Retrieved from Foundations for Economic Education: https://fee.org/articles/why-socialism-causes-pollution/

Discovery Communications, LLC. (2015). 1900s. Retrieved from Discovery Education: http://school.discoveryeducation.com/schooladventures/womenofthecentury/decadebydecade/1900s.html

Doder, D. (1993). Serbia's Inflations "Beyond Calculation" Life Savings Gone. Retrieved from *Baltimore Sun* online: http://articles.baltimoresun.com/1993-07-30/news/1993211045_1_yugoslavia-dinar-inflation

Dohmen, T., Falk, A., Huffman, D., and Sunde, U. (2012). Interpreting Time Horizon Effects in Inter-Temporal Choice. *IZA DP No. 6385*. Bonn, Germany: Institute for the Study of Labor.

Dugger, C. (2010). Zimbabwe Heath Care, Paid with Peanuts. Retrieved from *The New York Times* online: http://www.nytimes.com/2010/12/19/world/africa/19zimbabwe.html

Early, D. W. (2000). Rent Control, Rental Housing Supply, and the Distribution of Tenant Benefits. *Journal of Urban Economics*, 48(2), 185–204.

Edlund, L., and Korn, E. (2002). A Theory of Prostitution. *Journal of Political Economy*, 181–214.

Elborgh-Woytek, K., Newiak, M., Kochhar, K., Fabrizio, S., Kpodar, K., Wingender, P., and Schwartz, G. (2013). *Women, Work, and the Economy: Macroeconomic Gains from*

Gender Equity. Retrieved from International Monetary Fund: http://www.imf.org/external/pubs/ft/sdn/2013/sdn1310.pdf

Elliott, B. (2016). Economists Think 5-Star College Football Recruits Could Be Worth $500K Annually. Retrieved from SB Nation: http://www.sbnation.com/college-football-recruiting/2016/11/1/13418518/impact-recruit-college-football-team-performance-study-money-playoff (November 1).

Ellis, J. J. (2000). *Founding Brothers: The Revolutionary Generation*. New York: Vintage Books.

Employment in Agriculture (% of Total Employment). (2016). Retrieved from The World Bank: http://data.worldbank.org/indicator/SL.AGR.EMPL.ZS

European Commission. (2016). Competition: Cartels. Retrieved from European Commission: http://ec.europa.eu/competition/cartels/leniency/leniency.html

Fabian, J. (2010). Obama healthcare plan nixes Ben Nelson's "Cornhusker Kickback" deal. Retrieved from The Hill: http://thehill.com/blogs/blog-briefing-room/news/82621-obama-healthcare-plan-nixes-ben-nelsons-cornhusker-kickback-deal (February 22).

Fabian, J. (2016). Obama: "Hamilton" is the only thing Dick Cheney and I agree on. Retrieved from The Hill: http://thehill.com/blogs/in-the-know/in-the-know/272964-obama-hamilton-is-the-only-thing-dick-cheney-and-i-agree-on

Facing History and Ourselves. (2017). Inflated Weimar Currency (1923). Retrieved from Facing History and Ourselves: https://www.facinghistory.org/weimar-republic-fragility-democracy/economics/inflated-weimar-currency-1923-economics-1919-1924-inflation

Federation of American Scientists. (2000). "Russia's Physical and Social Infrastructure: Implications for Future Development." December.

Finkelstein, E., Trogdon, J. G., Cohen, J. W., and William, D. (2009). Annual Medical Spending Attributable to Obesity: Payer- and Service-Specific Estimates. Retrieved from Health Affairs: http://content.healthaffairs.org/content/28/5/w822.abstract#cited-by

Fisher, A. (2015). Should you still "dress for the job you want"? Retrieved from Fortune: http://fortune.com/2015/03/19/dress-job-promotions (March 19).

Fisher, J., and Smeeding, T. M. (2016). Income Inequality. The Stanford Center on Poverty and Inequality. Retrieved from: http://inequality.stanford.edu/sites/default/files/Pathways-SOTU-2016-Income-Inequality-3.pdf

Fixed Income, Bonds & CDs. (2017). Retrieved from Fidelity: https://fixedincome.fidelity.com/ftgw/fi/FILanding?imm_pid=700000001008518&immid=100082&imm_eid=e2027291546&gclid=COnLtP-I49ACFcieNwodEfYH0w&gclsrc=ds (March 27).

Fleming, P. (1973). The Politics of Marriage Among Non-Catholic European Royalty. *Current Anthropology*, 14(3), 231–249.

Forced Marriage Unit Statistics 2016 (2017). Retrieved from *Home Office* online: http://bit.ly/2m7SNx4

Forex Capital Markets. (2017). New York Stock Exchange (NYSE). Retrieved from FXCM: https://www.fxcm.com/insights/new-york-stock-exchange-nyse/

Fottrell, Q. (2015). Most Americans Have Less Than $1,000 in Savings. Retrieved from MarketWatch: http://www.marketwatch.com/story/most-americans-have-less-than-1000-in-savings-2015–10–06 (December 23).

Fox, E. J. (2015). Stanford Offers Free Tuition for Families Making Less Than $125,000. Retrieved from CNN Money: http://money.cnn.com/2015/04/01/pf/college/stanford-financial-aid (April 3).

Fox, E. M. (1997). US and EU Competition Law: A Comparison. *Global Competition Policy*, 339–354. Retrieved from: https://piie.com/publications/chapters_preview/56/10ie1664.pdf

Fox, J. (2016). *Government Statistics May Be Wrong, But They're Not Manipulated.* Retrieved from Bloomberg: https://www.bloomberg.com/view/articles/2016-08-09/government-statistics-may-be-wrong-but-they-re-not-manipulated

Francis, D. R. (2006). Why High Earners Work Longer Hours. Retrieved from July 2006 National Bureau of Economic Research Digest: http://www.nber.org/digest/jul06/w11895.html

Friedman, M., and Friedman, R. (1990). *Free to Choose: A Personal Statement.* New York: Houghton Mifflin Harcourt.

Friedman, M., and Schwartz, A. J. (1971). *A Monetary History of the United States, 1867–1960.* Princeton, NJ: Princeton University Press.

Friedman, R. (1977). Old San Juan: Vibrant City Life With a Style That's High and Low. Retrieved from *The New York Times* online: http://www.nytimes.com/1977/11/13/archives/old-san-juan-vibrant-city-life-with-a-style-thats-high-and-low.html?_r=1

Fryers, T. (2006). Work, Identity and Health. Retrieved from BioMed Central: http://cpementalhealth.biomedcentral.com/articles/10.1186/1745-0179-2-12 (May 31).

Fryers, T. (2006). Work, Identity, and Health. *Clinical Practice and Epidemiology in Mental Health: CP and EMH,* 2, 12. Retrieved from http://doi.org/10.1186/1745-0179-2-12

Full Fact Team. (2011). Does the UK Have the Toughest Laws on Strikes in the Developed World? Retrieved from FullFact: https://fullfact.org/news/does-uk-have-toughest-laws-strikes-developed-world

Gall, G. (2003). Employer Opposition to Union Recognition. In G. Gall, *Union Organizing: Campaigning for Trade Union Recognition.* London: Routledge, pp. 79–96.

Galley, J. (2014). *Stay–At–Home Mothers Through the Years.* Retrieved from Bureau of Labor Statistics: https://www.bls.gov/opub/mlr/2014/beyond-bls/stay-at-home-mothers-through-the-years.htm

Gartner, M. (1990). Nation Shrugs as Thugs Firebomb Freedom. *The Wall Street Journal.* November 29.

Gillen, T. (2005). *Winning New Business in Construction.* Aldershot: Gower Publishing Ltd.

Globalization and Monetary Policy Institute. (2011). *Hyperinflation in Zimbabwe.* Dallas, TX: Federal Reserve Bank of Dallas.

Goda, G. S., Levy, M., Manchester, C. F., Sojourner, A., and Tasoff, J. (2015). *The Role of Time Preferences and Exponential–Growth Bias in Retirement Savings.* NBER Working Paper 21482.

Goetzmann, W. N., and Rouwenhorst, K. (2005). *The Origins of Value: The Financial Innovations that Created Modern Capital Markets.* Oxford: Oxford University Press.

Goldin, C. (1993). Gender Gap. *The Concise Encyclopedia of Economics.* Retrieved from: http://www.econlib.org/library/Enc/GenderGap.html

Goldin, C. (2015). How to Achieve Gender Equality in Pay. Retrieved from Milken Institute Review: http://www.milkenreview.org/articles/how-to-achieve-gender-equality-in-pay (July 27).

Goldman, E. (1923). *My Disillusionment in Russia.* New York: Doubleday, Page and Company.

Goldstein, E. (2008). The Versailles System. In G. Martel (ed.), *A Companion to International History 1900–2001.* Hoboken, NJ: John Wiley & Sons.

Goodley, S. (2013). Dagenham Sewing Machinists Recall Strike That Changed Women's Lives. Retrieved from *The Guardian*: https://www.theguardian.com/politics/2013/jun/06/dagenham-sewing-machinists-strike (June 6).

Gould, E. (2016). Longer Hours, Not Higher Wages, Have Driven Modest Earnings Growth for Most American Households. Retrieved from Economic Policy Institute:

http://www.epi.org/publication/longer-hours-not-higher-wages-have-driven-modest-earnings-growth-for-most-american-households/

Green, R. K. (2013). Dress for the Career You Want, Not the One You Have. Retrieved from The Huffington Post: http://www.huffingtonpost.com/r-kay-green/career-future-advice_b_2583884.html (April 2).

Greenwood, J., Guner, N., Kocharkov, G., and Santos, C. (2014). Marry Your Like: Assortative Mating and Income Inequality. Retrieved from The National Bureau of Economic Research: http://www.nber.org/papers/w19829 (January).

Grolier Multimedia Encyclopedia (2015). "Union of Soviet Socialists Republic." Retrieved November 12, 2015.

Guo, J. (2014). Mexican Immigrants Will Move for Low-Skill Jobs. No One Else Will. Retrieved from *The Washington Post* online: https://www.washingtonpost.com/news/storyline/wp/2014/08/06/mexican-immigrants-will-move-for-low-skill-jobs-no-one-else-will/?utm_term=.90d5f611c53e

Haab, T. C., and McConnell, K. E. (2002). *Valuing Environmental and Natural Resources: The Econometrics of Non–Market Valuation.* Northampton: Edward Elgar Publishing. Retrieved from http://s1.downloadmienphi.net/file/downloadfile8/200/1375235.pdf

Hall, C. (2005). It's Official: Scientists Prove Why Accountants Are Boring. Retrieved from *The Telegraph* online: http://www.telegraph.co.uk/news/science/science-news/3342652/Its-official-scientists-prove-why-accountants-are-boring.html (August 24).

Hanemann, W. M. (2005). The Value of Water. Manuscript, University of California at Berkeley. Retrieved from http://are.berkeley.edu/courses/EEP162/spring05/valuewater.pdf

Harrison, G. W., Lau, M. I., and Williams, M. B. (2002). Estimating Individual Discount Rates in Denmark: A Field Experiment. *American Economic Review*, 92(5), 1606–1617.

Haucap, J., Heimeshoff, U., and Schultz, L. M. (2010). *Legal and Illegal Cartels in Germany between 1958 and 2004.* Düsseldorf Institute for Competition Economics Discussion Paper No. 08. Retrieved from: http://www.dice.hhu.de/fileadmin/redaktion/Fakultaeten/Wirtschaftswissenschaftliche_Fakultaet/DICE/Discussion_Paper/008_Haucap_Heimeshoff_Schultz.pdf

Hertsgaard, M. (1999). *Earth Odyssey: Around the World in Search of Our Environment.* New York: Broadway Books.

Hertz, T. (2016). Overview. Retrieved from United States Department of Agriculture Economic Research Service: https://www.ers.usda.gov/topics/farm-economy/farm-labor/

Historical Timeline – Farmers and the Land. (2014). Retrieved from Growing a Nation: The Story of American Agriculture: https://www.agclassroom.org/gan/timeline/farmers_land.htm

History.com. (2009). Ford's Assembly Line Starts Rolling. Retrieved from History.com: http://www.history.com/this-day-in-history/fords-assembly-line-starts-rolling

History.com Staff. (2009). J.P. Morgan. Retrieved from History.com: http://www.history.com/topics/john-pierpont-morgan

Hobson, W., and Rich, S. (2015). Playing in the Red. Retrieved from *The Washington Post* online: http://www.washingtonpost.com/sf/sports/wp/2015/11/23/running-up-the-bills/?utm_term=.946193568a37

Holzer, H. J. (2011). *Immigration Policy and Less–skilled Workers in the United States: Reflections on Future Directions for Reform.* Washington, D.C.: Migration Policy Institute.

Howe, N. (2014, April 22). The Unhappy Rise of The Millennial Intern. Retrieved from *Forbes* online: https://www.forbes.com/sites/realspin/2014/04/22/the-unhappy-rise-of-the-millennial-intern/#72ce2cea1328

Hubbard, R. G., and O'Brien, A. P. (2016). *Microeconomics.* London: Pearson.

Huffman, D., Maurer, R., and Mitchell, O. S. (2016). *Time Discounting and Economic Decision–making among the Elderly*. Ann Arbor: Michigan Retirement Research Center. Retrieved from http://www.mrrc.isr.umich.edu/publications/papers/pdf/wp347.pdf

Hutton, M. J. (2001). *Russian and West European Women, 1860–1939: Dreams, Struggles, and Nightmares*. Lanham, MD: Rowman & Littlefield.

Hyperinflation in Zimbabwe. (2011). Retrieved from Globalization and Monetary Policy Institute.

IBDB. (2017). *Fiddler on the Roof*. Retrieved from Internet Broadway Database: https://www.ibdb.com/broadway-production/fiddler-on-the-roof-3213

Jacobs, J. (2011). Downtown is for People (Fortune Classic, 1958). Retrieved from Fortune: http://fortune.com/2011/09/18/downtown-is-for-people-fortune-classic-1958 (September 18).

Jacobson, L., and Wogan, J. (2012). Ryan and the Simpson–Bowles Commission: the full story. Retrieved from Politifact: http://www.politifact.com/truth-o-meter/article/2012/aug/30/ryan-and-simpson-bowles-commission-full-story (August 30).

Jeffrey, T. P. (2015). 7,231,000 Lost Jobs: Manufacturing Employment Down 37% From 1979 Peak. Retrieved from CNSNews.com: http://www.cnsnews.com/news/article/terence-p-jeffrey/7231000-lost-jobs-manufacturing-employment-down-37-1979-peak (May 12).

Jenkins, B. (2009). Rent Control: Do Economists Agree? *Econ Journal Watch*, 6(1), 73–112. Retrieved from: https://econjwatch.org/file_download/238/2009-01-jenkins-reach_concl.pdf

Jones, C. I., and Klenow, P. J. (2016). Beyond GDP? Welfare across Countries and Time. *American Economic Review*, 106(9), 2426–2457.

JP. (2012). 5 College Degrees that Aren't Worth the Cost. Retrieved from U.S. News: http://money.usnews.com/money/blogs/my-money/2012/06/22/5-college-degrees-that-arent-worth-the-cost (June 22).

Kahneman, D., and Deaton, A. (2010). High income improves evaluation of life but not emotional well-being. *Proceedings of the National Academy of Sciences*, 107(38), 16489–16493.

Kain, J. F. (1965). The Commuting and Residential Decisions of Central Business District Workers. *National Bureau of Economic Research*, 245–274. Retrieved from: http://www.nber.org/chapters/c7058.pdf

Kane, S. (2017). Highest Paying Legal Jobs. Retrieved from: https://www.thebalance.com/highest-paying-legal-jobs-2164341

Kaufmann, D., and Kraay, A. (2002). *Growth Without Governance*. World Bank Policy Research Working Paper No. 2928. Washington, D.C.: The World Bank.

Keynes, J. M. (1963). Economic Possibilities for our Grandchildren. In J. M. Keynes, *Essays in Persuasion*. New York: W. W. Norton and Co., pp. 358–373. Retrieved from http://www.econ.yale.edu/smith/econ116a/keynes1.pdf

Keynes, J. M. (2003 [1936]). *The General Theory of Employment, Interest, and Money*. London: Palgrave Macmillan.

Killewald, A., Pfeiffer, F., and Schachner, J. (2017). Wealth Inequality and Accumulation. *Annual Review of Sociology*, 43, 379–404. Belmont, CA: Thomson Wadsworth.

Knox, D., and Schacht, C. (2007). *Choices in Relationships: Introduction to Marriage and the Family*.

Kohler, T. C., and Getman, J. G. (2005). The Story of NLRB v. Mackay Radio and Telegraph Co.: The High Cost of Solidarity. Retrieved from Boston College Law School Faculty Papers: http://lawdigitalcommons.bc.edu/cgi/viewcontent.cgi?article=1161&context=lsfp

Koster, K. (2017). 17 Facts About Sexual Violence and Sex Work. Retrieved from: http://www.huffingtonpost.com/katherine-koster/16-facts-about-sexual-ass_b_8711720.html

Krugman, P. (2011). *Oh! What A Lovely War!* Retrieved from *The New York Times* online: https://krugman.blogs.nytimes.com/2011/08/15/oh-what-a-lovely-war (August 15).

Krugman, P. (2012). How to End This Depression. Retrieved from *The New York Review* online: http://www.nybooks.com/articles/2012/05/24/how-end-depression/

Kuhn, P., and Lozano, F. (2008). The Expanding Workweek? Understanding Trends in Long Work Hours Among U.S. Men, 1979–2006. *Journal of Labor Economics*, 26(2), 311–343.

Laing, K. (2011). DOT Limits Hours Truck Drivers Can Work Per Week, But Not Per Day. Retrieved from The Hill: http://thehill.com/policy/transportation/201083-dot-limits-hours-truck-drivers-can-work-per-week-but-not-per-day (December 22).

Lam, B. (2015). How Much Do Waiters Really Earn in Tips? Retrieved from *The Atlantic* online: https://www.theatlantic.com/business/archive/2015/02/how-much-do-waiters-really-earn-in-tips/385515/

Lechtenberg, S. (2013). Should Tipping Be Banned? Retrieved from Freakonomics: http://freakonomics.com/podcast/should-tipping-be-banned-a-new-freakonomics-radio-podcast/

Leonhardt, D. (2008). What Makes People Give? Retrieved from *The New York Times* magazine online: http://www.nytimes.com/2008/03/09/magazine/09Psychology-t.html (March 9).

Linn, M. W., Sandifer, R., and Stein, S. (1985). Effects of Unemployment on Mental and Physical Health. *American Journal of Public Health*, 75(5), 502–506. Retrieved from http://ajph.aphapublications.org/doi/pdf/10.2105/AJPH.75.5.502

Linnane, C. (2016). Exxon Mobil's downgrade leaves just two AAA-rated companies in the U.S. Retrieved from Market Watch: http://www.marketwatch.com/story/exxon-mobils-downgrade-leaves-just-two-aaa-rated-companies-in-the-us-2016-04-26 (April 27).

Lino, M. (2014). *Expenditures on Children by Families, 2013*. Miscellaneous Publication Number 1528–2013. Washington, D.C.: U.S. Department of Agriculture, Center for Nutrition Policy and Promotion.

List, J. A., and Shogren, J. F. (1998). The Deadweight Loss of Christmas: Comment. *The American Economic Review*, 88(5), 1350–1355.

Makinen, G. (1981). *Money, Banking and Economic Activity*. New York: Academic Press.

Mankiw, N. G. (2011). *Principles of Economics*, 6th edn. Boston, MA: Cengage Learning.

Mankiw, N. G. (2016). I Paid $2,500 for a "Hamilton" Ticket. I'm Happy About It. Retrieved from *The New York Times* online: https://www.nytimes.com/2016/10/23/upshot/i-paid-2500-for-a-hamilton-ticket-im-happy-about-it.html?_r=0 (October 21).

Massey, D. S., and Denton, N. A. (1993). *American Apartheid: Segregation and the Making of the Underclass*. Cambridge, MA: Harvard University Press.

Mateer, D., and Coppock, L. (2014). *Principles of Microeconomics*. New York: W. W. Norton and Company, Inc.

Matos-Rodriguez, F., and Hernandez, P. (2001). *Pioneros; Puerto Ricans in New York City 1896–1948*. Charleston, SC: Arcadia Publishing.

Matthews, C. (2012). The Unemployment Report Wasn't Rigged, but It's Not Accurate, Either. Retrieved from TIME: http://business.time.com/2012/10/16/the-unemployment-report-wasnt-rigged-but-its-not-accurate-either (October 16).

McElroy, W. (2014). The Economics of Marriage and Divorce. Retrieved from Foundation of Economic Education: https://fee.org/articles/the-economics-of-marriage-and-divorce/

McGinty, J. C. (2016). Why the Government Puts a Dollar Value on Life. Retrieved from *The Wall Street Journal* online: https://www.wsj.com/articles/why-the-government-puts-a-dollar-value-on-life-1458911310

McGinty, T., and Mullins, B. (2012). Political Spending by Unions Far Exceeds Direct Donations. Retrieved from *The Wall Street Journal* online: https://www.wsj.com/articles/SB10001424052702304782404577488584031850026 (July 10).

Melby, C. (2011). Brutally Honest Accountants Confess to Being Boring. Retrieved from *Forbes* online: https://www.forbes.com/sites/calebmelby/2011/06/17/brutally-honest-accountants-confess-to-being-boring/#570b8fa36332 (June 17).

Military Advantage. (2017). Hire a Veteran – Employ America's Greatest Asset. Retrieved from Military.com: http://www.military.com/hiring-veterans/

Mirsky, J. (2012). Unnatural Disaster: "Tombstone: The Great Chinese Famine, 1958–1962," by Yang Jisheng. *The New York Times Sunday Book Review*, BR22. Retrieved from *The New York Times* online: http://www.nytimes.com/2012/12/09/books/review/tombstone-the-great-chinese-famine-1958–1962-by-yang-jisheng.html (December 7).

More than 200,000 children married in US over the last 15 years (2017). Retrieved from *The Independent* online: https://ind.pn/2sRg66d

Morin, A. (2014). Want to Be Happier? Change Your Commute or Change Your Attitude. Retrieved from *Forbes* online: https://www.forbes.com/sites/amymorin/2014/12/07/want-to-be-happier-change-your-commute-or-change-your-attitude/#1285826e7417 (December 7).

Murphy, R. (2009). *The Politically Incorrect Guide to the Great Depression and the New Deal.* Washington, D.C.: Regnery Publishing.

Nafziger, S., and Lindert, P. H. (2012). Russian Inequality on the Eve of Revolution (No. w18383). The National Bureau of Economic Research. Retrieved from http://www.nber.org/papers/w18383

National Center for Education Statistics. (2015). Bachelor's Degrees Conferred by Postsecondary Institutions, by Field of Study: Selected Years, 1970–71 Through 2013–14. Retrieved from National Center for Education Statistics: https://nces.ed.gov/programs/digest/d15/tables/dt15_322.10.asp?current=yes (September).

National Multifamily Housing Council. (2017). The High Cost of Rent Control. Retrieved from National Multifamily Housing Council: http://www.nmhc.org/News/The-High-Cost-of-Rent-Control/

National Public Radio (NPR). (2011). How To "Thrive": Short Commutes, More Happy Hours. Talk of the Nation. Retrieved from http://www.npr.org/2011/10/19/141514467/small-changes-can-help-you-thrive-happily

Nearing, S. (1911). Wages in the United States, 1908–1910; A Study of State and Federal Wage Statistics. New York: Macmillan Co. Retrieved from https://archive.org/details/wagesinunitedsta00near

Newman, J. (2014). Coaches, Not Presidents, Top Public-College Pay List. Retrieved from *The Chronicle of Higher Education* online: http://www.chronicle.com/blogs/data/2014/05/16/coaches-not-presidents-top-public-college-pay-list/

Newport, F. (2013). In U.S., Most Would Still Work Even if They Won Millions. Retrieved from Gallup: http://www.gallup.com/poll/163973/work-even-won-millions.aspx (August 14).

Norton, S. (1998). Property Rights, the Environment, and Economic Well-Being. In P.J. Hill and R.E. Meiners (eds.). In *Who Owns the Environment?* Maryland: Rowman and Littlefield Publishers, Inc., pp. 37–54.

Norwood, S. H. (2002). *Strikebreaking and Intimidation: Mercenaries and Masculinity in Twentieth–Century America.* Chapel Hill, NC: UNC Press.

Occupational Employment and Wages, May 2015. (2016). Retrieved from Bureau of Labor Statistics: https://www.bls.gov/oes/current/oes372012.htm (March 30).

OECD. (2017). *Russian Federation*. Retrieved from Better Life Index: http://www.oecdbetterlifeindex.org/countries/russian-federation/

Ogden, C., Carroll, M., Fryar, C., and Flegal, K. (2015). *Prevalence of Obesity Among Adults and Youth: United States, 2011–2014*. Retrieved from NCHS data brief: https://www.cdc.gov/nchs/data/databriefs/db219.pdf

Ornstein, M., Stevenson, H., and Stevenson, M. (2003). Politics and Ideology in Canada: Elite and Public Opinion in the Transformation of a Welfare State. Retrieved from https://books.google.com/books?id=iMfy8i4wvf4C&dq=strikebreaking+legislation&source=gbs_navlinks_s

O'Roark, B. (2012). Molasses to Rum – From the Musical 1776. Retrieved from Critical Commons: http://www.criticalcommons.org/Members/oroark/clips/molasses-to-rum.mp4 (October 15).

Palairet, M. (2000). *The Four Ends of the Greek Hyperflation of 1941–1946*. Copenhagen, Denmark: Museum Tusculanum Press.

Pannell, R., Ewanouski, K., Gupta, V., and Koduru, V. (2013). *Athletic Footwear Industry*. Cornell University. Retrieved March 19, 2017, from https://faculty.cit.cornell.edu/jl2545/4160/presentation/2013presentations/Athletic Footwear.pptx

Parming, V. P. (2013). *Competition and Productivity in the U.S. Trucking Industry Since Deregulation*. Massachusetts Institute of Technology. Retrieved from Transportation @MIT: http://transportation.mit.edu/sites/default/files/documents/MIT_Trucking_Productivity_Report_2013.pdf

Payscale. (2016). Best Graduate Business Schools by Salary Potential. Retrieved from Payscale: http://www.payscale.com/college-salary-report/best-schools-by-type/mba?page=13

Payscale. (2017). Immigration Attorney / Lawyer Salary. Retrieved from Payscale.com: http://www.payscale.com/research/US/Job=Immigration_Attorney_%2f_Lawyer/Salary

PBS. (2000). People & Events: Alexander Hamilton. Retrieved from American Experience: http://www.pbs.org/wgbh/amex/duel/peopleevents/pande06.html

Percentage of Students With Internship Experience Climbs. (2015). Retrieved from National Association of Colleges and Employers: http://www.naceweb.org/s10072015/internship-co-op-student-survey.aspx (October 7).

Perry, M. (2016). Some Thoughts on Equal Pay Day and the 23% Gender Pay Gap Myth. Retrieved from AEIdeas: http://www.aei.org/publication/some-thoughts-on-equal-pay-day-and-the-23-gender-pay-gap-myth/

Perry, M. J. (2015). "Equal Pay Day" This Year is April 14; the Next "Equal Occupational Fatality Day" Will Be on July 29, 2027. Retrieved from AEIdeas: https://www.aei.org/publication/equal-pay-day-this-year-is-april-14-the-next-equal-occupational-fatality-day-will-occur-on-july-29-2027/

Pew Research Center. (2010). The Return of the Multi-Generational Family Household. Retrieved from Pew Research Center: http://www.pewsocialtrends.org/2010/03/18/the-return-of-the-multi-generational-family-household/

Piketty, T. (2014). *Capital in the Twenty–First Century*. Cambridge: The Belknap Press of Harvard University Press.

Playbill. (2016). *Hamilton Wins 2016 Pulitzer Prize; Miranda Reacts*. Retrieved from Playbill: http://www.playbill.com/article/hamilton-wins-2016-pulitzer-prize-com-347196

Posey, K. G. (2016). Household Income: 2015 – American Community Survey Briefs. United States Census Bureau. Retrieved from Census.gov: https://www.census.gov/content/dam/Census/library/publications/2016/demo/acsbr15-02.pdf

Powell, J. (2003). *FDR's Folly: How Roosevelt and His New Deal Prolonged the Great Depression.* New York: Three Rivers Press.

Ramsey, D. (2017). How Teens Can Become Millionaires. Retrieved from Ramsey Solutions: https://www.daveramsey.com/blog/how-teens-can-become-millionaires

Rane, J. (2015). U.S. Tipping Guide: Expert Advice on When, Where, How Much – and Why. Retrieved from CNN: http://www.cnn.com/2015/03/02/travel/experts-guide-to-tipping-in-the-united-states/

Rastogi, S. (2014). *Ayurvedic Science of Food and Nutrition.* New York: Springer-Verlag.

Ratner, J. (2008). Education, Family Background, Key Factors Determining Economic Mobility. Retrieved from The Pew Charitable Trusts: http://www.pewtrusts.org/en/about/news-room/press-releases/2008/09/18/education-family-background-key-factors-determining-economic-mobility

Reeves, R. V. (2014). Saving Horatio Alger, Equality, Opportunity, and the American Dream. The Brookings Essay. Retrieved from http://www.brookings.edu/research/essays/2014/saving-horatio-alger

Richardson, B. (2015). Paul: Nobody Read the $1.1 Trillion Omnibus Bill. Retrieved from The Hill: http://thehill.com/blogs/blog-briefing-room/news/263836-paul-nobody-read-the-11-trillion-omnibus-bill

Ridker, R. G. (1967). *Economic Costs of Air Pollution: Studies in Measurement.* New York: F.A. Praeger.

Ritholtz, B. (2013). 18th Century Debt (UK Consols to 1742). Retrieved from The Big Picture: http://ritholtz.com/2013/05/18th-century-debt-uk-consols-to-1742/

Ross, C. E., and Mirowsky, J. (1999). Parental divorce, life-course disruption, and adult depression. *Journal of Marriage and Family*, 61(4), 1034–1045. Retrieved from The University of Texas System.

Rousu, M. C. (2015). Economic Lessons for Children from The Hunger Games. Retrieved from the Library of Economics and Liberty: http://www.econlib.org/library/Columns/y2015/Rousuhungergames.html

Sally, D. F., and Jones, G. T. (2006). Game Theory Behaves. In A. K. Schneider, and C. Honeyman, *The Negotiator's Fieldbook.* Chicago: American Bar Association, p. 87.

Samuelson, P. A. (1976). *Economics*, 10th edn. New York: McGraw-Hill.

Schakowsky.House.Gov. (2017). Bowles-Simpson. Retrieved from Congresswoman Jan Schakowsky: Representing the 9th District of Illinois: https://schakowsky.house.gov/bowlessimpson

Schiavone, J. (2013). Record-Setting Demand Projected for Accounting Graduates: AICPA Report. Retrieved from American Institute of CPAs: http://www.aicpa.org/press/pressreleases/2013/pages/record-setting-demand-for-accounting-graduates-aicpa.aspx (June 18).

Schneider, D. (2011). Wealth and the Marital Divide. *American Journal of Sociology*, 117(2), 627–667.

Schramm, D. G. (2006). Individual and Social Costs of Divorce in Utah. *Journal of Family and Economic Issues*, 27(1), 133–151.

Schulze, W. D., Brookshire, D. S., Walther, E. G., Kelley, K., Thayer, M. A., Whitworth, R. L., and Molenar, J. (1985). *The Benefits of Preserving Visibility in the National Parklands of the Southwest, Volume VIII of Methods Development for Environmental Control Benefits Assessment.* United States Environmental Protection Agency. Retrieved from https://yosemite.epa.gov/ee/epa/eerm.nsf/vwGA/237F44550B79EABD8525644D0053BE5E

Sherman, E. (2015). America Is the Richest, and Most Unequal, Country. Retrieved from *Fortune* online: http://fortune.com/2015/09/30/america-wealth-inequality/

Simpson, B. P. (2010). *Keynes's Theory of Depression: A Critique*. La Jolla, CA: National University.

Singh, R. P., and Heldman, D. R. (2001). Food Freezing. In *Introduction to Food Engineering*. Glasgow: Academic Press, pp. 410–446.

Smith, A. (1776). *The Wealth of Nations*. New York: Random House Inc.

Smith, H. (2012). *The Russians*. New York: Random House.

Smith, R. M. (2003). *From Blackjacks to Briefcases: A History of Commercialized Strikebreaking in the United States*. Athens: Ohio University Press.

Smith, V. K., Zhang, X., and Palmquist, R. B. (1997). Marine Debris, Beach Quality, and Non-Market Values. *Environmental and Resource Economics*, 10(3), 223–247. Retrieved from doi:10.1023/A:1026465413899

Smith-Barrow, D. (2016). U.S. News Data: Job Rates, Starting Salaries for MBA Grads. Retrieved from U.S. News and World Report: https://www.usnews.com/education/best-graduate-schools/top-business-schools/articles/2017-03-23/us-news-data-salary-prospects-job-rates-for-mba-grads

Solnick, S. J., and Hemenway, D. (1996). The Deadweight Loss of Christmas: Comment. *The American Economic Review*, 5, 1299–1305.

Sommers, C. (2017). *There Is No Gender Wage Gap*. Retrieved from PragerU.com: https://www.prageru.com/sites/default/files/courses/transcripts/sommers-there_is_no_gender_wage_gap-transcript.pdf

Spence, M. (1973). Job Market Signaling. *The Quarterly Journal of Economics*, 87(3), 355–374. Retrieved from: http://www.econ.yale.edu/~dirkb/teach/pdf/spence/1973%20job%20market%20signalling.pdf

Statistic Brain. (2016). Arranged / Forced Marriage Statistics. Retrieved from Statistic Brain Research Institute: http://www.statisticbrain.com/arranged-marriage-statistics/

Stevenson, B., and Wolfers, J. (2008). Economic Growth and Subjective Well-Being: Reassessing the Easterlin Paradox. Retrieved from The National Bureau of Economic Research: http://www.nber.org/papers/w14282

Stiglitz, J. E., Sen, A., and Fitoussi, J.-P. (2010). *Mismeasuring Our Lives: Why GDP Doesn't Add Up*. New York: The New Press.

Stringham, E. P. (2015). *Private Governance: Creating Order in Economic and Social Life*. New York: Oxford University Press.

Stroup, R. (2016). *Eco-nomics: What Everyone Should Know about Economics and the Environment*. Washington, D.C.: Cato Institute.

Stuart, H. (2014). 9 Reasons We Should Abolish Tipping, Once and for All. Retrieved from The Huffington Post: http://www.huffingtonpost.com/2014/10/17/abolish-tipping_n_5991796.html

Stutzer, A., and Frey, B. S. (2004). *Stress That Doesn't Pay: The Commuting Paradox*. Institute for Empirical Research in Economics, University of Zurich, Working Paper No. 151, 10, 22. Retrieved from University of Zurich: http://www.econ.uzh.ch/static/wp_iew/iewwp151.pdf (August).

Swärdh, J. E. (2009). *Commuting Time Choice and the Value of Travel Time*. Kållered, Sweden: Örebro University. Retrieved from https://www.diva-portal.org/smash/get/diva2:278104/FULLTEXT02.pdf

Szurmak, J. (2017). *Perspectives in Science Fiction and Cultural Narratives*. Retrieved from University of Toronto – Faculty Pages: http://sites.utm.utoronto.ca/szurmak/content/research

Table 303.10. Total Fall Enrollment in Degree-Granting Postsecondary Institutions, by Attendance Status, Sex of Student, and Control of Institution: Selected Years, 1947 through 2024. (2015). Retrieved from National Center for Education Statistics: https://nces.ed.gov/programs/digest/d14/tables/dt14_303.10.asp?referrer=report

Taleb, N. N. (2005). *Fooled by Randomness: The Hidden Role of Chance in Life and in the Markets*. New York: Random House, Inc.

Tanner, M. (2012). *The American Welfare State: How We Spend Nearly $1 Trillion a Year Fighting Poverty – and Fail*. Washington, D.C.: Cato Institute.

Teachout, T. (2015). "Hamilton" Review: The Revolution Moves Uptown. Retrieved from *The Wall Street Journal* online: http://www.wsj.com/articles/hamilton-review-the-revolution-moves-uptown-1438907400

The Associated Press. (2014). Majority of Economists Back Federal Reserve Policy on US Economy. Retrieved from *The Guardian* online: https://www.theguardian.com/business/2014/aug/25/economists-back-federal-reserve-policy-us-economy

The Associated Press. (2016). Where Business Economists Split on Fed Policy. Retrieved from CBS Money Watch: http://www.cbsnews.com/news/where-business-economists-split-on-fed-policy

The Bureau of Labor Statistics. (2000). Changes in Women's Labor Force Participation in the 20th Century. Retrieved from The Bureau of Labor Statistics: https://www.bls.gov/opub/ted/2000/feb/wk3/art03.htm

The Bureau of Labor Statistics. (2017). Consumer Expenditures in 1999 Through 2014. *Consumer Expenditure Surveys*. Retrieved from https://www.bls.gov/cex/csxreport.htm

The Bureau of Labor Statistics. (2017). Occupational Employment and Wages, May 2016: 53–3032 Heavy and Tractor-Trailer Truck Drivers. Retrieved from The Bureau of Labor Statistics: https://www.bls.gov/oes/current/oes533032.htm

The College Board. (2017). Average Published Undergraduate Charges by Sector, 2016–17. Retrieved from College Board: https://trends.collegeboard.org/college-pricing/figures-tables/average-published-undergraduate-charges-sector-2016–17

The Economist. (2014a). Sex, Brains and Inequality. Retrieved from *The Economist* online: http://www.economist.com/news/united-states/21595972-how-sexual-equality-increases-gap-between-rich-and-poor-households-sex-brains-and (February 8).

The Economist. (2014b). Nice Work If You Can Get Out: Why the Rich Now Have Less Leisure Than the Poor. Retrieved from *The Economist* online: http://www.economist.com/news/finance-and-economics/21600989-why-rich-now-have-less-leisure-poor-nice-work-if-you-can-get-out (April 22).

The Economist. (2014c). More Bang for Your Buck: How New Technology Is Shaking Up the Oldest Business. Retrieved from *The Economist* online: http://www.economist.com/news/briefing/21611074-how-new-technology-shaking-up-oldest-business-more-bang-your-buck (August 7).

The Economist. (2014d). I Dither: Most Women Still Want to Marry Men With Money. Retrieved from *The Economist* online: http://www.economist.com/blogs/democracyinamerica/2014/09/marriage-market (September 24).

The Government of Quebec. (2017). *C–27 – Labour Code*. Retrieved from Legis Quebec: http://legisquebec.gouv.qc.ca/en/ShowDoc/cs/C-27

The Hoover Institution. (2017). *What Are Property Rights?* The Hoover Institution. Retrieved from http://media.hoover.org/sites/default/files/documents/0817939121_1.pdf

The National WWII Museum. (2016). Primary Sources: Rationing. Retrieved from The National WWII Museum online: http://www.nationalww2museum.org/learn/education/for-teachers/primary-sources/rationing.html?referrer=https://www.google.com/

The U.S. Bureau of the Census. (1981). *Money Income of Households in the United States*. Washington, D.C.: U.S. Government Printing Office. Retrieved from https://www2.census.gov/prod2/popscan/p60–126.pdf

The U.S. Bureau of the Census. (1982). *Money Income of Households, Families, and Persons in the United States: 1980.* Washington, D.C.: U.S. Government Printing Office. Retrieved from https://www2.census.gov/prod2/popscan/p60-132.pdf

The U.S. Bureau of the Census. (1987). *Money Income of Households, Families, and Persons in the United States: 1985.* Washington, D.C.: U.S. Government Printing Office. Retrieved from https://www2.census.gov/prod2/popscan/p60-156.pdf

The U.S. Bureau of the Census. (1991). *Money Income of Households, Families, and Persons in the United States: 1990.* Washington, D.C.: U.S. Government Printing Office. Retrieved from https://www2.census.gov/prod2/popscan/p60-174.pdf

The U.S. Bureau of the Census. (1993). *Statistical Abstract of the United States.* Washington, D.C.: U.S. Government Printing Office. Retrieved from https://books.google.com/books?id=EMSbFBP_s0AC&lpg=PA457&dq=1910%20household%20income%20united%20states&pg=PA457#v=onepage&q=1910%20household%20income%20united%20states&f=false

The U.S. Department of Labor. (2001). *Report 949: Consumer Expenditures in 1999.* Retrieved from https://www.bls.gov/cex/csxann99.pdf

The U.S. Department of Labor. (2010). *Report 1021: Consumer Expenditure Survey, 2006–2007.* Retrieved from https://www.bls.gov/cex/twoyear/200607/csxtwoyr.pdf

The U.S. Department of Labor. (2015). Women of Working Age: Civilian Noninstitutional Population by Sex, Race and Hispanic Ethnicity. Retrieved from The United States Department of Labor: https://www.dol.gov/wb/stats/latest_annual_data.htm#labor

The United States Census Bureau. (2017). State by 6-Digit HS Code and Top Countries. Retrieved from United States Census Bureau: https://www.census.gov/foreign-trade/statistics/state/data/index.html

The Wall Street Journal. (2016). Is It Time to End Tipping? Retrieved from *The Wall Street Journal* online: https://www.wsj.com/articles/is-it-time-to-end-tipping-1456715614

The Week Staff. (2011). Top 5 'Pay to Play' Scandals Rocking College Football. Retrieved from *The Week* online: http://theweek.com/articles/488252/5-pay-play-scandals-rocking-college-football

The World Bank Group. (2016). GDP Per Capita (Current US$). Retrieved from The World Bank: http://data.worldbank.org/indicator/NY.GDP.PCAP.CD

The World Bank Group. (2017). *GDP Ranking.* Retrieved from The World Bank: http://data.worldbank.org/data-catalog/GDP-ranking-table (February 1).

Tony Awards. (2016). *Quick Facts.* Retrieved from Tony Awards: http://www.tonyawards.com/en_US/history/facts (June 1).

Travis, A. (2013). *National Archives: Margaret Thatcher Wanted to Crush Power of Trade Unions.* Retrieved from National Archives: https://www.theguardian.com/uk-news/2013/aug/01/margaret-thatcher-trade-union-reform-national-archives (July 31).

U.S. Army. (2017a). Civilian Jobs & Careers in the U.S. Army. Retrieved from U.S. Army: http://www.goarmy.com/careers-and-jobs/army-civilian-careers.html

U.S. Army. (2017b). Army STEM: Careers & Jobs; Science, Technology, Engineering and Mathematics. Retrieved from U.S. Army: http://www.goarmy.com/careers-and-jobs/about-army-stem.html

U.S. Department of the Treasury. (2010). *About: Alexander Hamilton (17891795).* Retrieved from https://www.treasury.gov/about/history/pages/ahamilton.aspx (November 11).

United States History. (2017). *The New Deal.* Retrieved from United States History: http://www.u-s-history.com/pages/h1851.html (July 6).

Usual Weekly Earnings of Wage and Salary Workers First Quarter 2017. (2017). Retrieved from Bureau of Labor Statistics: https://www.bls.gov/news.release/pdf/wkyeng.pdf

Voth, H.-J. (2001). The Longest Years: New Estimates of Labor Input in England, 1760–1830. *The Journal of Economic History*, 61(4), 1065–1082.

Waldfogel, J. (1993). The Deadweight Loss of Christmas. *The American Economic Review*, 83(5), 1328–1336.

Wall Street Oasis. (2013). 2013 WSO Compensation Report Has Arrived. Retrieved from WallStreetOasis.com: https://www.wallstreetoasis.com/blog/2013-wso-compensation-report-has-arrived (July 9).

Warneck, W. (2007). Strike Rules in the EU27 and Beyond. Retrieved from European Trade Union Institute: http://www.etui.org/Publications2/Reports/Strike-rules-in-the-EU27-and-beyond

Washington State Department of Licensing. (2017). Commercial Driver License (CDL). Retrieved from Washington State Department of Licensing: http://www.dol.wa.gov/driverslicense/cdl.html

Wegge, T. C., Hanemann, W. M., and Loomis, J. (1996). Comparing Benefits and Costs of Water Resource Allocation Policies for California's Mono Basin. Economic institutions and increasing water scarcity. In D. C. Hall (ed.), *Advances in the Economics of Environmental Resources. Volume 1: Marginal Cost Rate Design and Wholesale Water Markets*, Greenwich, CT: JAI Press, pp. 11–30.

Weiss, M., and Gaffney, P. (2015). *The Business of Broadway*. New York: Allworth Press.

Whalen, C. J., and Reichling, F. (2015). *The Fiscal Multiplier and Economic Policy Analysis in the United States*. Working Paper Series: Congressional Budget Office, 1–12. Retrieved from https://www.cbo.gov/sites/default/files/114th-congress-2015-2016/workingpaper/49925-FiscalMultiplier_1.pdf

Whaples, R. (2001). *EH.Net Encyclopedia*. Retrieved from Hours of Work in U.S. History: http://eh.net/encyclopedia/hours-of-work-in-u-s-history (August 14).

Wilde, P. (2015). America's Hunger Problem: What's Really Going On. Retrieved from Politico: http://www.politico.com/agenda/story/2015/09/americas-hunger-problem-whats-really-going-on-000222

Wilson, C. A. (2013). *Public Policy: Continuity and Change*, 2nd edn. Long Grove, IL: Waveland Press, Inc.

Woetzel, J., Madgavkar, A., Ellingrud, K., Labaye, E., Devillard, S., Kutcher, E., and Krishnan, M. (2015). How Advancing Women's Equality Can Add $12 Trillion to Global Growth. Retrieved from McKinseyandCompany: http://www.mckinsey.com/global-themes/employment-and-growth/how-advancing-womens-equality-can-add-12-trillion-to-global-growth

Wollan, M. (2015). The Great American Kidney Swap. Retrieved from *The New York Times* online: https://www.nytimes.com/2015/05/03/magazine/the-great-american-kidney-swap.html?_r=1

World Health Organization and UNICEF Joint Monitoring Programme. (2015). Progress on Sanitation and Drinking Water 2015 Update and MDG Assessment. WHO/UNICEF. Retrieved from http://www.who.int/water_sanitation_health/monitoring/jmp-2015-update/en/

Wright, E., and Rogers, J. (2009). *In American Society: How It Really Works*. Retrieved from Chapter 15: Gender Inequality: https://www.ssc.wisc.edu/~wright/ContemporaryAmericanSociety/Chapter%2015%20-%20Gender%20inequality%20-%20Norton%20August.pdf

INDEX